At Home in the Chinese Diaspora

Also by Kuah-Pearce Khun Eng

SOCIETY AND RELIGIOUS ENGINEERING: Towards a Reformist Buddhism

REBUILDING THE ANCESTRAL VILLAGE: Singaporeans in China

VOLUNTARY ORGANIZATIONS IN THE CHINESE DIASPORA (*edited with Evelyn Hu-DeHart*)

CHINESE WOMEN AND THEIR SOCIAL NETWORK CAPITALS (*editor*)

WHERE CHINA MEETS SOUTHEAST ASIA (*edited with Grant Evans and Christopher Hutton*)

Also by Andrew P. Davidson

E-COMMERCE IN TOURISM: Use of Websites by Small Regional and Urban Tourism Enterprises (*with Stephen Burgess*)

PRIVATIZATION AND THE CRISIS OF AGRICULTURAL EXTENSION: the Case of Pakistan (*with Munir Ahmad*)

IN THE SHADOW OF HISTORY: the Passing of Lineage Society

DAIRY INDUSTRY RESTRUCTURING (*edited with Harry K. Schwarzweller*)

At Home in the Chinese Diaspora

Memories, Identities and Belongings

Edited by

Kuah-Pearce Khun Eng
University of Hong Kong

and

Andrew P. Davidson
University of New South Wales

palgrave
macmillan

First published 2008 by
PALGRAVE MACMILLAN
Houndmills, Basingstoke, Hampshire RG21 6XS and
175 Fifth Avenue, New York, N.Y. 10010
Companies and representatives throughout the world

PALGRAVE MACMILLAN is the global academic imprint of the Palgrave Macmillan division of St. Martin's Press, LLC and of Palgrave Macmillan Ltd. Macmillan® is a registered trademark in the United States, United Kingdom and other countries. Palgrave is a registered trademark in the European Union and other countries.

ISBN-13: 978-0-230-50698-5 hardback
ISBN-10: 0-230-50698-4 hardback

This book is printed on paper suitable for recycling and made from fully managed and sustained forest sources. Logging, pulping and manufacturing processes are expected to conform to the environmental regulations of the country of origin.

A catalogue record for this book is available from the British Library.

Library of Congress Cataloging-in-Publication Data
At home in the Chinese diaspora : memories, identities and belongings
/ edited by Kuah-Pearce Khun Eng and Andrew P. Davidson.
p. cm.
ISBN 0-230-50698-4 (alk. paper)
1. Chinese—Foreign countries—History. I. Kuah-Pearce Khun Eng.
II. Davidson, Andrew P., 1951–

DS732. A8 2007
305.895′1—dc22 2007039533

10 9 8 7 6 5 4 3 2 1
17 16 15 14 13 12 11 10 09 08

Printed and bound in Great Britain by
CPI Antony Rowe, Chippenham and Eastbourne

Contents

List of Figures

List of Tables

Preface

The journey to this book has been a long and pleasurable one indeed. It first began when Kuah-Pearce organized a panel on 'Power of Memories: Negotiating Belongingness in the Chinese Diaspora' for the Third International Convention of Asian Scholars, held in Singapore in 2003, where several of us presented papers addressing the issues surrounding memories, sense of belonging and identity in the Chinese diaspora. Subsequently, the editors discussed the possibility of working on a book project on this topic. We invited various scholars to participate in this project and we have been privileged that they have taken up the challenge of writing for this project.

In this book project, we have tried to bring together various issues and interrogate the debates regarding how memory, identity and sense of belonging helped shape migrants' understanding of self, the diasporic community(ies) and the wider society in which they lived, as well as to account for the local and transnational challenges they faced in their daily lives. We looked at issues of how memories were reproduced, how they served as social and cultural capital, how they created tensions and conflicts and how memories changed and impacted on the individuals and communities across generational bars. We also explored the role of place in situating memories and how the media, films and music portrayed and reinforced the understanding of identity.

We are very grateful to our contributors who have taken the time to write and contribute to this edited book. Without their contributions, this book would not have taken shape, especially in its present form. Both editors have worked hard on this book, especially AD who undertook to contact the publisher and carried out editorial work on the chapters. We would also like to thank Md. Nazrul Islam for his assistance with the index.

Our efforts were made especially difficult as the editors and contributors were scattered across the globe. While the Internet and email made the completion of this project possible, the editors managed to work through the themes and details of the book early on in Hong Kong before AD returned to work in Vietnam. For this reason, our special and heartfelt thanks go to the contributors for their patience and persistence.

There are also many people we would like to thank for helping to make this book project a pleasurable endeavour. We would like to thank Jill Lake at Palgrave Macmillan for her support, patience and confidence in us and our project. AD would also like to express his gratitude to Lydia (Chuen Tai) Ngai and his children for emotional and other support. KP would like to thank her husband and daughter for their emotional support and trust in her ability. Lastly, as most of the contributors are transnational migrants and part of one diaspora or another, we dedicate this book to all migrants and hope that this book resonates within the memories of their own experiences.

Kuah-Pearce Khun Eng
Hong Kong, SAR China
Andrew P. Davidson
Dong Hoi, Quang Binh, Vietnam

Notes on the Contributors

Darryl Accone, Lecturer, Wits School of Arts, University of the Witwatersrand.

M.K. Esther Cheung, Associate Professor, Comparative Literature, School of Humanities and Director, Centre for the Study of Globalization and Cultures, University of Hong Kong.

Sheena Choi, Associate Professor, Social Foundations, School of Education, Indiana University-Purdue University Fort Wayne.

John Clammer, Professor of Comparative Sociology and Asian Studies, Sophia University, Tokyo.

Rosa Dai, doctoral candidate, School of Sociology and Anthropology, University of New South Wales.

Andrew P. Davidson, Senior Lecturer, Department of Sociology, University of New South Wales.

Karen Harris, Professor, Department of Historical and Heritage Studies and Director of the Archives, University of Pretoria.

David Ip, Associate Professor/Reader, Programme Director, Master of Development Practice, School of Social Science, the University of Queensland.

Kuah-Pearce Khun Eng, Associate Professor and Head, Department of Sociology and Honorary Academic Director, Centre for Anthropological Research, University of Hong Kong.

Walter F. Lalich, Associate, Australian Centre for Cooperative Research and Development, University of Technology Sydney.

Amy Wai-sum Lee, Assistant Professor, Department of English Language and Literature, Hong Kong Baptist University.

Maggi Leung, Humboldt Research Fellow, Department of Geography, University of Bonn, Germany.

Lucille Ngan, doctoral candidate, School of Sociology and Anthropology, University of New South Wales.

1
Introduction: Diasporic Memories and Identities

Andrew P. Davidson and Kuah-Pearce Khun Eng

Introduction

As the Chinese diasporic communities expanded throughout the world with the settling down of migrants as permanent residents or citizens of the nation state, a sojourner's mentality soon gives way to a sense of permanence, marking the transition from migrant to becoming a fully fledged member of the host society. In this sense, Georg Simmel's stranger finds home, fashioned from two worlds, similar yet disparate. As such, the diasporic communities take root in a land away from the original home. The extent to which the diasporic communities become fully integrated into the host society will allow us to understand the process – and success – of nation-building and citizenship development in a world where nation states are becoming increasingly multicultural and pluralistic in orientation. It is also a world where multiculturalism is becoming progressively more problematic as cultural identities confront the dictates of the nation state and dominant social groups. The presence of diasporic communities thus reveals the intense interchange of community and nation.

This chapter examines how diasporic communities are defined but redefined through the need to reformulate this as a conceptual category of community that is formed through the interplay of memories and identities. Nevertheless the concept of diasporic community quickly reveals congeries of meaning that are often difficult to disentangle and clearly delineate, or what Brubaker (2005, p. 1) terms 'The "diaspora" diaspora'. Yet the theoretical importance of community as the confluence of habits, customs and beliefs demands such a discursive exercise. Diasporic communities, by their very nature, suggest the idea of dispersal and fragmentation, of an enduring albeit often ephemeral connection between the diasporic community and what is generally termed the country of origin and host country. Nevertheless meanings do matter. In a certain manner, when a migrant becomes integrated into the host society, can we still continue to speak of a diasporic community? Or should we continue to understand the diasporic community in terms of their historical and contemporary migration routes and migrant roots? Then too what role does the state play in shaping migrants' feelings of home? And what of the migrants themselves; is there a compelling need, some form of autochthonous call, to recreate the past in the present, even at the cost of marginalization? Likewise, how do the migrants themselves look at the issue of 'self' in its search for an identity that straddles historical memory and contemporary demands (Kuah-Pearce 2006, pp. 223–39)?

Redefining diasporic communities

Communities are living entities that evolve through time and space in response to the social, communal and individualistic needs of their members and the contextual pressures of the wider nation state in which they are embedded. Then too diasporic communities change against the varying circumstances of trajectories and outcomes of resettlement, adjustment, adaptation and integration, pointing to the risk of attributing a self-actualizing, homogenizing logic to the diasporic communities, just as we cannot for the exaggerated claim of the nation states as the great unifier (Brubaker 2005). Diasporic narratives, like narratives of the nation state, are fraught with contentions over belonging, difference and diversity. In some of the literature on diasporas: 'We find an almost primordial conception that such collective identities are stable attributes that migrants take with them and insert into the country of settlement' (Koopmans et al. 2005).

On the contrary, just as memories are subject to the 'dialectics of remembering and forgetting' (Cattell and Climo 2002, p. 1), identities are malleable and subject to the putative concept of what Homi Bhabha, Stuart Hall, Gayatri Spivak and Paul Gilroy term 'hybridity'. While acknowledging the problematic nature of hybridity (see Werbner and Modood 1997), it is a useful term to reveal the interplay of memories on identity construction and the creation of transnational identities. In this volume we deploy a syncretized notion of hybridity, one informed by the discursive framework of specific cultural intersections. Specifically, we look at hybridity, or what Mudrooroo (1990, p. 24) propounds as 'the contestational weave of cultures'. Revolution in communication technologies and the affordability of long-distance travel facilitate the creation of hybrid identities and transnational communities and, for us, diasporic communities and their continued relevance as point of entry.

It is for these reasons that we choose to define community through the nexus of memory and identity as memories of regional, linguistic, ethnic and religious identities confront a larger imagery of identity, in this case 'Chineseness'. In other words, how memories and identities are racialized, if not overtly then flowing just beneath the surface of political correctness (see, for example, Stratton and Ang 1994). As Alexander and Knowles (2005) so eloquently note, race does matter and in many ways is the cornerstone of diasporic identities. Racially charged memories are bittersweet, providing succour to the migrant while serving to further differentiate. On the other hand, some migrants eschew the identities and memories of the diasporic community, rejecting the idea of their cultural authenticity and seek instead inclusion in the wider community. Still, memories run deep, however fractured they are, and inscribe themselves upon migrant identity in the shifting contours of identity politics.

In this book, we initially define diasporic communities according to the migration trajectories where migrants moved in search of better lives in the economic, social, political and ideological arenas. But migration is never so simple a matter of self-betterment. In the complex realities of migration, migrants experience a sense of deterritorialization and dislocation where the break with the country of origin with its familiar social practices and cultural icons means these are no longer available to these migrants in their adopted country. Diasporic communities thus conscientiously seek to retrieve and reproduce some of these social practices and cultural icons in order that migrants 'remember' and reconstruct the customary meanings migrants find in their daily lives. It is for this reason that diasporic communities engage in the production of diasporic collective and social memories; that is, as social constructions. Such reproduction can prove essential as it provides liminal communities with a sense of continuity of their cultural traditions, so necessary for the restabilization of their identity – their sense of social self – in a foreign land. Cultural familiarity is also imperative for its members to reterritorialize themselves as Chinese, however defined.

Diasporic community thus also refers to the core values, deep cultural memories and ideational self that inform migrants' biographies. According to Benedict Anderson's (1991) *Imagined Communities*, 'Communities are to be distinguished, not by their falsity/genuineness, but by the style in which they are imagined.' It is in this sense that the diasporic community leads migrants to fix in their minds a mental image of their amorphous communal affinity and bind it together with cultural artefacts and social constructs. Of course neither memory nor identity is static. Diasporic communities, like Anderson's nations, are subject to what Homi Bhabha (1990) calls 'the impossible unity of the nation as a symbolic force' as 'Nations, like narratives, lose their origins in the myths of time and only fully realize their horizons in the mind's eye.' So too with the diasporic community as the act of narration is lost in its ambivalent emergence. It is thus the symbolic artificiality of identity and plasticity of memory that shape and reshape the diasporic community, tightening communal bonds for some while loosening them for others, or what Brubaker (2005, p. 6) designates *'boundary-maintenance* and *boundary-erosion'*. Hence the diasporic community (like the nation), is never uncontested or unaltered.

Although many diasporic migrants do receive it (for us through Chineseness) as a primordial 'fact', its form and content are continuously subject to disputation, especially over its authenticity and meaning. We agree with Brubaker (2005) on the futility and similarly question the need to enumerate specific numbers for the various diasporas and that it is better to focus on it as a process. In short, the diasporic community, while problematic, offers a site to explore such questions. Diasporic community, as used here, refers to physical locations and/or imagined constructions where migrants come together from shared memories and a perceived common identity, albeit loci that are located in varying cultural, social and historical situations. This community of shared needs and solidarity (Gilroy 1993), however, points to the limitations of deploying diasporic discourse. We concur with Clifford (1997, p. 267) that diasporic communities are more than 'a "changing same", something endlessly hybridized and in process but persistently there – memories and practices of collective identity maintained over long stretches of time', but in a way that while indicating modes of belonging, transcends a presumed postcolonial condition (see Dunn 1998).

Nevertheless, and for analytical purposes, there is latitude for cautious generalization about diasporic communities as a lived form of social cohesion, but one indisputably cross-cut by long-standing structural issues. Clearly too, in this volume, we are arguing against an absolute or unitary Chinese culture and consequently challenge essentialist notions of Chineseness. And certainly we recognize migrants' feelings of alienation and insulation, but also acknowledge that not all are marginalized. Lastly, we note that diasporic communities are continually constructed, debated and reimagined through the intersection of memories and identities.

Diasporic memories and identities

Halbwachs and others explored the significance of social and collective memories in identity formation for all social groupings. Individuals and communities as a whole consciously choose what they want to remember and pass down to their future generations. This process of selection is a personalized choice on the part of the individuals and a collective choice for the community as a whole, depending on what cultural elements the individual and community view as key to the survival of their identity. As a result of the subjective choices of the cultural elements that are selected, Halbwachs (1992) argued that the reproduction of social memories is a fragmented process at best. As such, diasporic memories comprised only those sociocultural elements that the migrants selectively remembered and wanted to reproduce in their new home and community. This is often interlaced with their own social experiences, both in their original home and the host society.

At the same time, diasporic memories are also shaped by various sets of social experiences. First, there are the social experiences before the migrants left their home of origin. Second, there are the migration experiences that occurred during the interstitial or liminal period where the migrants moved from one locality to the next. Third, there is the experiential existentialism of a diasporic community where migrants often are subjected to a sense of marginality, discrimination and social exclusion in the host society (Alexander 2003). Here we see Simmel's stranger writ large (Heinke n.d.):

> The attributes of that stranger are his differences of time and place of his origin, his socially not belonging to the host society and also his independence in moving, staying and in his way of behaviour compared to the rest of society which he enters. If we communicate with strangers we have – at the same time – the impression of being close to someone from a distance and of being far away from someone who is in our immediate environment.

Within the diasporic communities, as the migrants settled into a new environment, it is imperative also for us to explore the significant social and cultural elements that the diasporic Chinese stashed in their personal and collective memories that they would reproduce as they work themselves into the host society. Among the key elements that they remembered and sought to reproduce are the Chinese social institutions such as the family, voluntary organizations (dialect and clan associations), the social ties and networks, *guanxi* and *guanxi-wang*, aspects of Chinese social customs and religious practices such as the continuing significance of the Lunar New Year, the Mid-autumn Festival with its attendant display of lanterns and mooncake eating, the *Duan-Wu* Festival and the consumption of rice dumplings and the dragon-boat race, the Hungry Ghost Festival, to name the few common ones. There is also the attempt to try to remember the Chinese language through the speaking of the Chinese dialects and Mandarin within the home environment as well as establishing Sunday Chinese language classes for the younger generation of Chinese. In some diasporic communities, formal schools were set up for the purpose of educating the children in order that they understand the Chinese culture and customs in the hope that they would continue to identify themselves as Chinese.

As each set of diasporic memories is affected by the migration process during various times, it is thus inevitable that the social customs and religious practices practised by each diasporic community take on an accentuated culturalized and localized form that is governed by migrants' peculiarities and their understanding of the significance and values attached to these practices in a highly contextualized environment that is unique to that group at that particular point in time. Hence, localization inevitably takes place. In this sense, what we are witnessing is a variety of Chinese diasporic communities emerging from within the diasporic outflow (see Song 2005).

All these experiences challenged the migrants' sense of belongingness on the one hand and cultural affiliation and identity on the other. Here we locate the creation of a diasporic memory that facilitates the (re)making of a diasporic culture. This diasporic culture is a distinctive one that specifically caters to the need of the diasporic community. Among the Chinese, the diasporic culture serves as a social cushion for Chinese migrants to anchor themselves during the early years of migration. As they started settling down sinking roots in the diasporic community, this set of memories and culture aided them in their relationship with the wider host society and their interethnic relationship with other groups of migrants.

The politics of memory and identity

Memories are not only culturally charged, they are often subjected to political interference that creates motivated representations of the past. This is particularly so with collective memories of a public kind where the remembrance process is carried out by a whole community. War memories constitute one important element of a publicly based kind of collective memories. It is thus not surprising that the way this set of memories is portrayed is highly dependent on the political climate of the community or nation state at that point in time and on how the dominant communities manipulate it to ensure political control.

Likewise, within the diasporic community, the dominant faction often wields much control and dominates the selection of elements for memorial reproduction. As such, there is often a struggle between different groups who contest to rewrite the memories of their community and gain ascendancy on cultural and mnemonic interpretation. There may be a notion of an authentic Chineseness but within the diasporic Chinese community the notion of whose Chineseness is authentic and questions authenticity as unmediated and genuine. Written Chinese language, for example, provides a sharp divide among diasporic Chinese migrants with Simplified Chinese characters replacing Classical, marginalizing migrants coming now from Hong Kong and Taiwan.

Memory, as Yelvington (2002, p. 236) cogently notes, 'is often used quite loosely' and too frequently is invoked 'as an unproblematic, possessable, recollection of an authentic past'. We concur with Koopmans et al. (2005, p. 114) that there is no primordial identity and thus no unchallenged and stable memories. On the contrary, memory functions within social, collective circumstances (Halbwachs 1992), and thus are imaginative reconstructions that bear the friction of cross-cutting structured processes. Here ethnicity, gender, generation and regional circumstances suggest difference in the way memories are recalled, articulated and situate meaning. Chinese (however defined) while perhaps coming by similar routes certainly do not possess a singularity of roots. Thus, 'cross-cultural memories are not only due to differences in interests, but also in differences in the way things are recalled' (Yelvington 2002). By representing distinct and different interpretations of the past, migrants re-member themselves differently in the diasporic community. Here 'identities appear as sites of transit between layers of historical experience' (Mageo 2001, p. 2), cross-cut with hierarchies of gender, generation, and regional interests. With respect to generation, for example, each cohort must reinterpret memories in forms that are most suitable to them, and each fashions an identity most appropriate to them.

In conjunction with these, class situation also affects variant migration outcomes that shape, discipline and position the way migrants think and act. While not seeking to reprivilege class or invoke the structuralist eschatology associated with earlier class theories (see, for example, Poulantzas 1975; Wright 1985), accounts of class relations are important (see, for example, Anthias 1998, 2001a, b). The hegemonic postmodern discourse on culture and identity needs to be reopened to materialist accounts of social and economic inequality and the complex intersections of variant hierarchies of power. Somewhere at the linguistic turn material accounts (i.e. class) have been jettisoned with the privileging of cultural discourse. Nevertheless, that class has seemingly fallen from grace is surprising in a world where capitalism is now global in stretch and so much of social life is commoditized. Thus a corresponding set of identity demands addressing class issues that goes to the core of social inequality and exclusion and thus the continuous unfolding of the geometries of power relations. As Anthias (2001a, p. 368) so coherently argues, we need to 'rethink social stratification away from the polarity between the material and the symbolic, and argue that material inequality, as a set of outcomes relating to life conditions, life chances and solidary processes, is informed by claims and struggles over resources of different types, undertaken in terms of gender, ethnicity/race, and class' and to which we add, generational difference.

So too with the politics of memory and identity. As within the larger nation state, interpreting memories that locate identity represent sites of conflict and contestation. These challenge the national embeddedness of identity, point to the stretch of memory across national borders, and underscore the need to understand the forces of differentiation within the diasporic communities. Such a project enables a more nuanced understanding of diasporic communities.

Overview

This collection explores individual and collective memory and its role in identity construction through the lived experiences of Chinese migrants, the places they create in space, and how time tempers self and society. In many respects, this collection is eclectic in that it does not include specific nation states, most notably the United States and Great Britain. This omission is purposeful as there are a large number of books, volume collections and articles that do so. Instead we focus on areas that have been under-researched. Moreover, two chapters do not deal with diasporic communities in the nation state but explore the Chinese diaspora and issues of identity and memory through discursive text and film whose interplay imposes new silences while pointing to new directions.

What the chapters share in common is the expression of memories as a connection between collective and individual identities, and between origins, heritage and history. Memory clearly has an impact on our identities, but identities also reconstruct the recollection of memories. This dialectic of memory and identity is punctuated by the all too familiar question typically asked of any migrant: 'Where do you come from?' Responses vary, but inevitably provide an image of origin, but an origin filtered through the lens of the present home such that the diasporic individual frequently has a double consciousness of belonging. The essays in this volume reflect on the movements of diasporic Chinese and the diverse experiences of the diasporic communities in several countries.

Four chapters pick up on this theme through examining diasporic communities in Australia. Davidson explores the interplay between identity and memory and how diasporic migrants devise a sense of belonging. For Ip, this stretch of home is noted as transnationalism and how diasporic communities often project themselves in relation to specific origins that do not inevitably weaken transnational connections such that identity construction and its management are in fact globalized. Lalich analyses the importance of communal built environment – sites – for the perception of Chineseness and the significance of community organizations for stabilizing and refixing identity. Diasporic communities are different, especially over time, as Ngan notes in her chapter on third- and fourth-generation Chinese migrants through her use of hybrid identities. Davidson and Dai deploy memory work to develop an understanding of how immigration policy influenced Chinese movements to New Zealand and analyses their strategies and transnational social networks that facilitated migration.

Although some theorists suggest that we are in an era of globalization that undermines any concern with roots, Kuah-Pearce examines how the Fujianese Chinese in Singapore negotiate their memories and narrate their social experiences and argues that these memories propel them to reproduce what they regard as desirable social values and 'authentic' Chinese culture. Choi turns her attention to South Korea and traces the manner in which perceptions of China and the presence of a Chinese diaspora in Korea at the turn of the twentieth century influenced the development of Korean awareness of 'self' and 'other'. Clammer focuses on the complex intersections where memory and belonging are forged, and where notions of space, place and time converge. He details the relations between contemporary Chinese communities and the Japanese out of which have emerged or been constructed both memories and narratives of exile and belonging, as well as the gendered aspects of Chinese settlement in Japan and the ways in which this influences social memory.

Migration is as much about mobility as it is home-making, as both a subjective sense of belonging as well as the ability and opportunity to secure a living. From this premise, Leung probes the diverse nature and functions of memories and nostalgia in the negotiation of belonging and sense of home among Chinese migrants in contemporary Germany. Accone and Harris, through the use of narratives, illustrate the absence of a sense of belonging of the Chinese diasporic community in South

Africa throughout its turbulent history. As they note, during the build-up to and during the rule of apartheid they were not white enough, while now they are not sufficiently black.

Lee's reading of text illuminates how signifying practices of memory are mediated through the specific mechanisms of identification and recognition that are produced in the intimate interaction of gender and generation. She further argues that the result can be a fractured psychological state, in which the individual cannot find a confirmed orientation to feel a sense of belonging. Then too she notes that understanding the value of human contact more than one's original culture as a shaping force in the understanding of identity. Cheung examines two major patterns of Chinese diasporas, both of which focus on Hong Kong as the focal location of dispersal and gathering. Through 'musical landscape' which moves across geopolitical boundaries, she deftly argues that while diaspora is intimately associated with the development of a cosmopolitan consciousness, a study of Hong Kong films shows how a sense of belonging is negotiated by the flows of different cultural artefacts in a transnational context.

References

Alexander, A. and Knowles, C. (eds) 2005, *Making Race Matter: Bodies, Space and Identity*, Palgrave Macmillan, New York.

Alexander, M. 2003, 'Local Policies toward Migrants as an Expression of Host–Stranger Relations: a Proposed Typology', *Journal of Ethnic and Migration Studies*, vol. 29, no. 3, pp. 411–30.

Anderson, B. 1991, *Imagined Communities: Reflections on the Origin and Spread of Nationalism*, revised and extended edn, Verso Books, London.

Anthias, F. 1998, 'Evaluating "Diaspora": beyond Ethnicity', *Sociology*, vol. 32, no. 3, pp. 557–81.

Anthias, F. 2001a, 'The Material and the Symbolic in Theorizing Social Stratification: Issues of Gender, Ethnicity and Class', *British Journal of Sociology*, vol. 52, no. 3, pp. 367–90.

Anthias, F. 2001b, 'New Hybridities, Old Concepts: the Limits of "Culture"', *Ethnic and Racial Studies*, vol. 24, no. 4, pp. 619–41.

Bhabha, H. 1990, *Nation and Narration*, Routledge, London.

Brubaker, R. 2005, 'The "Diaspora" Diaspora', *Ethnic and Racial Studies*, vol. 28, no. 1, pp. 1–19.

Cattell, M. and Climo, J. 2002, 'Introduction: Meaning in Social Memory: Anthropological Perspectives', in J. Climo and M. Cattell (eds), *Social Memory and History: Anthropological Perspectives*, Altamira Press, Walnut Creek, pp. 1–38.

Clifford, J. 1997, 'Diasporas', in J. Clifford (ed.), *Routes: Travel and Translation in the Late Twentieth Century*, Cambridge University Press, Cambridge, London, pp. 244–77.

Dunn, R. 1998, *Identity Crisis: a Social Critique of Postmodernity*, University of Minnesota Press, Minneapolis.

Gilroy, P. 1993, *The Black Atlantic: Modernity and Double Consciousness*, Harvard University Press, Cambridge, London.

Halbwachs, M. 1992, *On Collective Memory*, Chicago University Press, Chicago.

Heinke, J. n.d., *Georg Simmel, Strangeness, and the Stranger*, viewed 14 Nov. 2006 <http://www.postcolonialweb.org/australia/malouf/jh2.html> .

Koopmans, R., Straham, P., Giugni, M. and Passy, F. 2005, *Contested Citizenship: Immigration and Diversity in Europe*, University of Minnesota Press, Minneapolis.

Kuah-Pearce, K.E. 2006, 'Transnational Self in the Chinese Diaspora: a Conceptual Framework', *Asian Studies Review*, vol. 30, no. 3, pp. 223–39.

Mageo, J.M. (ed.) 2001, *Cultural Memory: Reconfiguring History and Identity in the Postcolonial Pacific*, University of Hawaii Press, Honolulu.

Mudrooroo, N. 1990, *Writing from the Fringe: a Study of Modern Aboriginal Literature*, Hyland House, Melbourne.

Poulantzas, N. 1975, *Classes in Contemporary Capitalism*, trans. D. Fernbach, NLB, London.

Song, M. 2005, 'Global and Local Articulations of Asian Identity', in A. Alexander and C. Knowles (eds), *Making Race Matter: Bodies, Space and Identity*, Palgrave Macmillan, New York, pp. 60–75.

Stratton, J. and Ang, I. 1994, 'Multicultural Imagined Communities: Cultural Difference and National Identity in Australia and the USA', *Continuum: the Australian Journal of Media and Culture*, vol. 8, no. 2, pp. 124–58 < http://wwwmcc.murdoch.edu.au/ReadingRoom/8.2/Stratton.html > .

Werbner, P. and Modood, T. 1997, *Debating Cultural Hybridity: Multi-Cultural Identities and the Politics of Anti-Racism*, Zed Press, London.

Wright, N. 1985, *Classes*, Verso, London.

Yelvington, K. 2002, 'History, Memory and Identity: a Programmatic Prolegomenon', *Critique of Anthropology*, vol. 22, no. 3, pp. 227–56.

2

The Play of Identity, Memory and Belonging: Chinese Migrants in Sydney

Andrew P. Davidson

> I think in my heart, I know I will never live there (Shanghai) permanently, but it is still in my dreams, in my memories. But Australia, I feel like I am just living here. That is a very strange feeling.
>
> Interview with Mai (2003)

Reality is a mercurial construct, fixed by what a person knows and, perhaps more importantly, by what they believe. In a world that is constantly changing, people are confronted with the social events, occurrences and circumstances of quotidian life that demand to be situated, made sense of. Whatever people experience is given signification and representation that prises a play 'between objective givenness and subjective meanings ... constituted by the reciprocal interaction of what is experienced as outside reality ... and what is experienced as being within the consciousness of the individual' (Berger et al. 1974, p. 12). It is in this sense that migration is powerfully evocative of the ambiguities and contradictions of beginnings and ends, the fixity and efflorescence of cultural identities, and sense of belonging and dislocation. Migration is strategically interruptive, decentring the boundaries and borders of place and identity. The capricious swirl of movement is what defines the migrant while masking an elusive paradox of being and becoming, polysemy and multivocality, alterity and mimesis. Nevertheless, locally defined contexts produce a range of strategic choices and attendant pragmatic frameworks by which subject-actors – migrants – make sense of the world around them as well as their fit in that locally defined world (Chun 1996). In other words, migrants negotiate a feeling of belonging based on their perceptions and memories of their social situations.

It is in the migrant's world that we begin to navigate the ambiguities of movement and identity, and with how migrants locate a sense of belonging, contest boundaries and attempt new spaces of identity and control for themselves in the 'host' country. The construction and configuration of identities have significant import for migrants, for their feelings of belonging and in their adjustment process in their new 'homes'. Unquestionably, memories – fragmentary moments – provide an intimate means of connecting a migrant's life worlds, in dealing with homesickness, security, social dissonance and cultural dislocation. Memory fragments, however, are not simply disassociated shards of past events but are actively (re)constructed to provide a new take on the old, (re)fashioned to provide a different perspective. In other words, memories are not static but are dynamic, emergent, and produced interactionally in the dialogical interlude between subject and location and as such impel a recursive relationship between the personal and the social.

But just how do migrants begin to feel at home and develop a sense of self, including a sense of belonging? As Amit-Talai (1998) reminds us, home is not a matter of being stationary but of being centred, creating a personal space of identification and belonging. This chapter raises questions about the notion of 'home' and belonging in its various and contradictory representations. It also poses questions about memory and how memories interpolate migrant motives, adjustments and desires and under what conditions and contingencies. Memories, after all, are the stuff of dreams as well as the substance of nightmares, they comprise representations of the past, provide signification of the present and open portals into the future. It is through cultural, symbolic, personal and collective memories that migrants derive a framework of meaning and locate a sense of belonging, and of identity. And in this study, with the role Chinese migrants play in their own migration, specifically with how migrants deploy memories through an interrogation of agency, discourse and practice in an effort to elucidate the role of memories in shaping the migration experience. It should also be noted, that while not all Chinese (People's Republic of China, hereafter referred to as PRC) can be considered diasporic, many can. But here we are not interested in diasporic numbers but in diaspora as a process and social construction such that the play of memory and identity provide a sense of belonging.

This chapter explores the migration experiences of Chinese migrants in Sydney, Australia. The limited nature of the sample, particularly its size and lack of representativeness, militates against making strong claims, however suggestive. The chapter is based on in-depth interviews with 16 female and 12 male migrants and proceeds with a dialogical approach rather than a monological narrative. As Bakhtin (1981, p. 284) insightfully notes, 'Discourse lives on the boundary between its own context and another, alien context' and that 'verbal discourse is a social phenomenon – social throughout its entire range ...' (Bakhtin 1981, p. 259). Moreover, dialogic practice entails an interplay between critique and reflexivity, turning both inwards and outwards, replacing 'self-effacement ... with a heightened self-consciousness – not to indulge our narcissism but to look squarely at our own relationship to our research' (Bucholtz 2001, p. 181). This approach assisted in enabling a more nuanced understanding of how Chinese migrants derive a feeling of belonging in the coalescence of identity flows that occurs in the spaces of memory.

Context

Chinese have a long history of migration (Chan 1999; Skeldon 1996; Wang 1991). Few countries do not have at least a small ethnic Chinese population (Brown and Foot 1994); Australia is no exception. Of particular interest is that the Chinese-born population continues to concentrate in large cities, primarily Sydney (56.2 per cent) and Melbourne (24.8 per cent) (DIMIA 2002). Nevertheless, in spite of a higher educational level and better qualifications, the labour force participation of China-born migrants is relatively low compared with the total Australian population (DIMIA 2003). One reason for this is that their level of English proficiency is relatively low; 44.1 per cent do not speak English well or speak no English (DIMIA 2002). Compounding adjustment difficulties, the educational qualifications of migrants are not always recognized and tertiary-trained workers often end up in menial jobs, find it necessary to retrain, or resit part of their degrees. Of course racism, both manifest and subtle, also cannot be discounted.

Of greater interest is the fact the majority of Chinese migrants entering Australia during the 1990s were females, migrating increasingly as single immigrants (DIMIA 2002). And although the role social networks play in facilitating migration is well documented, until recent years insufficient attention has been accorded to women's participation in migration, particularly with their actual experiences. When women migrate, for too long it was assumed that they did so as dependants of males or that they tapped into already established male networks (Huang et al. 2000; Kelson and Delaet 1999; Pessar and Mahler 2001). On the contrary, the number of single Chinese female migrants has surpassed that of males. While some Chinese male migrants leave Australia, probably to return to China, Chinese women seem more reluctant to do so. We do not believe that this can be relegated simply to a fear of 'loss of face' but perhaps what keeps these Chinese women migrants in Sydney, and despite the hardships faced by many, are the local social situations and opportunity structures, as well as 'escape' from the social constraints placed on middle-aged single women in China. As Min Tze (a middle-aged respondent) commented:

> Chinese men are stubborn, they are not as flexible as women, and they cannot change themselves to meet new situations. And besides, Chinese men can always go back [to PRC] and marry a younger woman, women can't do that. And they [men] may get help from the family [when they return], we don't usually, they think we should have a husband taking care of us, or be independent. Not a burden to the family.

Stereotypes and the play of cultural identities

> The stranger is ... the person who comes today and stays tomorrow. He is, so to speak, the *potential* wanderer: although he has not moved on, he has not quite overcome the freedom of coming and going. He is fixed within a particular spatial group, or within a group ... But his position in this group is determined, essentially, by the fact that he has not belonged to it from the beginning, that he imports qualities into it, which do not and cannot stem from the group itself.
>
> Simmel (1950, p. 402)

Discourse is generally used to designate the forms of representation, codes, conventions and habits of language that produce specific fields of culturally and historically located meanings. As Chun (1996, p. 115) perceptively notes, 'The self-effacing character of cultural discourse, in spite of its obvious authorial nature, is precisely what makes identity appear to be a value-free construct, when in actuality it is quite the opposite.' In other words, 'successful' discourse is that which is not critically encountered consciously in daily activity, its edicts are taken as given, as commonsensical – naturalized. Thus, in the end what matters is that which people believe to be true and how these 'self-evident truths' are employed in the course of their everyday lives. While it is important to understand how identity is socially constituted and constructed, it is equally germane to ask how and under what circumstances certain identities are invoked. And for our purpose, what types of memories trigger, reify and validate those identities.

Having said this, we take up the challenge of exploring cultural identities through the disjuncture between discursive construct and historical practice. It is, after all, in the play of history, culture and power where migrants derive their understanding of 'who they are' and 'what is possible'. Identities are relational and inherently political and consequently address issues relating to power inequities, representations and their effects on migrants' understanding of home and attendant feelings of belonging. Identities, as Hall (1997) reminds us, 'are constructed through, not outside, difference'. Then, too, identities require recognition and validation by others (Taylor 1992). More often than not this involves some form of stereotyping which entails questions of representation and discourses of power, imposing order on an unruly social world, fixing meaning and significance as natural and given (Pickering 2001). In his efforts to come to terms with the contingencies of being 'Australian Chinese', William Yang (2001, p. 29) comments: 'People tend to think that their attitudes and ideas come from some kind of innate instinct or are guided by divine power, when really they are more the result of cultural conditioning, and often quite biased. I support multiculturalism and a diverse society.' But while there is no balance sheet of what person is what identity(ies), nevertheless stereotypes flourish, people continue to tenaciously cling to their defining contours and routinely categorize, and in this ideational moment accept or dismiss through the cultural genealogies such labels invoke. As an issue of ethnic supplementarity, the concept of Chineseness is one such powerful, albeit at times subtle, stereotype (see, for example, Ang 2001; Chow 1998; Chun 1996). The point of the matter is that terms (or labels) are important in that they culturally and ideationally locate the subject, fix them.

Although the migrants in this study came to Australia from afar, they were not unknown prior to their arrival; their Chineseness preceded them. Within Australia, there is 'longevity of the Orientalist perception of Asia as female, submissive, emotional, immoral, alluring, repulsive, exploitable, and treacherous ...' (Broinowski 1992, p. 201). In response to a question about pejorative stereotyping, Ching, another young male migrant replied:

> Yes indeed. Take the SARS situation. This disease isn't something that every Chinese person carried just because they're Chinese. It's a disease, the one thing that doesn't discriminate against race or religion. Everyone was susceptible to it if they're exposed to it. Most of the other times, I like to think otherwise, but the occasional instances of prejudiced mindsets helped keep that view in check.

Or in the words of Chinyin, a young female migrant:

> Do you remember this rather old movie, *Big Trouble in Little China*? Chinese having magical powers, able to fly and cast fireballs and

lightning bolts onto their enemies? All within this secret dimension called Chinatown? And of course, the evil Asian warlord tried to turn two white beautiful ladies into his consorts, placing them in huge costumes and painted faces, making them look like geishas. Or the phenomenal rise of *Crouching Tiger, Hidden Dragon* with Chinese flying from roof to roof.... Talk about exoticising Orientalism.

Images of and Chinese as outsiders, not 'real' or 'authentic' Australians, never seems far from the surface. Of course it is not a simple straightforward matter but reflects the complexity of Australian culture itself. Certainly the last vestiges of the 'White Australia Policy' have been swept away. Now 'racism' is far more subtle. Although Pauline Hansen's 'One Nation' was overtly culturally exclusive, John Howard's migration policy developed a differentiation based on categories of neo-liberalism; wealthy and highly educated entrepreneurs or professionals are welcomed while poor, displaced or uneducated Asians such as Afghanis and Iraqis refused entry. Then too there is a political split between the conservative and rural 'bush' and the few major cities identified with Australia's 'multiculturalism' policies. This imprints on the particular shaping of the Australian immigration regime and hence on the disciplining of migrants it implies. One critical consequence is the tension between Australian neo-liberalism and the state's multiculturalism policies to the effect that cultural difference is highlighted, and not always in a positive way (e.g. Sydney's Lebanese community). Another male migrant bitterly complained about recurrent themes of the 'yellow peril' and 'white panic' underlying Australian Orientalist discourse:

> Let us not forget how in a not so recent past countries like Australia and America imposed restrictions on immigration to prevent themselves from being 'swamped' by Chinese. Considering that the Chinese and other Asian cultures and societies see themselves being swamped by Westerners, they impose their values on us and buy up local businesses, or force traditional businesses out from the market. Asian societies have in many ways, already been swamped and overwhelmed by the West. Which is worse? To have 2 to 5 percent of Australia's population be Asian and the rest screaming that you are swamped by them, or to have another culture force their movies, their copyright laws, their businesses and food and dressing and laws right into your face?

Nevertheless, stereotyping, pejorative or otherwise, is not the sole prerogative of 'Mr White Man'. An understanding of the potency of

Chineseness and attendant stereotyping would not be complete without recourse to recurrent sets of stereotypes among the migrants. As Rey Chow (1998, p. 6) argues, Chineseness resonates as a 'habitual obsession' among many Chinese – what she terms 'sinocentricism' – such that 'Everything Chinese ... is fantasized as somehow better – longer in existence, more intelligent, more scientific, more valuable, and ultimately beyond comparison.' This flips over and turns into derogatory accounts of an essentialized Australian. A number of migrants interviewed considered the 'typical' Australian as 'lazy', 'coarse', 'drinks too much' and 'too laid-back, they don't think about the future and save money' (of course there were positive stereotypes as well). It is this recourse to stereotypes that reifies difference within multicultural societies and essentializes ideational attributes.

The stretch of home and the quest to belong

At first glance, the concepts of home and belonging seem paradoxically at odds with the world of movement, swept away in the currents of distance and time. Both 'home' and 'belonging' represent imaginings that are at once both spatially expressed and emotively realized. Home traditionally has been located as the lived experience of locality, the place (home) where one usually lives and typically inferred consanguine relations (Rapport and Dawson 1998). To the contrary, the concept 'home' must be opened up in explorations of space in terms of social relations (Massey 1994) such that identities are then constructed through a complex of social relations within overlapping spaces and places (Ryan 2003). As Keith and Pile (1993, p. 4) note, 'space cannot be dealt with as if it were merely a passive, abstract arena on which things happen'. Similarly, Massey (1994, p. 3) argues that such a way of conceptualizing the spatial, and by implication home, 'inherently implies the existence of a simultaneous multiplicity of spaces: cross-cutting, intersecting, aligning with one another, or existing in relations of paradox or antagonism'. This understanding of space enables home as spatiality to be stretched, to be multifocal, in that people conceptualize and act on different contexts of home, and thus are connected to 'home' through variant social relations. Precisely because of its slipperiness, notions of home can be unfixed, contested and multiple.

The migrant, embodied and imagined, condenses our concerns with identity, home and the politics of belonging. For the Chinese migrants in this chapter, identity formation and reiteration involve the interplay of narratives of belonging and feelings of home. How home is deployed in migration narratives, how it is continuously worked on, reimagined and redefined, speaks to the poetics of belonging. Home as 'where we feel we belong' is a 'thick' concept, a panoply of performances that can serve to encapsulate while they transcend and link. And the particularity of feelings of belonging of home is constructed not by fixing its location in space and defining it through contrapuntal positioning to the other home left which lies beyond, but in interconnections that are open and porous (Fortier 2003). Feelings of home and belonging translocate the migrant both within Australia and China. Thus at any moment in the migration trajectory tensions are realized in different orders of home as well as different feelings of belonging. Nevertheless, in the images and relations of 'everyday home', 'roots', 'stability' and 'security' coloured the language of the migrants. And while home is both here and there, their lives are, for the most part, centred in Sydney. Interestingly, most of the migrants derived a sense of home and belonging to Sydney and not Australia (as a nation state), explaining in part the general reluctance of many Chinese migrants to take up Australian citizenship. Here too we see again the tensions played out in multiculturalism where some migrants are 'included out'.

But for Chinese migrants, at stake is how to find belonging, a sense of being at home, within the historical dominance and economic power of (male) Anglo-Celtic Australia. Migrants may, at least initially, draw on other Chinese for a sense of belonging in meaningful but diverse signifiers such as Shenzhen, Canton, China (and in its broader usage including Hong Kong, Macau and Taiwan) and Asia. This raises to the fore issues of essentialism and nationalism as framed in the discursive practice of national identity (or Chineseness). As in Derrida's (1988) notion of citationality, 'Chineseness' becomes an identity through its inerrability, through the reproducibility of 'cultural actions' in new contexts; in other words, remembering. In one respondent's words (a young female student):

> Many Chinese people like to often get together and have big lunches ... dinner parties. Usually it can happen from once a month to once a week. Groups of good old friends that they would have known for many years, and all are immigrants from China or Hong Kong. They gather together with their children to these parties normally at one particular family's house. Majority of the women/mothers play mahjong, four to a table and while they play, they talk about their work lives ... The other women/mothers will prepare Chinese tea and tea cake which is made of rice. Usually the tea is made by the mothers and brought around to the men and other adults by their younger daughters or sons. The men get together and talk about their work ... They get together to play Big Two, which is well known to all Chinese. Even if

> you were 12 you would be playing this game with children around your age. Dinner is usually served on a big table, and everyone takes turns to go to the table and get their dinner ... It is a very exciting time for all that participate in the gatherings ... because Chinese like to gossip and whine about their hard working lives and show off their wealth and lifestyle. These gatherings are very important to Chinese migrants. They like to stick in groups of old friends; some have known each other before they arrived in Australia. But they know each other anyway because all are migrants and have similar problems.

Remembering marks an awareness of the past in the present, creating a new 'narrative ordering of dispersed, disparate and perhaps unrelated events and personages to form a coherent, authoritative story' (Yelvington 2002, p. 235). It stretches while it redefines the boundaries of home. Similarly, Li Ping commented that all of her friends were Chinese or at least Asian as '["white"] Australians don't understand us. I don't feel comfort[able] with them, and they don't [with] us.' But while a sense of ethnic identity may recentre the migrant, it can also act as a straightjacket delimiting the range of possibilities (see, for example, Ang 2001). In the end, home and feelings of belonging are more a thing of relationships than physicality or territory.

The point is, although 'we feel we belong in our culture, because it constitutes a home of natural embeddedness and unthinking attachment – familiarity *tout court*' (Hedetoft 2002, p. 8), feelings of social disjuncture can lead to individual or collective 'soul searching', 'questionings that dissolve frozen identity images and fixed ideas about what people are or should be like' (Mageo 2001, p. 13). Thus, the stretch of home as the pull of Chineseness or the home of originary family is not infinitely elastic. Rather than invoke any essential identity of an individual or by the a priori privileging of any particular process of identity formation, the continuous transformation and vertiginous display of identities suggest a more complex and agonistic quest for belonging (Dean 1998). Rather it can be discontinuous and fractured. Tiffany felt much more at ease – 'at home', 'belong' – with non-Asian (especially non-Chinese) Australians:

> Chinese are always judging, too critical. I want to be independent, live my own life. My parents always treat me as a child, I hate it. I feel good visiting them but am happy when I come home [to Sydney]. And when I go back to China, I don't understand the people anymore. Everything is too different. Even my friends, they are like strangers. After a short time, nothing to talk about. Yes, it is always good to come home.

Lionel also had strong feelings of belonging to his new 'home', relating stories to me of sitting in the pub with friends, drinking a beer and watching rugby or cricket as is typical among many Australian men.

Then too this process of belonging is articulated through the availability and use of resources. Eventually migrants must find their way without a safety net or the chance of returning to the originary 'home'. What mediates and modifies the experience of migration is the first important social network within Australia – for many, the English class and/or the first job in a restaurant, invariably a Chinese restaurant. Here migrants from all over the world develop 'transethnic alliances' (Anthias 2001) and with different experiences share information about employment, housing, visas, government benefits and so on. While learning to speak English adequately proved too difficult for some, the information received from fellow English language students proved more invaluable than government services designed to assist new migrants. Migrants need to be able to adapt to multiple social circumstances, including cross-cultural competence (Castles 2002) in order to develop feelings of belonging. It is here where class position generally matters.

Not surprisingly, those migrants with better access to material resources typically had an easier time in 'adjusting', 'feeling at home', 'belonging'. San Teh stays with the daughter of his mother's sister's business partner in Sydney. Although a skilled carpenter his wages are not very good and he is struggling financially. He is resentful of everyone, especially those Chinese that are 'doing well'. He had been working in Japan for 10 years but with an expired visa he had to return to Nanjing. A man of 48, he does not want to return to Shanghai. Growing up during the tumultuous Cultural Revolution, he received little formal education and would be unable to secure a 'good job'. He feels isolated, alone. Without financial security, the dream of a better life can easily be replaced with feelings of despair, disillusionment and cynicism. On the other hand, Lu's parents provided him and his wife with the finances to purchase an apartment and buy an automobile. Although they are both students, they have scholarships and periodically receive additional funds from their parents. For them, 'Sydney is a very nice city. And it will be a good place to raise children. The air is clean and people are very friendly. We feel good here, it is a better life than back in Beijing.'

Issues of security repeatedly arose in discussions of belonging with migrants, especially with matters of financial security. Without some sense of economic security, migrants can experience significant stress and alienation, with both the wider Australian and Chinese Australian communities. The struggle to gain access to material resources is particularly acute among newcomers. Once in Australia, migrants can face an almost bewildering variety of 'blocks'. The English and educational skills Chinese migrants have in some respects are reflected in the occupations in which they work. With marginal English language skills, some migrants find themselves confined to low-paying unskilled jobs, even though they may have earned a tertiary degree and had job experience in China. Retraining or recredentializing, however, is rarely an easy decision, not only in terms of real costs and missed opportunities, but in anticipating the needs of the job market. Interestingly, older-aged females are more apt to return to school whereas males are more reluctant to study or quit before the completion of their degree.

Kim worked as an engineer in China and was married to a businessman. Both were divorced and each had one child. Kim, the primary immigrant applicant, moved with her husband and two daughters (the elder one is her stepdaughter) to New Zealand with the assistance of a migration agency. Lacking tertiary education qualifications, Kim's husband set up a small car repair garage. Unable to speak English, his business was restricted to Chinese speakers. Kim, on the other hand, enrolled in a language school and completed a year of English. Kim's marriage deteriorated as she fought continuously with her husband over his 'lack of ambition'. They divorced and Kim moved to Wellington with her daughter and began studying office administration. Her husband and his daughter returned to China. She met her new partner and they migrated to Australia. Kim's husband lost his job with the global economic downturn and after a few months of being unemployed, he too returned to China. Kim recently bought a small house-cleaning company. Her daughter went back to China to live with her ex-husband and now Kim lives alone. She supplements her income by renting one of the rooms in her flat and still claims unemployment family benefits. Without relatives in the area and only a few friends, Kim feels especially isolated and marginalized. In the words of Ching Man: 'It is difficult. I am a good accountant. I have experience. But the men in the office, they get the opportunities, they get the promotions. It makes me angry.'

For many the connection between belonging and monetary 'success' is unassailable. Yan is a 38-year-old divorced mother of one. She closed her small clothing trading company in Guangzhou and migrated to Sydney with her daughter to join her second husband. 'Even though my second husband had a home electrical installation certificate from TAFE, he never found a suitable job.' They currently rent a house and have started a small home business. 'I am working as a receptionist for my husband at home and so can also look after my stepson and daughter.

We earn about $1000 a week after tax. That is enough for us and I do not need to use my saving anymore.' Without English language skills, Yan found that it is hard to live in Sydney. 'I attended an English course in TAFE and meet lots of friends in the class. But my 12 year old daughter did not like living in Sydney, she misses her father and I had to send her to back to China. I miss her very much. It is a pain I live with.' Saving money to buy a house is Yan's sole working purpose now and rationale for staying in Australia.

The migrants' lives are not per se a struggle for social, economic or cultural justice, but an individual quest for opportunity and thus survival. Like Yan, Liu was a divorced 37-year-old woman with an 11-year-old daughter. Liu was introduced by her friend to her second husband, a taxi driver in Sydney. He was originally from Shanghai but migrated to Australia 10 years before as a student. Liu left her daughter with her parents in China and came to Sydney. 'I spent more than $200,000 dollars to buy this four bedroom house in Blacktown three years ago,' Liu said. She rents out three rooms but after making the mortgage payments finds there is little left. 'I can't look for a job, I have to do the cleaning, gardening and look after my three year old son at home. My husband is studying part-time, a computer course at UTS (University of Technology, Sydney), and works as a taxi driver on the weekend.' Liu intends to take an English course soon. 'I will try to find a good job. I want to save some money for my daughter. She might come in a few years when she is 16. If I had enough money I would sell this house and buy another near Ashfield. I would prefer to live in a Chinese community and look for an area where there is good education for my children.' What these three stories reveal is the power of home as house ownership and community as focal points of security and thus feelings of belonging.

The opaqueness of memory and the plasticity of imagined identity

> To be without a memory is to risk being without identity.
>
> McQuire (1998, p. 168)

Feelings of belonging are neither unsituated nor pure; rather they are also filtered through memories which shape an individual's images and perceptions of belonging by engendering meaning (Hedetoft 2002, p. 2) and thus facilitate the translocational stretch between here and there, however lasting or fleeting. Here memories weave together the multiple loci of home. Thinking in terms of memory also confronts an important element of power and releases memory from historiography in that memory is not about closure but enables people to reconceptualize and renegotiate the present, to 're-member' themselves. Lives, in other words, are made socially cohesive and imbued with meaning by the practice of memory. In the act of remembering, memory is renegotiated and reconstructed, allowing the individual self to merge into the social or collective self of the community.

People are everywhere acting on different memories but as sentient beings, memories are invariably suffused with emotions. Anthropological approaches to emotions typically define 'emotions as functional realms of action, as socially constructed categories, as culturally specific narratives, as evaluative judgements, and as ideological discourses which may reinforce power relations' (Svašek 2002, p. 10). According to Abu-Lughod and Lutz (1990, p. 15), 'emotional discourses are implicated in the play of power and the operation of a historically changing system of social hierarchy'. It is in the simultaneity or dialectical interplay between memory and emotion, the past and present, where events and practices are placed in relation to each other in such a way that new possibilities or futures are opened up (or closed down). The organization of memories, like emotions, is integral to the production of the social and not simply the results. Memories and emotions are therefore fully implicated in the migration experience, in the strategies devised to navigate the journey, palliatives to soothe the angst of the unfamiliar, signposts to situate the dislocated, and sinews for the ties that bind.

Memories can be seen in social interaction, triggered by social impulses and social play. Among most migrants in this study, migration was preceded by daydreaming; in the first instance the 'myth of elsewhere', or Australia. Excessive imagining constructed and directed the myth of elsewhere (Davidson 2004). Often this assumed the form of a type of romantic *Weltschmerz*, or painful encounter between the individual and their immediate world, engendering an emotive force; in this sense, releasing a homesickness for a place one has never been, a life potential that has not yet been realized. The imaginary world of elsewhere, here Australia, certainly played the sirens' song beckoning Chinese migrants to Sydney. For these migrants, when they were in China the imaginary world of elsewhere invoked a myriad of *If only I were* ... The myth of elsewhere, loosely assembled from afar, blurs the edges of fact and fiction, creating nascent memories where none existed. If memory cannot be forced, it wells up in sudden takes like little snippets from the cutting room floor, that are shot through with emotions and desire, what (Appadurai 1996) refers to as 'imagined nostalgia'. Memories too are refracted through local lenses so that Australia becomes the perceptual inverse of China. What was striking about the migrants' stories was the singular image of elsewhere as a better place than China to live and raise a family, an imagined world brimming with endless possibilities and unbridled opportunities in almost legendary proportions. The myth of elsewhere evoked desires and promised fulfilment of these. Stories of Chinese migrants living in Australia who were successful (earning high salaries and enjoying a modern lifestyle) were taken as the norm, stories of failure dismissed as individual shortcomings. In one migrant's words, Australia represented freedom of 'imagination' and 'being', as well as a surfeit of material promise – 'a golden garden' where 'life is easy', the 'golden mountain' where you can 'mine gold, become rich' (this has a long history among Chinese migrants in general). In many respects then, the myth of elsewhere was a reaction to compelling situations of symbolic immobility or, in fact, downwards mobility.

Finding home, fixing memories

> When 'leaving home' is the condition of possibility for finding a 'real' home, moving home establishes a clear distinction between the initial site of estrangement – home as not-home – and home as a new site of possibility.
>
> Fortier (2003, p. 8)

Changes in memories can present an entirely different set of expectations and understanding of present realities. It is through the myth of elsewhere that individuals construct and legitimate their desire (and thus compelling need) to migrate. Myths, or stories, rumours, images and disparate facts, are woven together into memories and thus there is frequently a tension within memories, between the interplay of perception and deception. The particular coalescence of memory flows that occur in given individuals is unique. It is possible, in the context of this discussion, to trace a line from memories addressing individual life crises to memories that involve family, lovers, community and nation states, illuminating the 'subjective meanings of historical experience' (Thompson 1999, p. 33). Jas, for example, recalled an early memory from 1966 when she was a little girl in Shanghai. Her mother was publicly criticized during the Cultural Revolution and was made to publicly wear a sign denouncing her 'sin' as a revisionist. Every night for a few months her mother returned home late following nightly readings of Mao's thoughts to exculpate her lack of revolutionary fervour. 'We never spoke about that time but the memory was always there. It always hurts me, makes me too sad.' In fact, most of the older migrants had unsettling memories of life during the Cultural Revolution and prior to the 'loosening up' of the economy. Miao, for example, was a successful entrepreneur back in Shanghai but was always fearful she would 'catch the eye' of the authorities as she lacked the necessary political connections and official papers. She eventually left in 1989, deciding to study English in Sydney. She, like many Chinese students, stayed on after the Australian government's immigration moratorium following the debacle of Tiananmen Square. She currently operates a small business in Sydney.

Once in Australia, it is often through memory that the migrant rationalizes their decision to stay or return. Migrants are not released from memories of the 'old home' and certainly these memories (and identities) inform them of who they are and where they came from, in effect co-defining their sense of belonging in the new 'home'. (If nothing else, people and institutions in the new home remind them.) Still, memories of the past must be understood, in part, in terms of the present local condition in which they are recollected and told. Man Yee was working in a large bank where she was having an 'illicit' affair with a married man. They were found out and ordered to the rural areas for 're-education'. She refused and instead migrated to Australia; the man spent several months in the Chinese countryside. When he returned to Shanghai he divorced and later remarried without ever contacting Man Yee again. Nevertheless, a sense of hope too can be a powerful articulation of belonging. Though initially sad, Man Yee is now content with her life in Sydney. In memory, forgetfulness is as important as remembering; memories are open to change and riddled with lines of flight.

Remembering home and fixing meaning is not about simply retrieving memories about an originate home, it is about defining and representing places and naming them home, it is a spatial context of momentary boundedness where relations are worked on and worked out (Fortier 2003). Ma arrived in Australia several years ago as a student. She was only 25 years old at that time and had completed her Bachelor of Engineering in hydraulic machinery at the Huazhong University. She intended to finish a postgraduate degree and return home to China. Shortly after arriving, however, she fell in love with another Chinese migrant she had met at an English language class barbecue. Ma's husband came from Shengzhen ten years ago as an overseas student. Upon completing his computer science degree he became an Australian permanent resident and has worked as a software engineer in a large company for the past four years. Ma completed a one-year language course and then went to the University of Sydney to study computer science, believing that the degree would make it easier to find a job in Sydney. One month after Ma finished her studies she began work. She and her husband presently live in a new two-bedroom unit and are planning to have a baby. Memories of the past are quickly being supplanted by memories of the present, and even the future. 'Husband, job and new unit! I am so lucky in Sydney. I will not go back to China anymore. Life is good, we go to Ashfield almost every weekend to buy fresh fish. My husband enjoys Chinese food. After we pay off the mortgage, we will buy a big house in Parramatta.' Ma is already imagining the large party they will have to celebrate their ten-year wedding anniversary.

Memories, however, are funny things. Memories are always unfixed, contested and multiple although people attempt to stabilize the meanings of particular envelopes of memory. People also routinely reconstruct events or delete them. As (Gardner 1999, p. 65) so aptly states, 'Memory is inherently revisionary', and for us, the focus is on the relation of the individual and memory, with what is remembered and how it is recalled (Küchler and Melion 1991). Errors and contradictions of memory illuminate the 'subjective meanings of historical experience' (Thompson 1999, p. 33), enabling people to understand the subjective meanings of historical experience and, as such, can be powerfully emotive. Nostalgia, for example, is frequently activated by movement. Given selective remembering and forgetting, narratives or memories must be understood, in part, in terms of the present local conditions in which they are recollected and told. Memories and particular ways of remembering people, places and events are tied up – directly and indirectly – with specific constructions of social relations. In their narratives, all of the migrants spoke with special reference to China. The China of their memories is shot through with localized expressions and experiences of family, friends and community. It is in this respect that we speak of moving between homes, but when migrants return to China, they invariable find that they must re-member home differently, especially with the passing of time. As noted, older migrants harbour mixed feelings with respect to China. A number mentioned that if the China of the past was the same as it is today, they would not have migrated.

Memory transits between the personal and the social, and between the past, present and future. As bell hooks (1990) notes, the struggle to remember is also a struggle against forgetting and the need to recreate spaces where one can redeem and reclaim the past. More importantly, hooks situates the politicization of memory, going from an indulgence in nostalgia or longing for what once was to a purposeful act of remembering that serves to illuminate the past to transform the present. It is here where Chineseness assumes importance as the migrants take pride in China's achievements. Eun-Ha married a ('white') Australian and had a son. She later divorced. She has sent her young son to study in Shanghai, not only to become fluent in Chinese, but she believes 'education there is better now than here'. Still, the logic of migration is rarely about movement per se. Rather it is an attainment of fixity and spatially bounded rootedness. 'As a rule, migrants do not have moving between points as their purpose', according to Hedetoft (2002, p. 17), 'but solely a means to an end'. In other words, migrants typically do not have movement as their source of identity, their *raison d'être*. Moreover, as migrants get older they are reminded of their increasing immobility (memories of youth are framed with independence, activity and freedom – 'the good old days').

Finally, memories are shaped by gendered experiences. The reiterated gender norm inscribed on the body separates the migrants immediately but with varying effects across time and place. For males, stereotypes are reminiscent of Chen's (1999, p. 589) images of American-Chinese men, including 'the shrieking martial arts expert, Armani-clad drug dealer, bumbling computer nerd, stone-faced patriarch'. Locating masculinity and dislodging the fixed identity constructions for many of the migrant men proved difficult. Kevin, for example, expressed frustration with his classmates who assumed that he studied social sciences because he was not 'smart enough to study finance or computer science'. He also had a sense that to '[white] Australians, I am just Kevin, they [especially females] don't see me as someone they would go out with and have a good time. Someone once, he said he was joking, said I was a 'tinted bit'. That was supposed to make me feel good, feel like I was a mate?' Female migrants, while subject to similar stereotypes, tend to be hyperfeminized, part of the (female) Asian mystique in the Western imagination. That is, excessively passive, dutiful, obedient and sensual (see, for example, Lee 1999). Pui Lam bitterly complained that at work, 'the men get promotion, or ['white'] Australian women, but not us, we are supposed to smile and work hard. And for lower pay. It makes me very angry.'

The stretch of home is thus gendered for the Chinese migrants. Women's ties to family in China, for example, are commonly more intense and carefully nurtured than those of men and are sustained more intimately over a longer period of time. Nearly all of the female migrants in this study regularly called family members while the men did so infrequently and then usually around Chinese New Year. On the other hand, males are more apt to foster business connections back in China, primarily by what Ong (1993, p.753) refers to as 'upper-middle class and upper-class … who have the resources to negotiate and exploit the varied conditions of commerce and family residence in China, Britain, and other countries'. Most migrants (male or female), however, do not; instead, like others in Australia, they are trying to make their way, find some sense of security and belonging in Australia. As one migrant commented, 'It is too difficult to live in more than one place, it is hard enough sometimes to just live here.'

Conclusion

> Between shark fin and bear foot.
> My home is where the good river and good mountain is.
>
> (Chinese sayings)

Migration, belonging and memory are enormously complicated topics and our intervention here is extremely modest. The stories we recounted remind us that the subjectivities, identities and practices of Chinese migrants are inflected with the mutually constitutive relationships between migrant Others and majority white Australians, as well as between other immigrant groups. For Chinese migrants (as with migrants in general), Australia is different from the imaginary world of elsewhere. For some the life is better, but for others the life is more difficult. The experience of a sense of downward mobility can be as common as upward. Although returning to China is a possibility, most realize that it is not tenable to pick up the life they have left, to fit easily back into their old relationships and lives. The first of the Chinese sayings above is well known. Most people can only afford one expensive dish when dining at a restaurant and once selected and the dish arrives, that is their choice. In other words, as Mai explained to me, 'Migration involves a cost, you give up something to gain something. Two good things you cannot have'. This simple metaphor epitomizes the migrant's dilemma. Most migrants in Australia remain and make a home for themselves and derive a sense of belonging as best they can.

The second saying points to a way to traverse the dilemma. Examined closely, the saying reveals a particular image of 'home' as a strong sign of identification of belonging. A home where the migrant is secure and all that security may mean; for them typically a stable family life, employment and friends centred around house ownership. Feelings of belonging were not located in spatial movement or in the processes of identity (re)formation but rather in security from movement and surety of the self in contradistinction to feelings of dislocation and instability. Rather than positing the capacity of migrant identities to flow endlessly, to inhabit multiple homes, the migrants in this narrative expressed their feelings of belonging as negotiable, but the grounding of a home is one of establishing a 'home' through which the feelings of belonging transpire. Of course memories shape the migrant's perceptions and images of home, direct performances of belonging. And the stretch of memory can connect the migrant across the expanse of time and space, giving meaning to the experiences of everyday day life. It is here where home, belonging and memory as both fixity and movement are interdependent modalities.

References

Abu-Lughod, L. and Lutz, C. 1990, 'Introduction: Emotion, Discourse, and the Politics of Everyday Life', in C. Lutz and L. Abu-Lughod (eds), *Language and the Politics of Emotion*, Cambridge University Press, Cambridge, pp. 1–23.

Amit-Talai, V. 1998, 'Risky Hiatus and the Limits of Social Imagination: Expatriacy in the Cayman Islands', in N. Rapport and A. Dawson (eds), *Migrants of Identity: Perceptions of Home in a World of Movement*, Berg, Oxford, pp. 41–59.

Ang, I. 2001, *On Not Speaking Chinese: Living between Asia and the West*, Routledge, London.

Anthias, F. 2001, 'New Hybridities, Old Concepts: the Limits of 'Culture', *Ethnic and Racial Studies*, vol. 24, no. 4, pp. 619–41.

Appadurai, A. 1996, *Modernity at Large: Cultural Dimensions of Globalization*, University of Minnesota Press, Minneapolis.

Bakhtin, M. 1981, *The Dialogic Imagination.*, trans. C. Emerson and M. Holquist, University of Texas Press, Austin.

Berger, P., Berger, B. and Kellner, H. 1974, *The Homeless Mind*, Vintage Books, New York.

Broinowski, A. 1992, *The Yellow Lady: Australians' Impressions of Asia*, Oxford University Press, Melbourne.

Brown, J.M. and Foot, R. 1994, *Migration: the Asian Experience*, St. Martin's Press, Oxford.

Bucholtz, M. 2001, 'Reflexivity and Critique in Discourse Analysis', *Critique of Anthropology*, vol. 21, no. 2, pp. 165–83.

Castles, S. 2002, 'Migration and Community Formation under Conditions of Globalization', *International Migration Review*, vol. 36, no. 4, pp. 1143–68.

Chan, S. 1999, 'What is This Thing Called a Chinese Diaspora?' *Contemporary Review*, vol. 274, no. 1597, pp. 81–3.

Chen, A. 1999, 'Lives at the Center of the Periphery, Lives at the Periphery of the Center: Chinese American Masculinities and Bargaining with Hegemony', *Gender and Society*, vol. 13, no. 5, pp. 584–607.

Chow, R. 1998, 'Introduction: On Chineseness as a Theoretical Problem', *Boundary 2*, vol. 25, no. 3, pp. 1–24.

Chun, A. 1996, 'Fuck Chineseness: On the Ambiguities of Ethnicity as Culture as Identity', *Boundary 2*, vol. 23, no. 2, pp. 111–38.

Davidson, A. 2004, 'Transnational Spaces and Sociocultural Networks', in K. Kuah-Pearce (ed.), *Chinese Women and their Cultural and Network Capitals*, Marshall Cavendish, Singapore, pp. 21–43.

Dean, K. 1998, 'Despotic Empire/Nation-State: Local Responses to Chinese Nationalism in an Age of Global Capitalism', in K. Chen, H. Kuo, H. Hang and H. Ming-Chu (eds), *Trajectories: Inter-Asia Cultural Studies*, Routledge, London, pp. 153–85.

Derrida, J. 1988, *Limited Inc*, Northwestern University Press, Evanston.

DIMIA 2002, *The China-Born in Australia in the 1990s*, Department of Immigration and Multinational and Indigenous Affairs, viewed 7 July 2003 <www.immi.gov.au/statistics/publications/community_profiles/ChinaNet.pdf>.

DIMIA 2003, *Multicultural Australia: the China-born Community*, Department of Immigration and Multinational and Indigenous Affairs, viewed 7 July 2005 <http://www.immi.gov.au/statistics/infosummary/textversion/china.htm>.

Fortier, A.-M. 2003, 'Making Home: Queer Migrations and Motions of Attachment', in S. Ahmed, C. Castañeda, A.M. Fortier and M. Sheller (eds), *Uprootings/Regroundings: Questions of Home and Migration*, Berg, Oxford, pp. 115–35.

Gardner, K. 1999, 'Narrating Location: Space, Age and Gender among Bengali Elders in East London', *Oral History*, vol. 27, no. 1, pp. 65–74.

Hall, S. (ed.) 1997, *Representation: Cultural Representations and Signifying Practices*, Sage, London.

Hedetoft, U. 2002, *Discourses and Images of Belonging: Migrants between 'New Racism', Liberal Nationalism and Globalization*, Aalborg University, Fibigerstraede, Denmark.

hooks, b. 1990, *Yearning: Race, Gender and Cultural Politics*, South End Press, Boston.

Huang, S., Teo, P. and Yeoh, B. 2000, 'Diasporic Subjects and Identity Negotiations: Women in and from Asia", *Women's International Studies Forum*, vol. 23, no. 4, pp. 391–8.

Keith, M. and Pile, S. 1993, *Place and the Politics of Identity*, Routledge, London.

Kelson, G. and Delaet, D. 1999, *Gender and Immigration*, New York University Press, New York.

Küchler, S. and Melion, W. (eds) 1991, *Images of Memory: On Representing and Memory*, Smithsonian Institution Press, Washington.

Lee, R. 1999, *Orientals: Asian Americans in Popular Culture*, Temple University Press, Philadelphia.

McQuire, S. 1998, *Visions of Modernity, Representation, Memory, Time and Space in the Age of the Camera*, Sage Publications, London.

Mageo, J.M. (ed.) 2001, *Cultural Memory: Reconfiguring History and Identity in the Postcolonial Pacific*, University of Hawaii Press, Honolulu.

Massey, D. 1994, *Space, Place and Gender*, Polity Press, New York.

Ong, A. 1993, 'On the Edge of Empires: Flexible Citizenship among Chinese in Diaspora', *Positions*, vol. 1, no. 3, pp. 745–78.

Pessar, P. and Mahler, R. 2001, 'Gender and Transnational Migration', *The Transnational Migration: Comparative Perspectives Conference*, Princeton University.

Pickering, M. 2001, *Stereotyping: the Politics of Representation*, Palgrave Macmillan, New York.

Rapport, N. and Dawson, A. 1998, 'The Topic of the Book', in N. Rapport and A. Dawson (eds), *Migrants of Identity: Perceptions of Home in a World of Movement*, Berg, Oxford, pp. 3–17.

Ryan, L. 2003, 'Moving Spaces and Changing Places: Irish Women's Memories of Emigration to Britain in the 1930s', *Journal of Ethnic and Migration Studies*, vol. 29, no. 1, pp. 67–82.
Simmel, G. 1950, *The Sociology of Georg Simmel*, trans. K. Wolf, Free Press, New York.
Skeldon, R. 1996, 'Migration from China', *Journal of International Affairs*, vol. 49, no. 2, pp. 434–55.
Svašek, M. 2002, 'The Politics of Emotions: Emotional Discourses and Displays in Post-Cold War Contexts', *European Journal of Anthropology*, vol. 39, pp. 9–27.
Taylor, C. 1992, *The Ethics of Authenticity*, Harvard University Press, Cambridge.
Thompson, A. 1999, 'Moving Stories: Oral History and Migration Studies', *Oral History*, vol. 27, no. 1, pp. 24–37.
Wang, G. 1991, *China and the Chinese Overseas*, Times Academic Press, Singapore.
Yang, W. 2001, *Australian Chinese*, National Portrait Gallery, Canberra.
Yelvington, K. 2002, 'History, Memory and Identity: a Programmatic Prolegomenon', *Critique of Anthropology*, vol. 22, no. 3, pp. 227–56.

3

Memories and Identity Anxieties of Chinese Transmigrants in Australia

David Ip

In the past decade there has been a major shift of paradigm in conceptualizing immigration. While earlier researchers saw immigration as a rupture between 'home' and 'host' countries, thus putting assimilation, acculturation, integration or incorporation of migrants into the adopted country at the centre of attention, recent scholars however see immigration as a process of spatial movements where migrants are not necessarily disconnected from, but continually remaining connected to, their place of origin while living at the site of migration (Basch et al. 1994). As many studies now contended, given the affordable air travel, cheap phone cards and easy access of the Internet, as well as the proliferation of channels for remittances and relaxation of laws in recognition of dual citizenship, it is more appropriate to talk of transnational migrants and transnationalism rather than migrants and immigration in an age of globalization and interconnectedness (Rouse 1991; Vertovec 2004). And today few would challenge what Basch et al. (1994, p. 7) proclaimed that transmigration is 'the processes by which immigrants forge and sustain multi-stranded social relations that link together their societies of origin and settlement'. They referred to these processes as transnationalism to emphasize that many immigrants today build social fields that cross geographic, cultural and political borders, maintaining multiple involvements in both home and host societies where they are engaged in patterned, multifaceted, multilocal processes that include economic, sociocultural and political practices and discourses. Subsequently in their view, many immigrants today are able to transcend the confines of the territorially bounded jurisdiction of the nation state; and they also make it an inherent part of their habitual lives (Guarnizo et al. 1999, p. 370). In short, these mobile migrants constitute a single social continuum between here and there.

This notion of transnationalism has also prompted many researchers to challenge the traditional assimilationist perspective where migrants are seen as a huddled mass whose cultural identity and political membership are defined by how well they have acquired new single identity, national allegiance, and representation in one national polity (Pickus 1998; Schuck 1998) while jettisoning those held previously (Alba 1985; Kessler 1998; Motomura 1998; Warner and Srole 1945). The transnationalism literature now concurs that a borderless identity and belonging among immigrants is not only common but also necessary because of the multiple options and unlimited mobility offered by a post-territorial and globalized socio-economic and sociocultural setting. For this reason, the identity construction among migrants today is frequently hybrid and channelled, multipositional and network-bound, transgressive and affiliative, freely formed albeit socially determined (Guarnizo and Smith 1998).

In these contexts, it is often observed that politicians, economists, journalists, researchers as well as cultural critics tend to accept the fact that migrants are 'at home' in more than one location, because they are able to negotiate and navigate a multiplicity of worlds when they move regularly between their place of origin and the site(s) of (im)migration or transmigration (Ho 2002; Kastoryano 2000; Portes 2001). They are thus transmigrants and heralded by many. For those who choose to perceive them as more privileged, the transmigrants are thus indicative of the arrival of a new era of transnationalism and transmigration. For others who readily see them as less privileged because of their circularity movements, they are also praised for their transgression on nationalisms and political boundaries (Ong 1999; Portes et al. 1999; Smith 2003; Vertovec 2003).

However, some researchers have also warned that the transnationalism perspective, in overemphasizing the migrants' multiple cultural and national attachments, and seeing their transnational movements as unproblematic, has overlooked many persistent obstacles, in particular the personal anxieties these transmigrants have to face in the process (Ip 2006; Kandiyoti 2003). Among them, a major concern is their problem in reassembling their identity when vacillating between 'here and there'. As Kandiyoti (2003) suggested, in transnational journeys, both 'here' and 'there' inherited particular social configurations however shot through by globalization, transnational networks or cross-cultural exchanges. These configurations include pre-given, localized definitions of class, culture, gender, race and religion that attempt to exclude or damage the personal identity of migrants. In their settlement and travels, transmigrants must confront and renegotiate those localized social, cultural and racist structures that are unsympathetic, and they also need to consider how they should reshape the localized definitions of belonging, which are not necessarily transcended or subverted by transnational allegiances and movements. In other words, while it is now common among researchers to acknowledge the identities transmigrants hold are multiple, fluid, plural, diverse, transnational, cosmopolitan or post-national (Hall 1992, p. 309), it is equally important to recognize the anxieties transmigrants have when constructing their identities while these identities are at once local and global and the activities they engage in are 'unbounded' and translocal (Brah 1996, p. 196), frequently requiring ongoing negotiation and mediation, involving agonizing ruptures of local constraints and social moorings as well as broader political and historical practices (Clifford 1994; Guarnizo and Smith 1998, p. 12).

Not surprisingly, research on the experiences of assembling and reassembling their identities between 'here' and 'there' has attracted much attention of late, especially in describing in general the factors that contribute to the making of their identities. What remains underexplored, however, is how multiple movements or migrations have affected their identities. As Windland (1998) maintained, in order to comprehend the content and parameters of such identities at specific moments in time in the lives of transmigrants, it is important to examine their inner world and the specific dimensions, contexts and idioms that constitute their definition of social and personal identities. The knowledge and understanding of this process, in his view, could very well shake up the ideological foundations and paradigms that are so commonly used for understanding immigration-based nations such as Canada or Australia because the identities of these countries can no longer be defined by a limited national and territorial locus, and they should be looked upon as a node in a post-national network of diasporas (Windland 1998, p. 567).

Understandably the study of the inner world of transmigrants has been gaining popularity. And one of the tools that enjoys increasing credibility and being taken most seriously is memories. As Chamberlain and Leydesdorff (2004, p. 228) aptly remarked, 'migrants, perhaps more than many people, are made by their memories of their birthplace, their homeland, those left behind – interruptions in their life narratives that require resequencing, remodeling and reinterpreting as the newcomers incorporate and surpass their pasts'. DeRoche (1996) further argued that accounts of personal memories are often a unique and frequently the only way to access migrant experience relating to identities, especially in understanding how memories are actively constructed, selected and distorted. Lambek and Antze (1996) similarly saw that memories were entrenched in the creation of meaning and thus, in turn, were fundamentally implicated in identity formation. Likewise, Parker (1995) also reminded us of the fact that memories, especially social or collective memories, could also provide the imagery and vocabulary for identity formation. And Kwok (2005) further emphasized that social memory is a form of collective identity as it is self-aware that what is 'remembered' (or represented in texts) is a locus of power and thus it has the ability to affect identity and self-definition.

However, it was Antze (2003) who boldly proclaimed that memories and the flashes that light up in our minds are scenes that shape our inner world and inform our identities. Chamberlain and Leydesdorff (2004) similarly concurred what is important about memories in identity construction is that as they move through the journey of their lives, they also engage themselves in a continuous revision of their memories as they revise their self and identity.

Method and sources

Following these works and the tradition that has long been established by Thomas and Znaniecki (1984, first published in 1918–21) and Mannheim (1952, first published in 1928), this chapter aims to explore in depth the inner world of a special group of transmigrants – recent Chinese migrants who have settled in Australia only since the early 1980s – specifically in terms of how their personal and social identities have been shaped and informed by their memories, especially when they live their lives regularly and frequently between 'here' and 'there'. The materials presented here are drawn from in-depth interviews of 20 Chinese informants from Hong Kong, Taiwan and China (PRC) that were conducted between 2004 and 2005. The informants were selected by means of a snowballing technique, starting at first from the researcher's own personal network before extending to a broader social arena introduced by the informants. The informants were also chosen on the basis of their sustained connections with and practices of transnationalism, i.e. either they had extensively and regularly travelled between their place of origin and Australia, or they had made it a regular routine of their everyday life to indulge in activities which allowed them to remain connected to their home countries (Ip et al. 2006). They were asked to reflect on how they defined and redefined their identities, whether memories had a particular role in negotiating their identities, especially when they were living 'here and there'. They were also asked to talk about the anxieties, if they had any, in imagining, remembering, representing and contesting themselves when moving across terrains.

Admittedly these are demanding and confronting questions that required informants to be most articulate, communicative and honest about their feelings and thoughts. For this reason, half of the informants found it difficult to continue with the interviews while the remainder were willing to describe in detail their memories and experiences of their journeys into renegotiating their identities when moving across borders. They also consented to be interviewed more than once to allow the researcher to verify and clarify their responses when necessary. Represented in this group of informants were three females and seven males, of whom three were from Taiwan, another three from the PRC and the remaining five from Hong Kong. They were all tertiary educated and engaged in either business (trading and restaurant) or provision of professional services (teaching, researching, travel and therapy).

Memories and anxieties of identities

At first glance, almost all the informants participating in this study did not seem to have any major problem with their personal or social identity, either living in Australia, or when they returned to their original terrain. Their response to the question of how they tended to identify themselves was overwhelmingly and convincingly positive and definite – many replied with little hesitation that they regarded themselves as both Australian and Chinese. Typically they gave statements such as 'I consider myself Chinese *and* Australian', 'I think I am half and half', 'I know I'm Chinese but I am also Australian', or 'when I'm in Australia, I see myself as Australian but when I return to my home country, I'll become Chinese again'. Based on these responses, one could not question what has been established by the transnationalism literature was correct – that nowadays the identity of migrants is hybrid, transnational, fluid and perhaps in some ways, cosmopolitan.

However, although identity is usually manifested by how people conceive of themselves, it is also other-referenced, or as Vertovec (2001, p. 573) put it, characterized by others. And it was when more questions were asked about the latter process that some informants began to reveal that beneath the facade lay some uncomfortable anxieties about their identities. Specifically, a number of informants candidly talked of the times when they had to renegotiate their identities because they felt how they defined themselves had been challenged.

Fay was born in China but migrated to Hong Kong with her family when she was very young. For this reason she always referred herself as a Hong Kong Chinese because 'my identity is deeply rooted in my memories of growing up in Hong Kong'. Like many with middle-class Chinese parents, upon completion of her high school education, she was sent to study in a university in the United States where she met her present husband who later obtained a teaching job in Australia. Soon after her arrival in Australia in the early 1980s, she found herself facing an identity crisis:

> Australia had a very different social environment. In the U.S., I was very comfortable with my identity as a Chinese-American, especially when people find out my husband is Irish-American. However, in Australia, I found myself ... no matter how hard I tried to fit in, learning and re-learning the lingo, socialising with the 'right' people, I was still regarded as an 'Asian'(!) who was only qualified to come to Australia because of my husband who is a 'Yank'. People questioned me whether my husband and I would settle down in Australia permanently. They asked me how I brought my kids up as if they had to grow up either as American or Chinese. That was the only way they saw me. I could not have a hyphenated identity in Australia – either I'm Australian, or not. I tried to convince myself that perhaps getting a postgraduate degree, and then a professional job, would help people to see me differently. But when I told them I was a speech therapist when people asked me what I did for a living, you should look at the expressions they had on their faces, they were like telling you, 'how *could* you do that job when your first language is not even English?' without knowing that speech therapy has nothing to do with it.

After years of frustrating experiences, Fay came to the conclusion that she had little option but to live her life as a Chinese in Australia and to reclaim her Hong Kong Chinese identity. She began making trips to Hong Kong regularly to explore Chinese arts and paintings. She wanted to learn Chinese cooking, preparing foods she remembered from her childhood. She started writing novels based on the memories she had about her family living in Hong Kong and stories her parents told her about China before the Communists took over. Furthermore, she developed an even keener interest in women and fashion during that era and started collecting women's clothing. However, people around her in Hong Kong could not understand her 'sudden' interest in all things Chinese, and found her behaviour strange and eccentric. Some even decided that she only wanted to be more Chinese than the (Hong Kong) Chinese, and therefore she was not normal at heart. Instead, she was regarded as a 'foreignized' Chinese who was interested and saw Chinese things tinted with Western taste.

Richard, another informant from Hong Kong, also spoke of similar incidents involving reconstructing his identity. After spending many years in the US and Canada finishing his postgraduate degrees, he obtained a teaching job in Australia:

> I'm normally not very conscious of my identity, or particularly worry about it. But when you're regularly reminded of it, then it becomes a nuisance. I remember when I first started teaching in Australia, because of my American accent, I was constantly asked why I had this 'funny' accent and some even claimed they could not understand what I said because they could not make out why I had a Chinese face and speaking English with an American accent. I decided that it would be easier to be accepted if I show people I consciously try to Australianise myself. I began reading Australian histories, listened to Australian rock bands, familiarised myself with Australian pop culture, did the pub thing, ate Chiko Rolls, tasted Vegimite, went to 'State of Origin' footie matches ... You name it. I'd give anything Australian a go.

However, during the first post-war 'race debate' spearheaded by one of Australia's most renowned historians, Professor Geoffrey Blainey, in the mid-1980s, who complained there were far too many Asian migrants settling in Australian too fast (Blainey 1984), Richard felt that wherever he turned, his identity was questioned as he experienced racial taunts and verbal abuse. Three years later in 1988, when another 'immigration debate' was sparked off by the then election candidate John Howard, arguing that Asian immigration to Australia must be curtailed (Heibert et al. 2003), he was furthered angered by the treatment he received from people around him:

> Suddenly I felt people around me didn't want to be seen with me. It didn't matter if that was real or imagined. The fact was, I was made to feel unwelcome because of my ethnicity and that was enough to make me feel offended.

And then, when Pauline Hanson in her maiden speech delivered at the Federal Parliament blaming Asian migrants in Australia for the nation's economic woes, ranging from taking jobs away from Australians, to 'ghettoized' Australia's major cities, causing a surge of anti-Asian sentiments nationwide in the late 1990s, he felt his identity since then had been totally transformed:

> I became very conscious of my ethnicity and also my identity, especially when it was racialised, labelled, and put on public trial. What

> most people did not realise was that suddenly, while Hansonism instrumentally forced the leaders of various Asian communities to come together and talk about what to do next, at the same time, there were so many ill feelings coming to the surface among the various Asian migrants. You know ... the Chinese would blame the Vietnamese, and the Vietnamese blamed the new boat people ... What was offensive to me was that on the one hand, I was turned into a homogenised and racialised 'Asian' by politicians, simultaneously I was also accused by them that I could not become Australian because everything I stood for, my physical appearance and my cultural background were 'foreign', or Asian.

During this time, he felt he was reminded repeatedly every day by newspaper headlines and television news of his identity in crisis. He began to explore his identity options and started to apply for jobs in Hong Kong because he thought he was still Chinese, and he also maintains his right of abode there. However, when he investigated more closely the possibility of returning to Hong Kong to work and live on his more recent trips, he also came to the realization that he was no longer considered a 'local':

> People kept telling me I had been away for too long, that I did not think the same way as the ordinary Hong Kong people, and that I would not be able to fit in anymore. People also seemed to see me as a threat as if I was intruding on their turf. I was hinted repeatedly that I should remain in Australia because that was my home now. Again I was reminded of my identity – what am I? I can't deny that I am Chinese because my memories of growing up in Hong Kong are an integral part of my existence and my identity. Yet I can't erase entirely the bad memories I had of the race and immigration debates. They also contributed to my identity, representing not only how I see myself, but also how others take me as an Australian. The irony is that it seems I now seem to be in a bind – I inherited and acquired memories in Hong Kong and Australia, yet my identities seem to be accepted by neither.

Richard's identity bind, however, was not shared by other informants. Ding, a Chinese migrant in Australia for nearly 17 years, was much more certain of his identity option. After completing a doctoral degree in architecture in Australia, and after working for an Australian architecture firm for two years, he set up his own private practice in both

Australia and China, and he travelled frequently between his homeland and Australia. When asked about his identity, he had little hesitation in declaring that he saw himself mainly as a Chinese living in two different countries. Pan (1990, p. 267) once observed that what made a Chinese define himself or herself as Chinese was 'not so much language, or religion, or any other markers of ethnicity, but some primordial core or essence of Chineseness which one has by virtue of one's Chinese genes'. Ding did not seem to agree entirely but knew that physically he did not 'look like an Australian [Caucasian]' and he confessed that he spoke 'English with a heavy Chinese accent'. Moreover, he felt he was 'not sure what made an Australian Australian', but he was more certain what it meant to be a Chinese, especially a 'mainlander' Chinese.

One particular notion he emphasized was that being Chinese had a different meaning for Chinese who came from Hong Kong, Taiwan or South East Asia. This he found out quickly when he first came to Australia, naively expecting all Chinese migrants, regardless of where they came from, to lend him a helping hand in finding employment, and getting him through difficult times. Instead, he realized that there existed an invisible subethnic hierarchy within the Chinese community in Australia, in that not only did both Hong Kong and Taiwanese migrants not embrace the 'mainlanders' warmly, they also looked upon the 'mainlanders' as 'backward, uncultured and aggressive'. Although he felt hurt, he believed that he would not hold any personal grudge against anyone from Hong Kong or Taiwan, but the memories he had of the discrimination he had received from what he called 'Chinese compatriots' eventually made him very aware of his own identity:

> I can now understand why other 'mainlanders' bonded with and found friendship among those who were previous *zhi qing* ('intellectual youth' sent down to the countryside for re-education during the Cultural Revolution), because they shared some common sufferings. I am sure other migrants from 'mainland' China would agree with me that the discrimination we have experienced is also something we remember that can define who we are.

Lily, a much younger and more recent PRC migrant who first came to Australia in the mid-1990s as an interpreter on a Chinese delegation and then returned as a migrant two years later when she turned 26 as a student and a migrant in an MBA programme, however, was less affronted by the treatment she had received from the Taiwanese and Hong Kong Chinese she met in her new 'home'. She admitted that she was made to feel distinctly 'mainland Chinese' when she first tried to make friends with them, 'like speaking about China as a country, and people from there being backward, unsophisticated and not knowing enough English to get by ...' However, once they learned her job in China was a Chinese–English interpreter for a European mining company and she had travelled frequently between Sichuan and the rest of the world, their attitudes towards her changed instantly. Some became very friendly while others seemed to bend over backwards to include her in their social circle, and she knew the reason for her sudden 'popularity' was mainly due to her ability to speak fluent and non-accented English, as well as having had a job that enabled her to travel so frequently that made it easy for other Chinese to equate her status almost to that of a 'diplomat'. For this reason, she was more forgiving of the initial discriminatory treatment she received in the university when almost every study group in her class refused to include her as a member working on a class project. What she found more hurtful and fearful was her daily experiences during the days of rapid emergence of One-Nation or Hansonism:

> I felt I was made unwelcome everyday when I read the newspapers, listening to the radio, or even walking in the streets. I felt I was made so conscious of my ethnicity that I was constantly being stared at, judged and policed. Like when I was waiting for a bus one day and some old white man sneaked behind my back and told me, 'There are too many of your kind in Australia.' I was totally in shock ... because he didn't look like an angry skinhead who was portrayed by the media as a typical racist ... In fact, he was quite well dressed and groomed, and for a minute I was not sure if I heard him correctly, or perhaps more correctly, I did not want to believe what he said to me. So I replied, 'what do you mean by that?' and he looked straight into my eyes and said in a tone that was at once cold and threatening, 'you know what I mean ... you're Asian, aren't you?' I remembered I felt so powerless and helpless that I had to run away immediately, and thought about my identity as a Chinese for months, constantly asking all kinds of questions, like, 'why am I staying here when I am not welcomed and accepted?' Perhaps when you're Chinese, you'll always be Chinese and that's something you can't do very much about.

Lily now frankly admits that the memories at that time have played a major part in affirming her identity as primordially Chinese, perhaps as a way to protect herself from the tension of dealing with racism from time to time, especially in that it gives her a sense of 'true' as opposed to 'promised belonging'. As she confessed freely during the interview, 'when things go bad again, at least I know I have a place to which I could return'. The feeling is particularly reinforced by the fact that since her graduation, she has been working as a Chinese liaison officer for a large multinational company and she is required to spend more and more time in China.

Yet Lin, a more recent PRC transmigrant who also spends much time travelling to China exporting Australia's education services, felt differently about what was important in defining his identity. Like Ding, he freely admitted that his identity was more Chinese than Australian, but his reasons were not the same. He did not feel other groups within the Chinese community particularly looked down on him 'perhaps because I had very little to do with them'. The reason why he felt more Chinese was mainly due to the fact that he had little symbolic identification with Australia as an imagined community occupying a particular place which is often nurtured through the construction of a social or collective memory (Osborne 2001, p. 7). He noted a number of episodes when he questioned his allegiance to Australia:

> There were times when I just didn't share the same feelings about things with Australians – like cheering for Australia's Gold Medallists, or singing the Australian national anthem, or having the same emotional involvement on Anzac Day ... When I thought about how involved I was emotionally when I learned Beijing beat other countries in the world to host the Olympic Games in 2008 and how I responded when I saw Ian Thorpe win all those swimming races in the last Games, I knew I was more Chinese, I felt as if there was something missing in me in claiming I was an Australian ... On the other hand, I remember when I travelled back to Shanghai, I felt so naturally comfortable and relaxed, like I knew everything about the place and its culture ...

Ling, a Taiwanese business migrant who moved to Australia in the early 1990s, also spoke of similar sentiments when she reflected on her business experiences. Without the necessary social and cultural capital as well as the knowledge of the business culture in Australia, she encountered enormous difficulties in getting her first business set up. Frustrated but not discouraged, she remembered what gave her strength was the collective memory she had about Taiwan being a nation made up of hard-working, flexible and innovative small and medium enterprises capable of making an impact in the global economy. She felt that with the same fearlessness and zeal, she could make her business equally successful as she did in Taiwan if she knew the Australian way of doing business better. In the following years, she actively sought and cultivated networks in the Australian business world and tried to identify herself as an Australian:

> I went to many business functions introducing myself to as wide a business circle whenever I could. I also thought by positioning myself as a Taiwanese business migrant eager to become a business woman and an Australian would be the best way to get Australians on my side and give me assistance. Things did not turn out the way I had expected ... perhaps because I was too eager and people did not believe me, or thought that I could become an Australian instantly, I ended up wasting a lot of time, money and effort.

Disappointed by the lack of profitable returns, Ling returned to Taiwan to resume her previous family business. Though holding Australian citizenship, she now visits Australia only for holidays while spending most of her time in Taiwan tending her business. Does this mean that she has given up her Australian identity completely? Her answer was not a simple 'yes' or 'no':

> When I was in Australia, I felt there was a part of me being Australian – like being able to share the best of what it could offer me as an entitlement, that I could access it freely and readily, you know, the open space, the clean air, the social stability ... And this often becomes the most pleasant memory I have about Australia whenever I return to Taiwan that somehow made me feel I am Australian. However, at the same time, when I was back in Taiwan, I was also surprised by how at ease I felt there and how little effort I had to make to fit in. I felt as if my heart and pulse had the same rhythm with the collective rather than only as an individual, and that I could relate to the social values, attitudes and ideals naturally with little effort of negotiation. I suppose this also means that I am at heart Taiwanese ...

However, Michael, who was a geography teacher in a high school in Hong Kong before he moved to Australia, found that the greatest anxiety he had as a transmigrant was not so much in determining his social identity as a Chinese or Australian or both, but his personal identity as a responsible provider for his family, especially when he looked back at the times when he was unemployed. He recounted that the major reason why he decided to move to Australia was because of the political situation after Hong Kong was returned to China – that the Special Administrative Region was under a government that was not only incompetent, but also unashamedly tied to powerful business circles and property developers. Out of a sense of outrage and disappointment, as well as concern for the future for his two young children, he decided to give up his secure government job and moved to Australia, expecting to find an inner peace that eluded him while working in Hong Kong. Unfortunately things did not turn out the way he had expected:

> Looking back, I must be extremely naïve about my own ability. I thought I could get another job easily in Australia but it turned out that it was impossible to get another teaching job unless I had Australian qualifications and experience. Suddenly I found myself not very employable because I could not bring myself just to take up another job for the sake of earning some income. I tried, like working as an insurance agent, selling real estate, but I simply could not perform well, and that meant that I could not make enough financially to provide for my family. I felt constantly like a loser, a failure ... and the fact that my wife, who was an English teacher in Hong Kong, had little problem in finding a job in an institution offering English classes to international students, made me feel even worse as she became the main income earner for the family.

He remembered that throughout those days, his memories in Hong Kong as a respected educator and a successful provider for his family haunted him incessantly. Furthermore, when he applied for jobs, he was made more aware of his personal and social identity crisis. Personally he questioned his own worth because he could not even get a job. Socially, whenever he wrote a job application, attended an interview, or even socialized with the Australian colleagues working with his wife, he found himself completely unprepared to 'act' as an Australian. He grew increasingly unhappy and demoralized and decided to return to Hong Kong to take up his old job while leaving his family behind in Australia. He intended to visit his family at least once a month and thought that was the best arrangement for him. However, he soon found that his personal and social identity anxieties grew deeper:

> I had my old job and income back, but upon my return people around me looked upon me as a failure, you know, not making it in Australia and had to return to Hong Kong. Some even commented on me being a 'failed Australian', especially when I had a different opinion

on things, they starting saying something like, 'oh, that's because Michael is different, he has become Australianised'.

Ultimately a year later, Michael left his job again and returned to Australia determined to stay permanently. Reflecting on what he experienced in Hong Kong, he felt that the one lesson he had learned was that when it came to identify himself, he had to treat it like a performance:

> I learn that if I wanted to be accepted socially, it really doesn't matter how I see myself, whether as an Australian or not, it all depends on how others see you and want you to be. Therefore I have little choice but to comply and perform what they expect of me. I learn that I'll have to perform a public identity if I want to be accepted, and keep my private or personal identity to myself. And sometimes that's not easy ...

The difficulty he found was that sometimes he could not 'perform' his public identity convincingly, like trying to pretend he knew Australian politics, or the popular gossip stories about celebrities in Hong Kong:

> That's when you felt completely like an outsider – like, when friends or colleague asked you, have you heard this big scandal about so and so? I just can't convince myself that I am very 'Hong Kong' anymore because honestly I don't know and I don't care! I have no memories of these scandals and therefore I don't have a script telling me how to act along. The same way in Australia ... when my neighbour asked me whether I am going to vote Liberals or Labour, I couldn't carry on a conversation with them because I didn't know what the parties stood for, and voting was never something very important to me. I had no basic knowledge or previous experience about the subject matter to guide me to continue with the conversation with my neighbour and I felt I simply wasn't Australian enough ...

Ironically this episode brings to mind the confession by Joe, who also came from Hong Kong, and who was an agent recruiting international students studying in Australia. When he was asked for the first time whether memories had a place in how he saw his personal or social identity, he thought the question made no sense and brushed if off. About eight months later after the interview, by chance he ran into the researcher in a café but decided to stay and had a chat about his latest trip back to Hong Kong. As expected, he raved endlessly about how exciting the shopping was and how impressed he was about the fine food he had sampled. However, in a quiet moment, he suddenly experienced an epiphany and said,

> You would not believe what happened to me in Hong Kong – I went to a Canto-pop concert with my cousin and there I was, with thousands of other fans there, trying to get into the swing of things. But then I realised that as other people started to sing along with him [the pop singer], I found myself not knowing the melodies, let alone the lyrics. While all these people were enthusiastically giving a 'yes' to what the singer asked them, do you remember this song? I was left stone cold because I had no memories of his songs; I was not part of the collective memories of that era in Hong Kong. Guess what? I just had to admit that my identity was no longer a bloody Hong Konger ...

Conclusion

It has been well accepted that for migrants, perspective and distance, tension and adjustment often jostle in the drama of belonging and identity (Chamberlain and Leydesdorff 2004, p. 227). However, despite the rapid proliferation of literature on transnationalism and identity, there has been relatively little attention on analysing the anxieties and struggles transmigrants may face in terms of identity formation and belonging in multiple sites when most researchers overemphasize their multiple cultural and national attachments as well as their seemingly unproblematic 'back and forth' movements and travels. More recent work on middling transnationalism (Chakravartty 2003; Ip 2006; Ip and Chui 2006; Lowell 2000a, b), however, has shown that the themes of difficulties of settlement, social mobility, discrimination and prejudice still feature prominently when transmigrants recounted their sensitivities, experiences and identities. Similarly there is further recognition that as transmigrants are enjoying their transnational existence, they also have to negotiate multiple traditions, ambiguities, inconsistencies and positions (Walsh 2004). These stories the transmigrants recounted are not only increasingly being acknowledged as a powerful window into understanding the subjective mentalities and shifts of transmigrants over time, but also into knowing intimately the dynamics of how their sense of selfhood, through participating in multiple sites, acquiring different statuses, playing different roles and internalizing different norms informs their identities (Gleason 1983).

In this chapter, through the personal accounts of a selected group of Chinese transmigrants from various backgrounds in Australia, we come to a clearer understanding of the dynamics and processes of how they structured and restructured their socio-biographical memory, that is, the mechanism through which they felt pride, pain, anger, uncertainties or shame with regard to events they went through in their lives (Olick and Robbins 1998). We come to the realization that as the transmigrants continued to move fluidly across nations and engaged in translocal activities, the traditional forms of belonging and identity they had experienced were destabilized, questioned and contested. Yet the valorization of multiple identities which transnational and disaporic theory claimed are not readily available to all transmigrants who maintain connections between multiple sites. On the contrary, more often than not, memory became a central, if not the central, medium through which their identities were constituted.

The life stories they provided in this chapter in many ways are affirmation of what (Hall 1994) proclaimed long ago – that identities are the means we give to the different ways by which we are positioned, and position ourselves, within the narrative of the past. And hence, 'identity is a matter of *becoming* as well as *being*. It belongs to the future as much as to the past' (Hall 1994, p. 394). In other words, both identity and memory should be recognized as ongoing processes, not possessions or properties (Olick and Robbins 1998, p. 122). As people are affected more and more by plural connections, and global movements and transnational identities are increasingly seen as a threat to the liberal, nation-bound concept of citizenship, nationhood and sovereignty, particularly in a climate so fearful of imagined or real terrorism, the importance of the ability to understand transnational identities, including their anxieties and options through the memories of transmigrants, cannot be underestimated. As Taylor (cited in Osborne 2001, p. 27; 1998, p. 341) heralded:

> We have to learn how to live with these multiplicities of identity and yet achieve some kind of common understanding. And this could only be done by recognising that our being together is important to us, that it enriches us, that it is something we all cherish.

References

Alba, R.D. 1985, *Italian Americans: Into the Twilight of Ethnicity*, Prentice-Hall, Englewood Cliffs.

Antze, P. 2003, 'The Other Inside: Memory as Metaphor in Psychoanalysis', in S. Radstone and K. Hodgkin (eds), *Regimes of Memory*, Routledge, New York / London, pp. 96–113.

Basch, L., Glick, S.N. and Blanc-Szanton, C. 1994, *Nations Unbound: Transnational Projects, Postcolonial Predicaments, and Deterritorialized Nation-States*, Gordon and Breach Publishers, Luxembourg.

Blainey, G. 1984, *All for Australia*, Methuen Haynes, Sydney.

Brah, A. 1996, *Cartographies of Diaspora: Contesting Identities*, Routledge, New York.

Chakravartty, P. 2003, *Symbolic Analysts or Indentured Servants?: Indian High-tech Migrants in America's Information Economy*, Centre for Comparative and Global Research, UCLA, California.

Chamberlain, M. and Leydesdorff, L. 2004, 'Transnational Families: Memories and Narratives', *Global Networks*, vol. 4, no. 3, pp. 227–41.

Clifford, J. 1994, 'Diasporas', *Cultural Anthropology*, vol. 9, no. 3, pp. 302–38.

DeRoche, C. 1996, 'I Learned Things Today that I Never Knew Before: Oral History at the Kitchen Table', *Oral History Review*, vol. 23, pp. 45–61.

Gleason, P. 1983, 'Identifying Identity: a Semantic History', *Journal of American History*, vol. 69, pp. 910–32.

Guarnizo, L., Sanchez, A. and Roach, E. 1999, 'Mistrust, Fragmented Solidarity, and Transnational Migration: Colombians in New York City and Los Angeles', *Ethnic and Racial Studies*, vol. 22, pp. 367–96.

Guarnizo, L.E. and Smith, M.P. 1998, 'The Locations of Transnationalism', *Comparative Urban and Community Research*, no. 6, pp. 3–34.

Hall, S. 1992, 'The Question of Cultural Identity', in S. Hall, D. Held and T. McGrew (eds), *Modernity and its Futures*, Polity Press, Cambridge, pp. 274–316.

Hall, S. 1994, 'Cultural Identity and Diaspora', in P. Williams and L. Chrisman (eds), *Colonial Discourse and Postcolonial Theory: a Reader*, Harvester Wheatsheaf, London, pp. 392–403.

Heibert, D., Collins, J. and Spoonley, P. 2003, *Uneven Globalisation: Neo-Liberal Regimes, Immigration, and Multiculturalism in Canada, Australia and New Zealand. Research on Immigration and Integration in the Metropolis*, Vancouver Centre of Excellence, Vancouver.

Ho, E. 2002, 'Multi-local Residence, Transnational Networks: Chinese "Astronaut" Families in New Zealand', *Asian and Pacific Migration Journal*, vol. 11, no. 1, pp. 145–64.

Ip, D. 2006, 'Conclusion: Middling Transnationalism and Chinese Transmigration', in D. Ip, R. Hibbins and W.H. Chui (eds), *Experiences of Transnational Chinese Migrants in the Asia-Pacific*, Nova Science Publishers, New York.

Ip, D., Hibbins, R. and Chui, W.H. 2006, 'Transnationalism and Chinese Migration', in D. Ip, R. Hibbins and W.H. Chui (eds), *Experiences of Transnational Chinese Migrants in the Asia-Pacific*, Nova Science Publishers, New York.

Ip, R. and Chui, W.H. 2006, 'Hong Kong Chinese Women as Resilient Migrants', in D. Ip, R. Hibbins and W.H. Chui (eds), *Experiences of Transnational Chinese Migrants in the Asia-Pacific*, Nova Science Publishers, New York.

Kandiyoti, D. 2003, *Multiplicity and Its Discontents: Feminist Narratives of Transnational Belonging*, Genders, viewed 30 December 2006 <http://www.genders.org/g37/g37_kandiyoti.html>.

Kastoryano, R. 2000, 'Settlement, Transnational Communities and Citizenship', *International Social Science Journal*, vol. 52, no. 165, pp. 307–12.

Kessler, C.R. 1998, 'The Promise of American Citizenships', in N.M.J. Pickus (ed.), *Immigration and Citizenship in the Twenty-First Century*, Rowman and Littlefield, Lanham, pp. 3–39.

Kwok, J.T. 2005, 'Postcolonial Methodology and the Significance of Social Memory', personal communication.
Lambek, M. and Antze, P. 1996, 'Introduction: Forecasting Memory', in P. Antze and M. Lembek (eds), *Tense Past: Cultural Essays in Trauma and Memory*, Routledge, New York, pp. xvi–xix.
Lowell, B.L. 2000a, 'The Demand and New Legislation for Skilled Temporary Workers (H-1Bs) in the United States', *People and Place*, vol. 8, no. 4, pp. 29–35.
Lowell, B.L. 2000b, 'Information Technology and Foreign-born Workers in Contingent Jobs', *The Metropolis Conference*, Vancouver, Canada.
Mannheim, K. 1952, 'The Problems of Generations', in *Essays in the Sociology of Culture*, Routledge and Kegan Paul, London, pp. 276–322.
Motomura, H. 1998, 'Alienage Classifications in a Nation of Immigrants: Three Models of Permanent Residence', in N.M.J. Pickus (ed.), *Immigration and Citizenship in the Twenty-First Century*, Rowman and Littlefield, Lanham, pp. 199–222.
Olick, J.K. and Robbins, J. 1998, 'Social Memory Studies: From "Collective Memory" to the Historical Sociology of Mnemonic Practices', *American Review of Sociology*, vol. 24, pp. 105–40.
Ong, A. 1999, *Flexible Citizenship: the Cultural Logics of Transnationality*, Duke University Press, Durham.
Osborne, B. 2001, 'Landscapes, Memory, Monuments, and Commemoration: Putting Identity in its Place', *The Ethnocultural, Racial, Religious and Linguistic Diversity and Identity Seminar*, Halifax, Nova Scotia.
Pan, L. 1990, *Sons of the Yellow Emperor: a History of Chinese Diaspora*, Secker and Warburg, London.
Parker, D. 1995, *Through Different Eyes: the Cultural Identities of Young Chinese People in Britain*, Avebury, Aldershot.
Pickus, N.M.J. (ed.) 1998, *Immigration and Citizenship in the Twenty-First Century*, Rowman and Littlefield, Lanham.
Portes, A. 2001, 'Introduction: the Debates and Significance of Immigrant Transnationalism', *Global Networks*, vol. 1, no. 3, pp. 181–94.
Portes, A., Guarnizo, L.E. and Landolt, P. 1999, 'The Study of Transnationalism: Pitfalls and Promise of an Emergent Research Field', *Ethnic and Racial Studies*, vol. 22, no. 2, pp. 217–27.
Rouse, R. 1991, 'Mexican Migration and the Social Space of Postmodernism', *Diaspora*, vol. 1, pp. 8–23.
Schuck, P.H. 1998, *Citizens, Strangers, and In-Betweens: Essays on Immigration and Citizenship*, Westview, Boulder.
Smith, M.P. 2003, 'Transnationalism, the State and the Extraterritorial Citizen', *Politics and Society*, vol. 31, no. 4, pp. 467–502.
Taylor, C. 1998, 'Globalization and the Future of Canada', *Queen's Quarterly*, vol. 105, pp. 331–44.
Thomas, W. and Znaniecki, F. 1984, *The Polish Peasant in Europe and America*, Dover, New York.
Vertovec, S. 2001, 'Transnationalism and Identity', *Journal of Ethnic and Migration Studies*, vol. 27, no. 4, pp. 573–610.
Vertovec, S. 2003, 'Migrant Transnationalism and Modes of Transformation', *International Migration Review*, vol. 37, pp. 641–2.

Vertovec, S. 2004, 'Cheap Calls: the Social Glue of Migrant Transnationalism', *Global Networks*, vol. 4, no. 2, pp. 219–24.

Walsh, A. 2004, 'Soa's Version: Ironic Form and Content in the Self-Account of a Transnational Métisse Narrator', *Global Networks*, vol. 4, no. 3, pp. 259–70.

Warner, W.L. and Srole, L. 1945, *The Social Systems of American Ethnic Groups*, Yale University Press, New Haven.

Windland, D.N. 1998, 'Our Home and Native Land? Canadian Ethnic Scholarship and the Challenge of Transnationalism', *Canadian Review of Sociology and Anthropology*, vol. 35, no. 4, pp. 555–77.

4
Chinese Collective Memories in Sydney

Walter F. Lalich

Introduction

Communal places comprise visible documents of the continuity of settlement. Like other ethnic groups in Sydney, Chinese immigrants developed communal places to satisfy a particular collectively perceived social need, either spiritual or secular. Collectively developed communal places identify perceived needs by a group of immigrants, urgency of need satisfaction, social objectives, settlement constraints, and patterns of collective engagement. Various places of worship, leisure, education and welfare denote arrival, transfer and maintenance of culture, established roots, community care and a new communal address.

Immigrants form groups on the basis of common ethnicity and settlement experience, but also according to place of origin, spiritual adherence, cultural and social differentiation, and enhanced social capital. Immigrants' particular interests become intertwined through their joint collective endeavour, materialized in a collective good, and the subsequent collective memory expressed through remembrance of people, events and things that mark their common experience. Hence, differences in collective memories emerge even among immigrants of the same ethnic and cultural origin.

Diverse immigrant groups develop needed communal places because the host society cannot or is not prepared to satisfy immigrants' disparate social needs. Heterogeneity of settlers irrespective of their ethnicity compounded by diversity of settlement experiences impacts on particularization of action. Consequently, immigrant collectives appropriate their own communal place to satisfy a particular collectively perceived social need, such as communication, spiritual adherence, recreation, socialization, culture transfer and maintenance, security and care for weaker community members. It is claimed by Hareven and Langenbach (1981, p. 119) that buildings derive historical importance, not only because of the time period of creation or aesthetic values, but also because of the social context in which they were developed and used, the functions fulfilled and experiences associated with them.

Communal places identify diverse collective engagements aimed to solve a collectively perceived social need. As tangible resources, as a part of the built environment and material world, ethnic communal places sustain myths and ideologies, evoke, locate and encapsulate collective memories (Halbwachs 1992; Hareven and Langenbach 1981; Irwin-Zarecka 1994; Laguerre 1999; Middleton and Edwards 1990; Radley 1990). People remember events in which they participate. These events are identified through their direct engagement in a particular communal place or building, grounding collective memory in the 'committed perspective of a group' (Wertsch 2002, p. 40). In these places, localized collective memories are formed, defined, displaced, altered, kept and transferred as they establish links between the past and present of a collective (Halbwachs 1992; Lowenthal 1985; Radley 1990).

The physical setting is important for people to remember past events as memories are generated out of group experiences. However, memories are not only inherited, refined and retained, but are recalled and transferred to the next generation. It is argued by Fernandez-Kelly (1995) that social networks do not exist separate from physical location, which in turn provides necessary tangible references in defining experiences and the character of reciprocity. This is underlined by the insights on the major role of Chinese places of worship, temples and churches, in community life in different contexts, including during settlement in a new social environment, in Sydney and other places of settlement (Chandler 1998; Jing 1996; Laguerre 1999; Mar 1993; Stephen 1997; Warner 1998; Yang 1999).

This chapter attempts to construct key identifiers of Chinese collective memories embedded in appropriated communal places. It is divided into three parts, starting with a brief theoretical discussion on collective or social memory that precedes considerations on public or communal places developed with the intent to facilitate comprehension of communal places as the key nodes of localized collective memories. The second part is constructed on the basis of data collected from Chinese ethnic organizations that have appropriated their own places in Sydney since the 1950s. The available data are used in the third part to develop observations on key memory landmarks localized in communal places and to explore probable patterns of Chinese collective memories in Sydney.

Collective memory

Collective memories evolve through direct and shared experience of people and establish reference points creating 'the most important symbolic resources' (Irwin-Zarecka 1994, pp. 54 and 67). Collective memory is intricately related to the sense of collective identity and a human place on earth. Weil (1996, p. 8) claims that 'a collectivity has its roots in the past' and adds that we have no other living sap, than 'treasures stored up from the past and digested, assimilated and created afresh by us'. More recently Cattell and Climo (2002, p. 4) interpret collective or social memory as a social reality, transmitted and sustained through the conscious efforts of groups and institutions. However, as social reality differs for diverse groups of people, so do their collective memories.

Social groups create memories and determine what is memorable and what is not, as individuals remember and identify with events of importance to their group. Collective or social memory considered as a social construct is the outcome of a process of organizational discourse, selection (of events) and mediation (Halbwachs 1992). To Radley (1990) social remembering is the collective recounting of a shared past experience as events are mediated and more significant ones selected to be remembered, communicated and transmitted between people and across generations. As collective memory is a dynamic category and not fixed, past events could be remembered and interpreted differently (Burke 1989; Cattell and Climo 2002; Halbwachs 1992; Irwin-Zarecka 1994; Laguerre 1999; Wertsch 2002). It is fostered by a collective act in the appropriation and subsequent consumption of a collective good, the communal place.

Immigrant collectives have their own experience of a 'lived' past that generates their own collective memory. A community is constituted by its 'own' past as people tend not to forget the past (at least the past they choose not to forget); as they remember together and share memories of events and objects that are social in origin (Middleton and Edwards 1990, p. 3). Hence a claim by Bellah and Madsen (1985) that a real community is a 'community of memory', as it has its own past. Stories of success and suffering, hopes and commitment, time and space, create a narrative and remembrance of past events and people directly related to a particular collective with shared cultural understanding and settlement experience. As a resource, collective memories help maintain social bonds, claiming authority for mobilizing and legitimizing current and future action (Irwin-Zarecka 1994; Radley 1990), and contributing to the creation of 'coherent individual and group identities' (Wertsch 2002, p. 31).

Inevitably, there is coexistence of ethnic communal places and generated collective memories. Collective memory is localized within a particular group (Halbwachs 1992, pp. 38, 51), but also in a collectively appropriated place, and reflects the experienced past within the given socio-spatial context. It is argued by Casey (1993) that memory is place-oriented as we summon up places in mind and memory. Moreover, Casey's formulation of 'place memory', meaning the stabilizing persistence of a place as a container of experiences that 'contributes so powerfully to its intrinsic memorability', is applied by Hayden (1995, pp. 46–7) in her claim that place memory can help 'trigger social memory' for people-insiders who have shared a common past, while at the same time it can represent a shared past to outsiders too. Places where events and things happened are stimuli to memory according to Archibald (2002), as there 'memories will pour out with irresistible force'. Moreover, Burke (1989, pp.106–7) argues that uprooted people have a very deep sense of social memory and use it to define their identity. The settlement experience is often particularized and, consequently, collective memories differ within any large ethnic group.

Communal places

Immigrants often do not access the existing public places due to cultural differences and preferences, inadequate information, and various social constraints. Most post-Second World War immigrant communities in Sydney neither inherited appropriate communal places nor had easy access to suitable public places. As a consequence, many immigrant groups established their own communal places to satisfy a particular collectively perceived need, appropriating urban space through collective action. Place is comprehended as a particular physical object established by human activity with a definite social intent. People and places are considered as mutually constitutive, as places and people cannot exist without each other (Relph 1976; Sack 2000).

The intricate idea of place is defined by Heidegger's (1993) use of *dwelling* to denote capacities for building, cultivation, construction and safeguarding. A particular place is endowed with utility that enables production and consumption, but it is also a symbolic representation of culture, and as symbols 'become endowed with meaning' (Parsons and Shils 1962). A place is marked by human experience, by living beings whose relation to that physical object is compounded by feelings and thoughts (Lefebvre 1991), and by place attachment accrued over time (Cresswell 1996; Tuan 1977). As the most visible aspects of settlement, communal places are the key ethnic resource, a 'tangible asset' (Barth 1969).

People perceive their own belonging and attachment to communal places as they perform obligations, services and commit their resources (Scherer 1972, p. 44). Similarly, Hareven and Langenbach (1981, pp. 114–19) claim that the present and past personal, and collective, experience is identified with buildings. Human attachment to places is real and symbolic, as it is intertwined with personal roles, associations with other people, mutuality and institutional ties. The symbolic value of a particular place evolves because of a way of life, its role in human lives, projected sense of continuity, and often because of its environmental quality and aesthetic value and style. These memory landmarks associated with a familiar way of life provide continuity of social as well as physical fibre, and 'the more mobile a society, the greater the value of the continuity symbolised by these buildings'.

As a social construct, place combines the spatial with the social and facilitates ideological and psychological attachments. The properties of a place are manifold, as they secure an anchor to stabilize personal and collective identities, or rootedness; locate local knowledge; enable social interaction; provide utility and the image of stability and permanence (Casey 1993; Smith et al. 1998; Tuan 1977). Also, Balshaw and Kennedy (2000, p. 6) indicate that places, through localized stories, images and memories, provide meaningful cultural and historical bearings for individuals and communities.

The practice of communal place-making is a fragmented activity that anchors diverse cultures or subcultures creating a new urban heterogeneity. This is very well expressed through the particularized experience of a large body of settlers identified by a common Chinese ethnic background in Sydney, but fragmented due to place of origin, linguistic, cultural, religious, political and social differentiation. It is indicated by Knox (1995) that the production of the built environment is not simply a function of supply and demand within the socio-economic system, but also a 'function of time- and place-specific social relations that involve a variety of actors or participants, including the State'. Such places are defined as collective goods rather than public goods because of the exclusive nature of their production and consumption.

Collective memories landmarks

Places or physical objects are the mode capable of encapsulating and transmitting collective memories (Burke 1989; Cattell and Climo 2002; Halbwachs 1992; Laguerre 1999). Places make memories cohere in complex ways (Hayden 1995, p. 43), as there is a direct link between physical settings and memory as places, built or 'fabricated environments', and the other artefacts which help us to remember the course of events that lead to the present (Radley 1990, p. 49). Diverse ethnic communal places are the source and the medium of transmission of the locally established collective memories. Through development of communal places immigrants establish their own 'landmarks of recollections' (Halbwachs 1992, p. 175) or 'physical memory markers' (Irwin-Zarecka 1994, p. 151), that is, signifiers of their past collective efforts and experience. Place-embedded collective or social memory is a social construct that evolves out of a shared settlement experience.

As a key ethnic resource with important utilitarian, symbolic and emotional meanings, communal places signify arrival, settlement, culture transfer and maintenance of ethnic identity in a new social environment. Communal places communicate to others about people that developed it, their values, aspirations, needs and desires (Ryan 1983; Thwaites 2000). They are tangible links with the shared past which helps to sustain identity, as people identify with places that provide tangible manifestation of individual and collective identity. The argument by Tuan (1977, p. 164) that many places built to satisfy practical needs could also appropriate the meaning of a *home* is supported by Bookchin's (1982) claims of acute human *sense of place* and that decentralized communities would most likely have a strong commitment to place. Immigrant communal places appropriate the status of a communal *home* as they remain a fixed object that anchors feelings and memories, besides its utility function as a location of social exchange, and the resistance against hegemonic structures (Cresswell 1996). This intricate importance of ethnic communal places is even more emphasized in society marked by social and spatial mobility.

Collective appropriations of places for common need differ between similar events even among collectives of the same ethnic background. Hence, such visible symbolic references to transferred culture and to the process of urban development are not only an addition to landscape, but also repositories of a particularized collective memory. Here, places are representative not of official histories, but of *common* or *popular* memories (Hareven and Langenbach 1981; Middleton and Edwards 1990) of people who settled in a new environment. Furthermore, various material artefacts, relics and construction material donated to communal places further expand not only the sense of attachment, but also the intensity of collective memory.

The culturally diverse population in immigrant societies creates unpredictable spaces of the public realm that become both sites and sights of new collective identities. Nevertheless, collective memory localized in a particular physical object, or node in social space, often transcends group, ethnic, urban and state boundaries. This adds to the totality of human experience as immigrant collective memories become linked both to the place of settlement and to the place of origin, being eventually embodied in multiple collective memories that extend beyond experiential, generational and spatial limits.

Chinese settlement in Sydney

Post-1950s Chinese immigrants arrived from 21 other countries (Lynch 1971, p. 10), not only from China, Hong Kong, Macau and Taiwan, which underlines the diversity of their settlement experiences in Sydney and Australia. This immigration stream is socially differentiated by language, dialect, place of origin, religious beliefs, ideology, education, age, class and transferred wealth, as well as by the diversity of the interim migration experience. However, similar to earlier settlers, new Chinese immigrants continued to develop their own organizations as they established at least 260 different non-profit organizations to satisfy their diversified spiritual and secular collective needs. This development reflects diversity of collective experiences in undertaking measures to satisfy social needs perceived by the fragmented Chinese ethnic segment of Sydney's population and the consequent plurality of their collective memories.

Sydney as destination city

Sydney is the most popular settlement destination in Australia for all immigrants, with 23 per cent or 906,954 settlers born overseas coming from over 220 national groups (ABS 2001; CRC 2003). There were 118,146 Sydneysiders in 2001 born in China and Hong Kong, and an additional 8977 residents in New South Wales born in Macau and Taiwan. The Chinese are the largest foreign-born community after British-born settlers in Sydney, as 248,756 of its inhabitants are of Chinese descent, although it is difficult to estimate precisely the number of ethnic Chinese in Australia (Burnley 2001; Hon and Coughlan 1997).

This recent Chinese settlement is characterized not only by structural differentiation but also by spatial dispersion. Among the Chinese in Sydney there are now more female immigrants (ABS 2001), as well as many transnational and 'astronaut' immigrants (Inglis and Wu 1992; Pe-pua et al. 1996). This differs from the immigration of predominantly male sojourners in the nineteenth century who arrived mostly from four districts in Quandong province (Choi 1975), and from the situation recorded in 1947 when there were only 9144 Chinese settlers or 0.12 per cent of the total Australian population as a consequence of the impediments established by the 'White Australia policy'.

The heterogeneous nature of Chinese immigration is indicated by census data on the incidence of home use of Chinese languages and dialects by at least 190,400 persons (CRC 2003), or over 17 per cent of all Sydney inhabitants using another language at home rather than English. Cantonese is used at home by 61 per cent, in comparison with 34 per cent who used Mandarin and 5 per cent who used other Chinese languages and dialects in 2001 (CRC 2003).

Chinese settlers are dispersed across the Sydney metropolitan area. In 18 out of 44 local government areas (suburbs), Chinese languages are used at home by more than 5 per cent of all inhabitants; in nine suburbs this ratio exceeds 10 per cent, the maximum being in Auburn with 16.7 per cent (CRC 2003). This differs from the situation in the first half of the last century when most Chinese in Sydney settled in and close to Chinatown (Fitzgerald 1997). This structurally and spatially differentiated settlement had consequent organizational implications as well.

Development of Chinese communal places

Approximately one-fifth of a conservatively estimated 260 Chinese ethnic communal organizations have appropriated their own facilities in Sydney since 1957, the year when the Chinese Presbyterian Church dating from the nineteenth century in the inner-city suburb of Redfern acquired larger premises (Mar 1993). These places were appropriated to satisfy spiritual and secular needs reflecting traditional linkages (origin, dialect and religion) and current structural social changes. Some, like childcare, welfare and aged-care facilities were developed with the support of public authorities reflecting changes in public policy. Schools were not constructed except within the premises of community organizations, while some organizations use the existing, and more accessible, public schools for language and religious education over the weekends.

A summary of the postwar appropriation of communal places in Table 4.1 indicates the intensity of the development of Chinese communal places in recent decades. These places are categorized as Buddhist temples, Christian churches, community centres, social clubs, and aged-care organizations. Although 90 per cent of the appropriation has occurred over the last 20 years, 50 per cent occurred during the 1990s, indicating not only continuous immigration, but also persistence of needs and affluence.

Chinese organizations situated their places across the metropolitan area. Besides spatial demographic dispersion, among the major location-determining factors are the availability of existing public buildings and accessible undeveloped land. The process of appropriation differed as some

Table 4.1 Development of Chinese communal places, Sydney, 1956–2000 (units)

Periods	*Buddhist temples*	*Christian churches*	*Social clubs*	*Community centres*	*Aged care*	*All communal places*
1956–60			2			2
1961–70		2	1			3
1971–80	1					1
1981–90	2	3	2	3	3	13
1991–2000	8	11	2	1	2	24
Total established	11	16	7	4	5	43

Source: Lalich (2004).

collectives purchased inadequately patronized and abandoned churches and masonic halls, while others built new buildings on purchased, donated and, in one case, even on land leased from the state over a long period. However, unlike in the earlier postwar decades when most places were established close to the CBD and in more densely inhabited inner (sub)urban areas, local government authorities now have more stringent development requirements for public places, particularly in relation to parking, safety and noise disturbance. It is estimated that 43 respondent Chinese organizations developed at least 30,000 square metres of communal space, of which just over 50 per cent were for religious entities.

Institutional framework

The development of Chinese communal places is a consequence of a socially stratified immigration, culture transfers, encountered social constraints and spatial dispersion. The outcome of direct human engagement in diverse collectives is identified by data on appropriated buildings, modes of human involvement and indicators of externalities. The differing experience of various Chinese collectives during the process of appropriation of communal places creates diverse localized collective memories.

It is estimated that Chinese communal places serve the current needs of over 31,000 persons or at least 15 per cent of the Chinese speakers in Sydney (Table 4.2). However, the available estimates do not provide complete information because of difficulties in ascertaining the full extent of participation as it does not fully record participation of spouses. Data do not include children attending Sunday and language schools, but do include attendance at childcare places and the residents of homes for the elderly, and this allows for possible further adjustments in the numbers of consumers.

Table 4.2 Chinese community organizations: community participation, Sydney, estimate 2001

Dimensions	*Buddhist temples* (n = *11*)	*Christian churches* (n = *16*)	*Regional clubs* (n = *6*)	*Community centres* (n = *5*)	*Aged care* (n = *5*)	*Total places* (n = *43*)
Participants	4,450	3,775	3,750	18,649	398	31,022
Actively engaged	336	1,359	381	1,128	250	3,454

Source: Lalich (2004).

Social value

The development of ethnic communal places, of new urban and community resources, is a final product of locally generated social capital. This mobilization of human and social capital created significant material value and generated immeasurable social value for the local Chinese communities over a short time span. The established social value can be perceived through the personal satisfaction of members or consumers of appropriated places acquired through satisfaction of social needs; provision of solutions to major family problems; creation of opportunities for communication, socialization and meeting with co-ethnics; enabling transfer and maintenance of culture and language; the development of a new sense of belonging and attachment; continuity of contacts with the place of origin; and establishment of links with the immediate social environment.

The grounds for continuous generation of activities within the functional description of a particular place are established, and communal places are imbued with a sense of dynamics, of life. Furthermore, a feeling of a *sense of place* is generated towards communal places, as they are not just any accessible place but places that have certain connotations of a *home* with localized human feelings of attachment outside the family home. The sense of attachment to a particular communal place could be derived from functional and relational reasons. Developed social values or attachment to religious and secular communal places among Chinese communities in Sydney are presented in Table 4.3.

Data in Table 4.3 are based on the average of approximately three relational indicators per organization. Social clubs and community centres generated 31 sense of attachment indicators, while religious organizations established 59 indicators. This compares with the total number of 641 indicators for all religious and 342 for all leisure ethnic organizations (Lalich 2005). Still, despite the small sample it is possible to separate

Table 4.3 Chinese religious and secular community organizations: dispersions of a sense of attachment indicators (%)

Relational signifiers	*Secular (31%)*	*Religious (59%)*	*Functional signifiers*	*Secular (31%)*	*Religious (59%)*
Feeling of home	38.7	13.6	Religious		32.2
Way of life		6.8	Meeting with friends	9.7	13.6
Involvement		6.8	Access to help	25.8	13.6
Relaxed	9.7		Social potential	6.4	8.4
Uniqueness	9.7		Education		5.0

Source: Lalich (2004).

indicators into functional and relational categories. Immigrants develop close relationships to communal places, where they establish roots in a new environment and acquire a sense of belonging and security, and many identify closely with the communal place they helped to establish and pertinent activities are being realized satisfying social needs. Among social clubs and community centres the most prominent response relates to the *feeling of home*. Although many respondent religious organizations also emphasized the importance of a feeling of home in their perception, functional indicators are nevertheless more prominently emphasized.

For many immigrants communal places are a real *home*, or home away from home. Moreover, the *communal home*, being collectively developed and consumed, provides landmarks for very intricate feelings and memories to people that developed it, and make it possible for any collective to reconstruct their past at any moment. These indicators provide insights into the patterns of attachments oriented towards established communal places, the apparent differences in developed relations and in the intent behind collective engagement. Collective memories differ as experiences vary during the lifespan of ethnic communal places. People directly related to a particular communal place do have a different set of memories than the other comparative groups, as 'the community of memory materializes in space and is supported by space' (Laguerre 1999). Their collective memory is localized in a particular place that they helped to develop and consume, where they bond with other participants and have acquired diverse external linkages. Such places appropriate important symbolic significance to particular groups of people that is embedded in a particularized collective memory as well. This is best described by the statement 'As three generations of my family have been involved in the affairs of the temple, I felt compelled to research and record its history' (see K. Fong in Sze Yup Society 1998, p. 30).

Landmarks of Chinese collective memories in Sydney

These communal endeavours were also facilitated by the change in local social circumstances, and hence it is an analysis of creation or construction and not of demise or destruction as it was in the earlier experience of Chinese collectives in Australia (Choi 1975; Mar 1993; Stephen 1997). Despite encountered constraints, postwar experience related the success in achieved collective aims reflecting the ability of groups of people to collectively respond to settlement challenges. This experience tells about self-reliance, collective spirit, voluntary engagement, appropriated communal places, locations, generated activities and feeling of belonging as major elements of perceived collective memories of many diverse Chinese collectives. New Chinese social and urban landmarks were created on the city map.

Through collective actions settlers solve social problems appropriating a place for communal use and create memory markers, landmarks, a very segmented field of experiences with diversely constructed experiential or memory frameworks (Halbwachs 1992). Most of the recent appropriation of Chinese communal space in Sydney occurred within a short time period, and in some cases it is still primarily the experience of a first generation. Nearly 50 diverse collective experiences localized in collectively appropriated communal places that could often have certain similarities and even direct linkages create a local field of Chinese collective memories.

This settlement experience defined by appropriated communal places, that is, in actions and everyday life, is now 'immobilized in clearly defined frameworks' (Halbwachs 1992, p. 151). The comprehension of presumed key aspects of collective memories located in communal places is necessarily very subjective. A dutiful immersion in a particular collective could produce a remembrance of the past collective experience and, probably, different insights into memory landmarks. Following Halbwach's emphasis that only experiences with a 'pedagogical character' would be retained by memory, an attempt is made to retain and analyse some registered and presumably representative experiences, like human engagement, inclusion, location and linkage effects, in addition to earlier discussed attachment to appropriated places.

Human engagement

The use of communal places and subsequent activities conducted at or from these places enable people to actively engage and to apply human and social capital, and material resources. People participants actively engage in the development, management and in the consumption of established communal places, either through leadership, management roles, voluntary work, use of capacities, participation in activities or provision of regular financial support. Through engagement in organizational life, people become socially and emotionally attached to their communal place. Chinese communal places in Sydney are managed by at least 600 volunteer committee members who are assisted by over 2500 additional volunteers in various functions, ranging from Sunday school teachers to organizers of sport activities and in cooking community Sunday meals. However, the number of volunteers is difficult to estimate and the data presented indicate the lowest estimate, since usually 'everyone is a volunteer' in smaller organizations. Finally, these organizations have generated employment opportunities for around 400 people, some of whom are non-Chinese.

People organize with the intention to collectively satisfy perceived needs, through the appropriation and the management of necessary physical objects. During that process, decisions are made and activities undertaken. This direct involvement in the life cycle of a communal place is recognized and recalled in the memory of participants of a particular collective. Through active participation, joint activities, communal meetings and other repeated actions (Halbwachs 1992, p. 47), individuals or participants recall their immediate past experience, creating a process of continuous recall and mediation. In many instances members of a collective pay tribute to people actively involved in the development; many ethnic facilities or publications have names of benefactors identified. Over the years this past joint experience constitutes the collective memory, and history, of that particular place and a group of people.

The process of decision making, and the ensuing financial burden and voluntary work, has its meaning and place in the collective memory. In many instances an individual is prepared to take on a higher burden and provide more resources. It is a collective decision to get involved with the intent to appropriate a suitable place and to carry the burden that becomes encapsulated in collective memory. Initially, only a few Chinese organizations benefited from acts of philanthropy, either by an external patronage, like the large Cabramatta Temple, or by the priests who started the development of several smaller temples, as in Cabramatta, Forrestville and Surry Hills. However, nowadays some people do appear as major donors (ACCA 1999). Furthermore, there is increased dependence on overseas funding, while some welfare service providers depend very much on government support. Hence, human engagement differs among organizations and generations, creating not only differences in the development path but of collective memories as well.

Financial engagement

Community engagement can be monitored through direct financial involvement in several phases of an organizational life cycle: the initial purchase of a physical object or undeveloped land, development of facilities, everyday financing and anticipated future upgrading and expansion. The appropriation of communal places was primarily possible because of the direct financial involvement by members of diverse collectives. It is estimated that members of diverse Chinese organizations donated at least 63 per cent of the estimated value of total investment of around 100 million Australian dollars (expressed in year 2000 dollar value). This direct involvement made possible additional financing from other sources. The additional sources of financing also became possible because of changes in public policy, recognition of newly formed ethnic organizational entities and increasing overseas affluence. As a consequence the needed financial resources were in some cases supplemented from diverse local and overseas sources with an impact on the construction of collective memories.

Various forms of community contributions (offerings, donations, fund-raising drives and internal loans) are the single most important sources for the investment and the repayment of loans or outside financial support, in particular for religious and leisure facilities. The most important source of financing of welfare places, aged care and childcare in community centres is public funding, as Australian governments have become supportive of the development of ethnic community welfare and education facilities since 1980 (Foster and Stockley 1988; Galbally 1978). Also, various religious organizations received financial aid from the affiliated organizational network to overcome initial investment obstacles, and as some organizations have branched out into new locations, the parent organization provided necessary capital for their initial development. The overseas support was mostly directed to the development of Buddhist temples and to a smaller degree of aged-care facilities. Financial institutions played a major role in financing the development of social clubs, and to a lesser degree of various religious and aged-care facilities.

This dependence on communal funding as a key source of investment indicates institutional embeddedness in their own community and in the new social environment where additional sources of public and commercial funding are generated. Consequently, current Chinese collective memories differ from former experiences when communities depended only on their own resources for social support and survival (Choi 1975). In comparison, the oldest Buddhist temples, Sze Yup and Yiu Ming, built in the late nineteenth century, were declared heritage objects and after decades of decay were reconstructed with financial and technical help by public authorities and commercial entities in the late twentieth century (Stephen 1997; Sze Yup Society 1998). It is recorded that the Yiu Ming Temple has served the religious and social needs of its community, maintaining their culture through the difficult decades of the 'white Australia' policy and into the multicultural present (Stephen 1997, p. 7).

Inclusion

Unlike the earlier period of settlement when the exclusion of Chinese was both the public attitude and policy, the recent period is marked with a difference. Cultural diversity and inclusion are a new paradigm in a culturally diverse society, although the evident ideological, cultural and linguistic differences impose certain limits. However, inclusion appropriates different significances and reflects relationships beyond the encounter with the immediate environment.

The recorded experiences of organizations differ. The development of the Buddhist and Tao Wong Tai Zin Temple in Ashfield encountered objections at the local level when it developed from a masonic hall, as evidently certain local property interests did not like this development. On the other hand, good and friendly relations with the immediate neighbourhood are the experience of the Kuan Zin Temple in Canley Vale. This development cleared the formerly unused property of local drug addicts. The landscape of this distant suburb is now firmly defined by the temple's Chinese garden, the Australian Chinese and Descendants Mutual Association (ACDMA) Retirement Home's Chinese pergola and the street ornaments of the Tien Hau Temple on the other side of the railway station.

Various collectives identify some form of government help in the recall of their development, and in particular by the child and aged-care organizations. Even more so, there is a marked difference between the oldest Chinese Christian church in Sydney, the Presbyterian Church established in 1893, that for years could not bring in a priest because of the official policy (Mar 1993) and the Western Sydney Presbyterian Church, that with the other four ethnic collectives (Khmer, Lao, Turkish, Vietnamese) developed on land leased for 60 years by the Government of NSW. This church is among several other Chinese churches and temples established in distant suburbs, and are, like many other ethnic communal developments, among the first public buildings erected in the area which was being intensively peopled in the second half of the last century.

There is also a specific form of inclusion by some postwar Chinese organizations that used the advantage of the formerly developed public space in the former Chinatown, in Surry Hills (Fitzgerald 1997). The old buildings were purchased and adapted for communal use. These organizations exploit the advantages of a known, easily understood and accessible place. This development preserved some features of the once proscribed Chinatown, adding a new quality and dimension to the inner city. Some of these functionally diverse places are, because of their accessibility, of major importance to many elderly Chinese residents who followed their children to Sydney through the family reunion immigration scheme. By providing meeting places for people living in different parts of the metropolitan area, these places extended the social significance of the new commercialized Chinatown. Continuous ethnic consumption of place extends the collective memory beyond the organizational beginning, incorporating memories from the former settlement experiences.

Locations

Respondent Chinese communal organizations are mostly satisfied with the location of existing facilities, but not necessarily with the developed premises. This enables continuous involvement and creation of new opportunities and modes of satisfaction, and of collective memories located in a particular place situated in social space, the immediate neighbourhood and in the (sub)urban environment. The location of a communal place often has a significant bearing on the quality of communal life. Spatial and social mobility of settlers within the metropolitan area affects the location of ethnic communal places, daily management, the quality of communal life creating various experiences, processes and collective memories. Such diversity of human engagement adds to the totality of the postwar history of Chinese settlement experience in Sydney.

Decisions on locations are crucial as they imply not only accessibility, organizational fixed abode and address, but also roots in a new environment. Considerations of locations are for some organizations a continuous process due to changes in circumstances and challenges, and some have to reflect on the sustainability of the current location, particularly in the light of spatial mobility and generational changes. Some organizations branched out, creating new communal places, new nodes, providing financial support and instigating new collective memory frameworks as well.

Traditionally, immigrants in Sydney choose locations close to railway stations for the development of their communal places to secure easy access. Out of the 19 clusters of ethnic communal places developed in the second half of the twentieth century only three did not form close to a railway station. The cluster of eight Chinese organizations in Surry Hills developed close to a railway station like some other spatially dispersed

Chinese communal places facilitating inclusion of the elderly immigrants in community life.

Many participants in communal functions often travel an hour or even more to attend religious activities that turn into day-long communal events with the additional forms of exchange and bonding. Consequently, some spatially dispersed organizations are faced with the challenge to move from the present, albeit, attractive addresses to one that is closer to transport hubs, more suitable locations or larger concentration of co-ethnics. To service their members some organizations rent public schools close to railway stations, like the Evangelical Free Church from East Lindfield and the Chinese Congregational Church from Padstow. Similarly, Hwa Tsang Temple in Homebush complements its limited capacities with the use of a nearby public school to realize its Youth Fellowship programme and diverse tuition, computer and adult English classes; only 40 per cent of students are of the Buddhist faith (Hwa Tsang Monastery Inc. 1996).

Finally, some ethnic communal organizations, like the Taiwanese Friendship Association, developed their facilities in semi-industrial zones. Development at such locations facilitates activities and avoids problems like parking, noise and other disturbance. Such locations are highly valued because of the ease of access and ample parking space over the weekends. Consequently, diverse spatial decisions create important landmarks in communal life and in the resultant collective memories.

Linkages

Diverse linkages established as a consequence of the defined function and generated activities provide diverse experiences and memory landmarks. Links are defined as frequency and purpose of visits and origin of visitors, established local and overseas contacts, sources of material help, received funding, contacts with youth. Further examples are events such as the Chinese New Year, dragon boat racing, organization of youth visits to the place of origin of their forebears, local visits, investment, or material aid. The existence of developed communal places makes such diverse patterns of linkages not only feasible but also sustainable.

However, there is no uniform pattern of established linkages, and these differences have far-reaching effects reflecting organizational ability to communicate at different levels with their own community, place of origin, immediate neighbourhood, transnationally and the second generation. The complexity of linkage effects is illustrated in the finding that ethnic religious and leisure places generate over 15 different activities and often more than one function per unit, while aged-care units record at least ten diverse activities (Lalich 2004). Such diversity puts additional emphasis on the variety of collective experiences and memories created through the process of appropriation and consumption of communal places by diverse Chinese immigrant collectives in Sydney as well.

It is found that Buddhist organizations have more intensive contacts with the place of origin than Christian religious organizations, which had more intensive contacts with the local social environment and the second generation. The latter emphasis is of particular significance because intrinsic to collective memory is its transgenerational character. Similarly, community centres have more intensive contacts with the local environment since to a certain degree they depend more on public support than social clubs, which are primarily oriented towards their own community and the place of origin, but not necessarily towards the next generation. The observed pattern of established relations defines the temporality of many ethnic clubs within the process of social and generational changes.

All ethnic collective organizations are repositories of transferred culture and memories from the place of origin. However, new memories are created that directly relate to the development and life of a particular ethnic communal place. Moreover, some have acquired public places developed by the earlier (non-Chinese) settlers through the process of 'ethnic succession' (Waldinger et al. 1990). Consequently, memory landmarks related to such communal places generated by diverse communities are defined by the continuity of their public significance and represent a totality of localized place memories. Memories are therefore not only transferred from home as some are inherited with the acquired building, while the most relevant experience of place, and henceforth memories, are created within a particular ethnic collective. An example could be provided through the story of the Chinese Evangelical Church which did not encounter any problems from their neighbours in East Lindfield, but the native Baptist community that built it 30 years before did meet serious obstructions.

During this period various postwar appropriated ethnic communal places were declared as heritage, being representative of the social development of various suburbs as well. Such communal places signify duality of heritage, being representative of reterritorialized (Deleuze and Guattari 1994) cultures and of the development in a particular (sub)urban area. They are a *popular* communal heritage embedding collective memories transgressing generational and cultural boundaries. These places are of importance not only to people who initiated, developed and sustained them, but also to their descendants, neighbourhood and country of origin.

While imposing communal places on not always a very friendly environment, important segments of public history are created by diverse particularized immigrant collective actions.

Conclusion

This insight into the patterns of collective memories of diverse Chinese communities in Sydney is constructed on the basis of collected information, and as it is systematized subjectively it does not reflect participants' perception. This attempt to develop a pattern of key collective memory landmarks tries to approximate possible story exchanges, recall and mediation in individual collectives. Still, it indicates the plurality of responses by immigrants to the constraints at the time of settlement in Sydney. This discourse based on a limited sample nevertheless underlines the argument by Halbwachs (1992, p. 141) on collective memories as a vector of initiated functions and generated activities. Postwar Chinese settler immigrants reacted differently when responding to their collectively perceived needs and, in accordance with their capability and available resources, materialized desired aims by appropriating and securing access to places that satisfy their social needs.

A localized collective memory establishes a very specific memory framework for a particular group of people, while others have a different set of experiences and memories about a particular ethnic communal place. Through discussion on appropriated communal places, investment and sources of funding, human engagement, inclusion, created sense of place attachment, location, and diverse linkage effects, an attempt is made to develop an assumed memory framework. It attempts to establish insights into the possible memory frameworks arising out of documented experience in the development of communal places by diverse Chinese religious and secular collectives in Sydney over the second half of the twentieth century.

This analysis indicates that diverse collectives have different experiences, although there are some similarities within the process of production and consumption and consequent collective memory patterns. Memories of many immigrants are firmly localized in a particular communal place, but their relevance often transcends generational, cultural and spatial boundaries. It is argued by Halbwachs that in collective memories many individual memories are located as well; however, some people would join and participate in the life of diverse communal places, develop and consume diverse places. This particular aspect of the settlement experience of structurally stratified postwar Chinese immigrants is mapped in diverse collective memories localized at different communal places. Collective memories that hinge not only on places, but also on the participants, necessarily differ among place-defined memories, creating communities of memory. This attempt to emphasize some probable landmarks of localized collective memories provides insights into the complexity of the development of communal life by heterogeneous postwar Chinese settlers in Sydney, and hence in the plurality of locally embedded Chinese collective memories.

References

ABS 2001, *Clib, Census 2001 Statistics*, Australian Bureau of Statistics, Canberra.

ACCA 1999, *News*, Australian Chinese Community Association of NSW Inc., Sydney.

Archibald, R.R. 2002, 'A Personal History of Memory', in J.K. Climo and M.G. Cattell (eds), *Social Memory and History*, AltaMira Press, Walnut Creek, pp. 65–80.

Balshaw, M. and Kennedy, L. (eds) 2000, *Urban Space and Representation*, Pluto Press, London.

Barth, F. 1969, *Ethnic Groups and Boundaries: the Social Organization of Cultural Difference*, University Forlaget/George Allen & Unwin, Oslo/London.

Bellah, R.N. and Madsen, R. 1985, *Habits of the Heart: Individualism and Commitment in American Life*, University of California Press, Berkeley.

Bookchin, M. 1982, *The Ecology of Freedom*, Cheshire Books, Palo Alto.

Burke, P. 1989, 'History as Social Memory', in T. Butler (ed.), *Memory: History, Culture and the Mind*, Basil Blackwell, London, pp. 97–113.

Burnley, I. 2001, *The Impact of Immigration on Australia: a Demographic Approach*, Oxford University Press, Melbourne.

Casey, E.S. 1993, *Getting Back into Place: Towards Renewed Understanding of the Place-World*, Indiana University Press, Bloomington.

Cattell, M. and Climo, J. 2002, 'Introduction: Meaning in Social Memory: Anthropological Perspectives', in J. Climo and M. Cattell (eds), *Social Memory and History: Anthropological Perspectives*, AltaMira Press, Walnut Creek, pp. 1–38.

Chandler, S. 1998, 'Chinese Buddhism in America; Identity and Practice', in C.S. Prebish and K.K. Tanaka (eds), *The Faces of Buddhism in America*, University of California Press, Berkeley, pp. 13–30.

Choi, C.Y. 1975, *Chinese Migration and Settlement in Australia*, Sydney University Press, Sydney.

CRC 2003, *The People of New South Wales: Statistics from the 2001 Census*, Community Relations Commission for a Multicultural NSW, Sydney.

Cresswell, T. 1996, *In Place Out of Place: Geography, Ideology and Transgression*, University of Minnesota Press, Minneapolis.

Deleuze, G. and Guattari, F. 1994, *What is Philosophy?*, trans. H. Tomlinson and G. Burchill, Verso, London.

Fernandez-Kelly, M.P. 1995, 'Social and Cultural Capital in the Urban Ghetto: Implications for the Economic Sociology of Immigration', in A. Portes (ed.), *The Economic Sociology of Immigration*, Russell Sage Foundation, New York, pp. 213–47.

Fitzgerald, S. 1997, *Red Tape, Gold Scissors: the Story of Sydney's Chinese*, State Library NSW, Sydney.

Foster, L. and Stockley, D. 1988, *Australian Multiculturalism: a Documentary History and Critique*, Multinlingual Matters Ltd, Clevedon/Philadelphia.

Galbally, F. 1978, *Migrant Services and Programs: Report of the Review of Post-Arrival Programs and Services for Migrants*, AGPS, Canberra.

Halbwachs, M. 1992, *On Collective Memory*, Chicago University Press, Chicago.

Hareven, T.K. and Langenbach, R. 1981, 'Living Places, Work Places and Historical Identity', in D. Lowenthal and M. Binney (eds), *Our Past Before Us*, Temple Smith, London, pp. 109–23.

Hayden, D. 1995, *The Power of Place: Urban Landscapes as Public History*, The MIT Press, Cambridge.

Heidegger, M. 1993, *Basic Writings*, Routledge, London.

Hon, H.C. and Coughlan, J.E. 1997, 'The Chinese in Australia: Immigrants from the People's Republic of China, Malaysia, Singapore, Taiwan, Hong Kong and Macau', in J.E. Coughlan and D. McNamara (eds), *Asians in Australia: Patterns of Migration and Settlement*, Macmillan Education Australia, Melbourne, pp. 120–70.

Hwa Tsang Monastery Inc. 1996, *Hwa Tsang Monastery and its Developments*, Sydney.

Inglis, C. and Wu, C.T. 1992, 'The "New" Migration of Asian Skills and Capital to Australia', in C. Inglis, S. Gunasekaran, G. Sullivan and C.T. Wu (eds), *Asians in Australia: the Dynamics of Migration and Settlement*, Allen Unwin/ISAS, Sydney.

Irwin-Zarecka, I. 1994, *Frames of Remembrance: the Dynamics of Collective Memory*, Transaction Publishers, New Brunswick.

Jing, J. 1996, *Temple of Memories: History, Power, and Morality in a Chinese Village*, Stanford University Press, Stanford.

Knox, P. 1995, *Urban Social Geography*, Longman, Harlow.

Laguerre, M. 1999, *Minoritized Space*, University of California, Berkeley.

Lalich, W.F. 2004, 'Ethnic Community Capital: the Development of Ethnic Social Infrastructure in Sydney', PhD thesis, University of Technology, Sydney.

Lalich, W.F. 2005, 'The Development of Chinese Communal Places in Sydney', in K.E. Kuah-Pearce and E. Hu-DeHart (eds), *Chinese Voluntary Organisations in the Diaspora*, Hong Kong University Press, Hong Kong, pp. 169–200.

Lefebvre, H. 1991, *The Production of Space*, Blackwell, Oxford.

Lowenthal, D. 1985, *The Past is a Foreign Country*, Cambridge University Press, Cambridge.

Lynch, P. 1971, *The Evolution of Policy*, Department of Immigration, Canberra.

Mar, W.L. 1993, *So Great a Cloud of Witnesses: a History of the Chinese Presbyterian Church Sydney 1893–1993*, The Chinese Presbyterian Church, Sydney.

Middleton, D. and Edwards, D. 1990, *Collective Remembering*, Sage Publications, London.

Parsons, T. and Shils, E.A. (eds) 1962, *Toward a General Theory of Action*, Harper & Row, New York.

Pe-pua, R., Mitchell, C., Iredale, R. and Castles, S. 1996, *Astronaut Families and Parachute Children: the Cycle of Migration between Hong Kong and Australia*, Centre for Multicultural Studies, University of Wollongong/BIMPR, Canberra.

Radley, A. 1990, 'Artefacts, Memory and a Sense of the Past', in D. Middleton and D. Edwards (eds), *Collective Remembering*, Sage Publications, London, pp. 46–59.

Relph, E. 1976, *Place and Placelessness*, Pion Ltd, London.

Ryan, A. 1983, 'Public and Private Property', in A.I. Benn and G.F. Gauss (eds), *Public and Private in Social Life*, Crooms Helm, London.
Sack, R.D. 2000, 'Place, Power, and the Good', in P. Adams, C.S. Hoelscher and K. Till (eds), *Textures of Place: Exploring Humanist Geographies*, Minnesota University Press, Minneapolis, pp. 233–45.
Scherer, J. 1972, *Contemporary Community: Sociological Illusion or Reality*, Tavistock, London.
Smith, J.M., Light, A. and Roberts, D. 1998, 'Introduction: Philosophies and Geographies of Place', in A. Light and J.M. Smith (eds), *Philosophies of Place*, Rowman & Littlefield Publishers, Lanham/London, pp. 1–20.
Stephen, A. (ed.) 1997, *The Lions of Retreat Street: a Chinese Temple in Inner Street*, Hale and Iremonger/Powerhouse Publishing, Sydney.
Sze Yup Society 1998, *Sze Yup Kwan Ti Temple: 100 Year Centenary*, Sydney.
Thwaites, K. 2000, 'Experential Landscape: Place, Neighourhood and Community in Landscape Architecture', in J.F. Benson and M.H. Roe (eds), *Urban Lifestyles; Spaces, Places, People*, A T Balkema, Rotterdam, pp. 49–55.
Tuan, Y.F. 1977, *Space and Place: the Perspective of Experience*, University of Minnesota Press, Minneapolis.
Waldinger, R., McEvoy, D. and Aldrich, H.E. 1990, 'Spatial Dimensions of Opportunity Structures', in R. Waldinger, H.E. Aldrich and R. Ward (eds), *Ethnic Entrepreneurs: Immigrant Business in Industrial Society*, Sage Publications, Newbury Park, pp. 106–30.
Warner, R.S. 1998, 'Immigration and Religious Communities in the United States', in R.S. Warner and J. Wittner (eds), *Gatherings in Diaspora: Religious Communities and the New Immigration*, Temple University Press, Philadelphia, pp. 3–34.
Weil, S. 1996, *The Need for Roots*, Routledge, London.
Wertsch, J. 2002, *Voices of Collective Remembering*, Cambridge University Press, Cambridge.
Yang, F. 1999, *Chinese Christians in America*, The Pennsylvania University State Press, University Park.

5

Generational Identities through Time: Identities and Homelands of the ABCs

Lucille Ngan

Introduction

Diaspora usually presupposes connections between multiple communities of a dispersed population who feel, maintain, revive or reinvent a connection with a prior home in various ways. Members of Chinese diasporic communities dispersed throughout the world often make gradual transitions from a migrant to becoming a fully integrated member of the host society as they take root in a land away from the original home. Scholars such as Phizacklea (2000), Ryan (2002) and Waters (2002) have given much attention to the notion of coexisting homes that link the homeland with the host country. As Clifford (1994, p. 311) highlights, the discourse of diasporas reflect 'the sense of being part of an ongoing transnational network that includes the homeland, not as something simply left behind, but as a place of attachment in a contrapuntal modernity'. As such, ties to homeland play a crucial, ongoing and often central role in informing not only notions of ethnicity but also of one's relationship to society. An important aspect of such connections are the ways migrants and their descendants construct notions of 'home' whereby a sense of self, place and belonging are shaped, articulated and contested. 'Home' is embedded with meanings, emotions, experience and relationships that create a sense of belongingness, vital to the well-being of human life. Traditionally, 'home' has been located as the 'lived' experience of locality, a concrete place where intimate familial relations are established (Rapport and Dawson 1998). However, due to intensified interconnectedness across national and cultural borders diasporic Chinese are able to sustain multiple identities and create new cultural forms using elements from a diversity of settings (Ma 2003). As different people are drawn into interconnections with each other, waves of social transformation cross virtually all over the world which impact on the links between homeland and identity. Consequently, contemporary images of 'home' intertwine origin, roots, cultural heritage, ancestral homeland and local residence as part of a wider spatial world that has become important in theorizing identity. In order to comprehend identity formation of diasporic communities, notions of home need to be opened up to spatial explorations where identities are constructed through a complex of social relations overlapping spaces and places. Davidson (2003, p. 12) suggests that by incorporating a spatial understanding it 'enables home as spatiality to be stretched, to be multi focal, in that people conceptualise and act on different contexts of home, and thus are connected to home through variant social relations'. It is precisely because of its fluid nature, notions of home can be unfixed, multiple and contested. 'Home' thus represents imaginings that are spatially expressed and emotionally realized. This is no different for ABCs or Australian-born Chinese, especially those who can trace their lineage in Australia for three or more generations.

Transnational practices have been regarded as crucial processes that shape the construction of Chineseness for Chinese diasporic communities linking them from the host country to their homeland. In particular is the growing awareness of inadequacy of the older theoretical frameworks which emphasize migration as being a one-off process of movement from the homeland to a new home where a unilateral process of assimilation[1] occurs (see also Alba and Nee 1999; Basch et al. 1994). Now it is widely acknowledged that separate places form a contiguous community 'through the continuations circulation of people, money, goods and information' (Rouse 1991, p. 14). The establishment of identity and belonging is not simply enhanced by the continuous movement across physical territories, but is also conditioned by transnationality which Ong (1999, p. 4) defines as the 'cultural interconnectedness and mobility across space'. The exploration into the flexible practices and strategies of the transnationality of Chinese subjects has given rise to figures such as the 'multi-passport holder'; the multicultural manager with 'flexible capital'; the 'astronaut', shuttling across borders on business; 'parachute kids' who can be 'dropped off in another country by parents on the trans-Pacific business commute and so on' (Ong 1999, p. 19; also see Pe-pua et al. 1996). The framework seeks to understand the migration experience through multi-levels of social, legal, political, economic, religious and educational linkages that are sustained by both migrants and non-migrants across national borders which have important ramifications for the construction of home and identity. The emerging impression is that the overall cultural orientation of diasporic Chinese has been predominately shaped by their transnational linkages, the host country to a pre-existing home (Ma 2003). Thus, Chineseness is assumed to be linked with the intensity of transnational bonds and cultural identification with homeland as 'China' becomes a defining factor of their Chineseness.

Most researchers have largely centred on the regular transnational practices of first- and second-generation migrants and the sojourner's sense of roots in a diasporic setting. While the transnational characteristic of systematic border crossings may be part of interconnection with homeland, 'multi-locale diasporas cultures are not necessarily defined by a geographical boundary' (Clifford 1994, p. 304). As Nonini and Ong (1997, p. 26) among others observe, although Chinese identities in diasporas are transnational in nature, they are increasingly independent of place as they are made up of patterns such as varied connections of family ties, kinship, commerce and sentiments which denote a common condition that is perceived to be shared by individuals separated by space. All diasporic communities are characterized by some form of differentiation; differences proliferate among diasporic 'Chinese' as each diasporic Chinese community has its own cultural construction and conception of Chineseness, which invariably differs from Chinese communities elsewhere. Where diasporic narratives are fraught with contentions over belonging and difference, identities are often subject to notions of hybridity. While the concept of hybridity confronts and problematizes the unsettling boundaries of identities, ethnic identification is still largely perceived to decrease over successive generations, resulting in acculturation and then assimilation. Such melting-pot concepts contribute to the underlying reasons behind the lack of in-depth research relating to the negotiation of identity of the subsequent generations of diasporic communities.

Specifically, somewhat lost in the debate over Chinese diasporas and identities is the experience of those with long-term residence and who have well established themselves outside mainland China or in regions inhabited by a majority of Chinese population. Many do not engage in transnational practices or have the deep cultural memories of Chinese subjects as highlighted in the migration literature. There is little room in the diasporic paradigm for the principled ambivalence about physical return and attachment to land which characterizes much of their experience. In a certain manner, when descendants of early Chinese migrants become integrated into the host society, can we still continue to include them as members of a diasporic community? Can a fully fledged member of society experience hybridity? How do we articulate their connections to a larger imagery of Chineseness when transnational linkages to homeland are absent? This chapter brings to light some important issues in relation to the cultural consciousness of the subsequent generations of early Chinese migrants in Australia by exploring the hybrid space in which their identities are mingled with a variety of memories, experiences and voices. Data for this chapter were derived from in-depth interviews with 43 Australian-born Chinese whose families have resided in Australia for over three generations. For sake of brevity, I will address those who were born in Australia and whose parents (either one) were also born in Australia, in other words third-generation ABC or more, as 'long-established' ABC.[2] Pseudonyms have been used to maintain anonymity of interviewees.

Redefining subsequent generations

Invariably subsequent generations do not have the cultural memories of first generations; consequently, physical and emotional ties with homeland as China are typically less intense. In the case of long-established ABC, their experiences reveal that they do not meet the diasporic paradigm of a strong attachment to and desire for literal return to a well-preserved homeland. Such feeling can be illustrated by Jane, a third-generation ABC: 'China is just a foreign place, it means nothing much to me.' Perhaps an even more vivid illustration is the rectification of the phrases 'going back' and 'returning' which I unconsciously referred to during the course of an interview. Rob insisted that his family has resided in Australia for three generations, he has never been to China and lastly that he has no intention of going there. He contends, 'we still have a traditional family house which I have no interest in. Realistically what's the point! I will never go there, I have no association. It's a bit bizarre! I often say just give it away, we don't need it.' While he is definite he will not return to China, connections with a Chinese identity can nonetheless clearly be highlighted:

> I am Chinese because by definition I am. My cultural roots are Chinese. If you ask me what country I come from, it's Australia but my cultural background is Chinese. That is by definition, but I consider myself as an ABC. If you are asking me what makes me think I am Chinese, I don't know!

The fact that he does not maintain physical and emotional links with China yet still defines himself as Chinese and more specifically as ABC illustrates that decentred connections may be just as important as those formed around a teleology of return and origin. As Clifford (1994, p. 306) notes, 'a shared ongoing history of displacement, suffering, adaptation or resistance may be as important as the projection of a specific origin'. The specification of 'ABC' suggests an exclusive social space of Australian-born Chinese who are able to share a past experience of adaptation and connection but innately connected to a larger imagery of Chineseness that is shared by diasporic Chinese. Those with a long settlement history particularly take on new dimensions in their construal of their Chineseness through decentred connections rather than a linkage to a specific locality as homeland.

The meaning of Chineseness inevitably varies across the Chinese diaspora; the experience of Chineseness for overseas-born recent migrants cannot be qualified with that of subsequent generations as the values and practices of a culture change at different points in time. While the construction and conception of Chineseness for recent migrants are more subject to effects of transnationalism, for later generations the construal of identity is often accentuated through political interference motivated by representations of the past by their parents and grandparents. This is particularly so because diasporic memories are often affected by the different periods of the migration process; as such, it is inevitable that traditions and customs take on localized forms that are governed by the peculiarities of the wider society in which they are embedded. Concisely, not only do the meanings of 'Chineseness' change, the cultural practices are also changing and within each locality. What needs to be considered are the decentred links to a distant 'homeland' that are maintained by the force of memory, nostalgia and imagination of the family as they become a part of daily life which continuously shapes identities. The memories and imaginations of previous generations play an important aspect in the establishment of identity for the next generations who are further distant from their 'origin'.

This chapter examines the problematics of a diasporic notion of 'hybridity' through the dynamic interplay of memory and identity as a means to understand the negotiation of Chineseness of long-established ABC. While the concept of hybridity has been utilized as a centring tool to understand the entanglement and complexity of diasporic communities, it has largely been formulated as a means to understand the experience of recent migrants. What is often neglected in the literature are those who have a long settlement history, who certainly negotiate Chineseness in different ways and have varied physical and emotional ties to the homeland. As Mageo (2001, p. 2) contends, 'identities appear as sites of transit between layers of historical experience crosscut with hierarchies of gender, generation, and regional interests'. With respect to generation, for example, 'each cohort must reinterpret memories in forms that are most suitable to them, and each fashions an identity most appropriate to them' (see Kuah Pearce and Davidson's Introduction to this volume). As such, the following section brings to light such dimensions in relation to the significance of intergenerational ties that bring in the force of imagination as both memory and desire that are shared by long-established diasporic ABC. It begins by examining the misconceptions of models of hybridity in its incorporation of the experience of long-settled communities. Secondly, it brings to light the important dimension of diasporic imagination through intergenerational influence of memory and nostalgia as a significant aspect in the construction of Chineseness.

Hybridized lives of subsequent generations

Due to the varying circumstances of trajectories and the contextual pressure of wider society, social and cultural elements reproduced through memories of homeland often lead to the development of hybridized lives for people in diasporas. Just as memories are subject to transformation through the passing of time, identities are fluid and subject to the process of hybridization. Hall (1996) explains that the formation of identity is a hybrid process where the self becomes a flexible zone, opening up multiple discourses. The self in this respect is made up of past memories and future anticipation linked to an ever-transforming present. In this sense, these processes exacerbate the blurring of 'boundaries' resulting in more volatile realities of ethnicity for diasporic communities. The putative concept of hybridity has largely been formulated as a means to problematize the complex process of identity formation of recent migrant communities, particularly challenging the ideal of homogeneity embedded in early assimilation models. The model projects that through a process of assimilation, ethnic and racial groups would be integrated into the majority of society's institutions and culture in which minority identities would eventually disappear (Cornell and Hartmann 1998, p. 44). However, due to transgressions of boundaries and dynamics of the social environment, the formation of identity of diasporic communities is increasingly complex and cannot be defined simply in bounded homogeneous notions.

Conventional static collectivist notions of identity are incapable of capturing the essence of the shifting cultural identities of diasporic Chinese, and the safety of sameness embedded in these constructs no longer suffices for the understanding of social relations. As Wang (2002, p. 67) eloquently articulates, 'individuals sought, sometimes found, their own cultural amalgam in which they lodge a Chinese ethnic loyalty – but for many of them, neither tradition nor modernity alone could explain the complex and changing world in which they found themselves'. Diasporic narratives fraught with contentions over belonging and difference consequently lead to situations where the negotiation of identity for migrants and their descendants occurs in a space of liminality and concepts of a decentred identity develop. In the case of diasporic Chinese in Australia, particularly for first, one point five (the children who straddle the old and new home) and second generations, a number of studies have highlighted their feelings of liminality and hybridized identities (see, for example, Ang 2001 correspondingly; Davidson 2003; Pe-pua et al. 1996).

While the notion of hybridity confronts and problematizes the unsettling boundaries of identities, ethnic identification is still largely perceived to decrease over successive generations, resulting in acculturation and then assimilation consequently, resulting in a lack of in-depth research relating to identity formation of subsequent generations of early Chinese migrants in Australia. The common assumption is that a natural linear process occurs that eventually leads to complete integration into the mainstream society, and the consequent erasure of 'ethnicity' such as Chinese is perceived as the price of assimilation. In common parlance, the perception is the more Australian one becomes, the less Chinese one will be. Furthermore, as a result of the paucity of in-depth analysis on the identity of subsequent generation their claims to ethnicity have generally been seen as inauthentic and unfounded. According to Gans's (1979, p. 9) study among third- and fourth-generation European immigrants in the United States, only 'symbolic ethnicity' is left after substantive ties have disappeared. Gans suggests the following about symbolic identity: 'It is characterized by a nostalgic allegiance to the culture of the immigrant generation, or that of the old country; a love for and a pride in a tradition that can be felt without having to be incorporated in everyday behavior' (1979, p. 9).

Gans contends that successive generations are able to be 'ethnic' through symbols, but not necessarily by participating in ethnic organizations or affiliating with ethnic groups or by living in ethnic enclaves. In other words, symbolic ethnicity does not require functioning groups and networks, it does not need a practised culture, but is instead dominated by nostalgic memories and preservation of symbols such as ethnic restaurants and festivals. Thus occasional ethnic behaviour is seen by Gans as an absence of 'real' ethnicity. In short, Gans conceptualized the weakening of ethnicity as 'symbolic ethnicity' and argues that ethnicity is a question of 'feeling ethnic' rather than one of being so.

Such melting-pot concepts of acculturation, assimilation and integration contribute to the underlying reasons behind the lack of in-depth research relating to the negotiation of identity of subsequent generations of the ABC community. However, through in-depth interviews with participants, it is evident that that complicated entanglement of cultural boundaries embodies their daily life. As Jenny, a sixth-generation ABC says, 'I don't feel I fit into the Chinese community, but I don't really feel like I fit into the White community either. I sort of feel I am floating in between but I am okay with it.' Such liminal feeling of inability to fully belong to the white as well as the Chinese community is typical of their experience. The reality of hybridity is illuminated in Malcolm's acknowledgement of an 'in-between' culture:

> I think there is a culture of in-between but it hard to know who belongs to that culture. A lot of people are marrying Western people, do you include them or not? Realistically I am a hybrid of both, but I would like to be more on the Chinese side.

While subsequent generations have a strong sense of belonging and identities grounded in Australia, their particular histories of their families criss-crossed with personal experiences often do not fit into the master narrative of the dominant 'white' Australian culture. For Jenny, despite the fact that the majority of her friends are Westerners, and being in a de facto relationship with an Anglo-Australian, she still feels difficulty in fully integrating:

> I feel I am different. It depends on who I am with and how comfortable I am. So with different people, I feel more Chinese or less Chinese depending on what they do. I remember my friend once said to me, 'sometimes I forget that you are Chinese'. I thought that was a weird thing to say. It made me think twice. It made me notice.

Although she sees herself as an Australian, she is continually viewed through a prism of otherness differentiating her from 'white' Australians because of the stereotypical images imposed by the broader social spectrum.

It is important to point out here that while a sense of otherness often differentiates long-established ABC from dominant white Australians, neither do they fully associate with Chinese communities in Australia. It was common among the majority of the participants to experience a sense of difference that separates them from other 'Chinese' groups in Australia. The liminal zone in which long-established ABC are situated can further be highlighted by Rob, a fifth-generation ABC. He recalls a conversation with his wife who is a Hong Kong-born migrant who came to Australia as a child:

> My wife still considers me to be Australian. She thinks I wear my Chineseness like a – something that I can put on and say 'oh I am Chinese I have a min larp[3] on' and then I take off. She doesn't think I am Chinese at all ... My wife says 'you are pretending to be Chinese and you are talking about things you don't know anything about. You are trying to take the best of both worlds. You are trying to be Australian but you are trying to be Chinese at the same time.'

Although racialized collectivities are stratified within a broader social spectrum where stereotypical identities are often imposed by the dominant groups, in-group members also play an important role in establishing their own hierarchy of identities. The way in which racialized groups shape their own identities is illustrated by the delegitimization of Rob's Chineseness by his Hong Kong-born wife. Such a reaction is often percolated from the ideology that China is the land of the ancestors of the people of Chinese descent and the original source of Chinese civilization. Such a challenge of authenticity coincides with Gans's (1979) notion of symbolic ethnicity where occasional ethnic behaviour is seen as an absence of 'real' ethnicity. Although Rob identifies himself as Chinese in certain situations, because of the hegemonic discourse of authenticity differentiating him from his wife, he is teased as being 'not a real Chinese' thus often situating him in a state of limbo. In this respect ABCs' claims to Chineseness are often referred to as lacking substantial cultural content and being culturally empty.

However, Chineseness, like any other racial collectivities, is not merely an inert fact of nature, but is 'ideas' that have histories and tradition of thoughts, imageries, memories and vocabularies that have given it reality (Said 1978). As such, the very suggestion locating ethnicity through notions of authenticity embodies the flaws of essentialism. The qualification of such 'ideas' then, I suggest, needs to be studied through the nexus of memories and identities as the negotiation of identities involves a complex response to the contextual pressure of environment in which individuals are embedded. Martin, who is the fourth generation of his family to depart from China, highlights the way in which intergenerational influence had a consequential impact on the way in which he (re)negotiated and (re)articulated his identity:

> My home village in China is a place that I definitely have to go to. I can picture myself. It will be so emotional ... I guess it is a sense that

> you are stuck in-between two cultures so you don't really belong to either. I can't really say that I feel like Australian. I definitely want to identify as Chinese but I can't say that because I can't even speak the language and I haven't been taught much about the culture. I just imagine if my grandparents didn't decide to migrate out of China, what would life have been. I just feel that I will have a sense of belonging that I don't feel in Australia.

The formation of identity of long-established ABC involves entering a state of hybridity where they maintain multiples identities and create new cultural forms using elements from a diversity of contexts, particularly through the intergenerational influence of memories. Martin explains that his interest in Chinese culture and heritage all stemmed from his relationship with his grandfather who played an important role in the establishment of his identity. His grandfather would tell him Chinese myths and legends and the people's way of life in China as he remembered them. Although his grandfather insisted on the maintenance of a Chinese identity, his parents however never really wanted to associate with their Chinese past because of the difficulties they had in establishing their life in the Western world. While both Martin's father and himself experienced racial assaults, for him they led to stronger affiliations with 'everything Chinese', whereas for his father they led to a concealment of his Chinese past in order to be accepted in the host country. He was struggling between his father's pursuit of integration and his own desire to maintain his Chinese heritage. As eloquently noted by Davidson and Kuah-Pearce's Introduction to this book, 'racially charged memories are bitter-sweet, providing succor to the migrant whilst serving to further differentiate ... some migrants eschew the identities and memories of the diasporic community, rejecting the idea of their cultural authenticity and seek instead inclusion in the wider community'. For subsequent generations, the formation of identity involves entering a state of hybridity – such that their sense of identity is often situated in-between different generational and locational points of reference – the previous generations and their own, as they display who they are to be or to be seen as in different contexts. The hybrid space they encounter is mingled with a variety of memories, experiences, voices, language and identities.

It is important to highlight the problematic nature of assimilationist assumptions, which considers integration of subsequent generations as a unified, linear and unidirectional process. Although long-established ABC have a strong sense of identity and belonging in Australia, their experience reveals that it is not a simple case of weakening ethnicity or a progressive assimilationist path to 'complete' integration, but rather complicated entanglements and negotiations between memories and identities through the generations. In the hybridized lives of subsequent generations, their negotiation of identity and belongingness is inevitably influenced by their family's imagination of 'homeland' and their experience of displacement. It is within the ambiguities of movement and identity that diasporic communities locate a sense of belongingness, contest boundaries and attempt new spaces of identity. The following section seeks to examine the hybridized life of subsequent generations through the interplay of memories of home and social experience of previous generations as they inscribe themselves upon their identities. Although there exists no unchallengeable authentic grounding of identity, notions of home through memories and imaginations are often designated as an authentic site for the migrants as a reaffirmation of identity.

Intergenerational ties, memories and identities

The establishment of Chineseness is often articulated through personal and collective memories in which social and cultural elements of traditions, myths, histories and languages are reproduced within the family, linking subsequent generations to their ancestral homeland. A number of studies have indicated that although first-generational migrant parents are more active in maintaining the relationship that directly links the homeland and the receiving country (Basch et al. 1994; Wolf 2002), children of immigrants, at the very least, maintain these ties at emotional levels through ideologies and cultural codes. In Wolf's (2002, p. 258) study on the struggles of second-generation Filipinos in California, she highlights the aspect of 'emotional transnationalism' whereby the 'migrant children are often situated between different generational and locational points of reference, both the real and the imagined – their parents, sometimes also their grandparents and other relatives, and their own'. Although they may not actively participate in transnationalism, the carving of identity is influenced by the transnational ties maintained by the older generations within the family. Furthermore, through intergenerational connections, memories of the family become a part of daily life which continuously shape identities and establish a sense of attachment with the 'homeland'. The autobiographic essays in 'Cultural Curiosity' (Khu 2001) reveal the power of intergenerational influence on the establishment of Chineseness for diasporic Chinese. As Chan (2001, p. 144) expresses, 'my feeling of alienation from and my rejection of my

Chineseness was most of all linked with and intensified by, the growing rift with my father' and for Chu (2001, p. 131) his mother would constantly remind him about 'the long glorious history of the Chinese people ... to make [him] feel proud of [his] heritage'. The diasporic experience thus is a dynamic process of interactions between places and ideologies as identities are not established in a vacuum but are intergenerationally influenced. Such circuits have been celebrated as a site of authentic meaning, value and experience, imbued with nostalgic memories and the love or pain of the home that was left by early migrants. Social and cultural elements reproduced within the family often play a crucial and ongoing role in informing not only notions of ethnicity but also their relationship to the receiving country. As such, memories provide an intimate means of connecting life worlds of the past and the present and are continually reshaped to provide different perspectives (Davidson 2003).

Memory is often linked with subjectivity but it is still often regarded as authentic, especially when it comes to eyewitness accounts that provide a record of the impact of significant moments on individual lives – increasing studies of personal testimony and cultural memory testify to this. However, memory fragments as a source of authenticity are problematic. Cook (2005, p. 3) explains that 'the fact that the eyewitness was actually present at the time invests their recollections with an aura that transcends the knowledge that their experience is reconstructed for the purposes of current agendas, and endows with it authority and emotional power'. Memories, therefore, are not simply dissociated pieces of past events but are continually reconstructed to provide a new take on the old and reshaped to provide different perspectives (Davidson 2003). In general, while communities and individuals cannot consciously choose what they want to remember, they can, however, choose what they want to pass down to their future generations. As highlighted in the Introduction to this volume, such a process of selection is a personalized choice on the part of the individuals and a collective choice for the community as a whole, depending on what cultural elements the individual and community perceive as important for the well-being of their children as they settle in the host country. Consequently, the subjective choices of the cultural elements that are reproduced are arguably fragmented pieces of social memories. As such, diasporic memories of subsequent generations often comprise those sociocultural elements that the previous generation selectively wants to reproduce in their new home, intertwined with their own social experiences before they left their home of origin and also their migration experience in the host country. Nevertheless, however fractured those memories are, they have a deep impact upon not only the migrants themselves but the subsequent generations as they inscribe themselves in the establishment of identities.

Nostalgic memories, in particular, impact not only the overseas-born migrants' construal of identity and home but also that of their descendants because of the power of intense emotions through intergenerational transmission. Nostalgia can be defined as 'a state of longing for something that is known to be irretrievable, but is sought anyway' (Cook 2005, p. 3). In so far as it is rooted in suspension of disbelief, nostalgia is generally associated with fantasy and regarded as even more inauthentic than memory. This intensity of longing inevitably impacts not only the overseas born migrant's sense of identity but also that of their descendants because of the power of emotions. For descendants of migrants, links to the homeland are largely shaped by nostalgic memories of previous generations. Chu (2001, p. 14) writes, 'this and other stories about my ancestors indeed made a deep impression on me. They reminded me of the great sacrifices that my ancestors had made to create a better life for their descendants ...' Although the distinction between memory, nostalgia and history which are the source of imagination is often blurred and dynamic, nevertheless notions of home are of much import in the construal of ethnicity for people in diasporas.

Nostalgic memories

For long-established ABC, nostalgic memories that are passed down from one generation to another within the family become a vital aspect in their construal of Chineseness. Their imagination of a notional homeland is often situated between different generational and locational points of reference percolating from their own parents, grandparents and other relatives. The power of memories through intergenerational connections can be clearly illustrated through Vera's experience. Vera is the third generation of her family to reside in Australia. Her paternal grandfather moved from China to Australia in 1917 for better financial opportunities while the rest of the family remained in China. As a result, although her grandfather resided in Australia, there was nevertheless the maintenance of intense transnational activities through constant physical returns, remittances and letters between the two places. Her father, who born in China, married her mother in China. After the initial years of marriage her father moved to Australia to assist her grandfather's market garden business. Her mother, while waiting for approval to migrate to Australia, was caught in the Chinese Cultural Revolution and was persecuted because the family owned properties in China. Her father tried hard to speed up the application process but due to the impact of the White Australia Policy, it took many years before her parents could reunite. Vera recounts her connections with China:

> I have only been to China several times over the many years. I don't have contact with any relatives over there. I don't know anybody there, but I don't mind going on visits. My mother doesn't want to go to China because she was tortured and basically suffered quite a lot so she never wants to go back again. Only my father went back to the village a few times after they came to Australia. My mother used to talk about what life was like in China and she still talks about it now. She suffers depression and it actually gets worse when she talks about how she was persecuted. But for my father, when he talks about it, he actually talks about the good times. So they have totally different perspectives in their memories.

This is a classic narrative that can undoubtedly be told in countless variations by many long-established diasporic Chinese throughout the world, articulating the shared experience of the weakening of social linkages with the homeland as a locality – that is, geographical China per se. Yet, there are intimate connections established through intergenerational passing of stories and myths which have significant impact on the diasporic imagery of Chineseness. Vera reveals that she has only been to China a few times throughout her life and does not have emotional ties with relatives, yet at the same time she has never lost a sense of certainty about the self-declared fact of her Chineseness. This can be clearly seen in the fascination she has about the land that her grandparents and parents left behind. She says, 'I hear different stories about life in China and I sometimes imagine what my life would be like if I was brought up there.'

Memories of previous generations become the basis for the imagination of the homeland, establishing a larger imaginary of Chineseness that works to inform not only notions of ethnicity but also of one's relationship to Australia. The connection with the 'Chinese race' can be further emphasized by the intensity of Vera's statement that 'a political attack on the Chinese community is like a personal strike' on herself. Although she claims to have successfully integrated, her stance on such issues highlights an identity which is established through intimate connection with an imagined 'Chinese' collectivity. As such, intergenerational influence often works as complex forces situating one in the nexus of memory and identity, as memories and imagination of the homeland confront the reality of life. She says, 'I feel I'm very lucky as I have a unique quality to my situation. I was born in Australia but of Chinese heritage.' This glimpse into one ordinary individual with a long history in Australia indicates that while subsequent generations may have relatively weaker physical and emotional linkages with the 'homeland', notions of ethnicity can nonetheless be articulated through imagined linkages with it. Through intergenerational connections, memories of stories, myths, events and old photos of the family become a part of daily life which continuously shape identities and establish a sense of attachment with the 'homeland'.

The power of intergenerational influence on the construal of homeland for subsequent generations can be further highlighted through Sunny who is the fourth generation of his family to reside in Australia:

> I don't consider China as my homeland because Australia is my home. But I have connections with it that is how I view it. I guess I do have some contact with cousins ... My mother always wants me to go back. The relatives want to see you and this and that. I say 'ok I'll go back and say hello'. For me it is a place where my family grew up and there is connection before me but it is not a total connection.

While, in general, subsequent generations do not personally maintain physical or emotional linkages with China to the same level of intensity as first-generation migrants, through intergenerational influence transnational linkages maintained within the family undoubtedly create a sense of ethnicity. The memories and ties of the previous generations not only become an allegiance to an imagined past for their children but also establish a sense of cultural heritage, linking them to China as the homeland.

The power of intergenerational influence on the establishment of identity can be further highlighted through Sean's experience. Similar to a number of other respondents, he maintains no physical or emotional linkages with China, but there is definitely a sense of certainty about his sense of Chineseness which is largely spatially constructed through imaginations. His connection with China was built by his grandparents' conscious effort in maintaining his Chinese identity through means of media particularly during his childhood years. Sean explains that the Kung Fu movies that his grandparents encouraged him to watch as a child played a major role in his establishment of Chineseness through which he developed an interest in Chinese traditions, history and pride:

> I think my grandparents were worried about our Chinese so they got us Kung Fu movies to watch. The videos! I think they wanted us to

> watch the soaps but I didn't like them so they had to settle with the Kung Fu movies. I still watch them on occasions, if someone has got all the tapes then I will borrow them and watch them. But I guess I don't watch them as much now because my wife can't speak Chinese. But definitely during uni times and the first couple of years after uni, I listened to tapes, CDs, Chinese songs. Even though I didn't understand I still listened to them ... I think my love of Chinese history comes from those Kung Fu movies. All the armies fighting, the emperors, I wanted to understand the culture behind the empires of China, one country three kingdoms, the classic stories!

An important aspect of the media is the reinforcement of the stereotypes by which Chinese is represented. As (Said 1978, p. 26) articulates, 'all the media's resources have forced information into more and more standardised modes'. Although Sean had never been to China until recently, the ideology of an imagined China as the homeland was largely developed through the reinforcement of stereotypes in movies, TV, music and also through intergenerational influence throughout his life course. The interest in Chinese Kung Fu movies was due to his grandparents' conscious effort in maintaining attachment to his Chinese roots. Consequently, he developed a cultural attachment to a long glorious history of the Chinese race which contributed to his pride in his Chinese heritage. His diasporic imagination of 'being Chinese' has direct ramifications for the way he wants to raise his children:

> I want my raise my kids definitely with a Chinese identity. It is a conscious thing. I am proud to be Chinese and I want them to think that way. I am not going to teach them that the Chinese are better but definitely that the Chinese have contributed to world development. And I will teach them the key historical facts about Chinese history, that the Chinese empire was better than the Roman empire!

The diasporic experience is a dynamic process of interactions between places and ideologies as identities are not established in a vacuum but are intergenerationally influenced through memories and imaginations. Although the distinctions between memory, nostalgia, history and imagination are often blurred and dynamic in the passing of generations, nevertheless they are of much import in the construal of ethnicity for people in diasporas. Thus, highlighting that contemporary images of the homeland often intertwine between origin, roots, cultural heritage, ancestral homeland and local residence which form a significant part of the diasporic imagination of Chineseness.

Moreover, the family represents a fundamental context for childhood socialization and plays a major role in the development of culture across generations (Tan 2001). The point is, the status of Chineseness is a discursive construct rather than something that can be taken as natural and thus is a matter of subjective experience and not solely a question of theory. The point is not to argue about the adequacy of a particular type of linkage as a condition of Chineseness, which would be a futile assertion as individuals are bound to have different opinions, but to recognize that significance of intergenerational influence. The establishment of identity for long-established ABC is not a simple process of gradual transition but a reflection of the sociocultural elements that the previous generations selectively want to reproduce in their new home intertwined with the pressure of changing social circumstances.

Conclusion

Successive generations who are well dispersed from the original homeland often do not engage in transnational practices or have the deep cultural memories of recent migrants; their principled ambivalence about physical return and attachment to the homeland characterizes much of their experience. Consequently, under the current diasporic paradigm, their claims to ethnicity are often considered as lacking substantial cultural content. While the diasporic framework is certainly important in understanding the relationship between transnational linkages and identity, it is often bound to particular localities as well as concentrating largely on the experience of recent migrants. As such, the prevailing theoretical diasporic framework of using transnational linkages as a centring device for the construction of ethnicity and attachment is problematic.

Furthermore, while notions of hybridity problematize the unsettling boundaries of identities, and the focus has been on the experience of recent migrants, ethnic identification is still largely perceived to decrease over subsequent generations. However, imaginary and subjective relationships to the homeland through intergenerational passing of memories become an important part of their construction of identity. Links with the 'homeland' are largely influenced by the nostalgia and memories of their parents and grandparents. As deployed in narratives of long-established ABC, the construction of identity often involves interplay of memories, intergenerational influence and imagination of China as the homeland as they respond to the social, contextual pressure of the wider society in which they are embedded. Their stories illuminate the precarious establishment of Chineseness in a hybrid space through which is often neglected under the current diasporic paradigm.

Since the diasporic experience of those with long settlement cannot be adequately incorporated in the diasporic paradigm as their negotiation of ethnicity is invariably different from recent migrants, it is worthwhile exploring decentred connections to home through the interplay of memories and identity. Intergenerational influence in the form of stories, myths, secrets, photographs, language, etc. actively shapes the construal of an 'imagined' homeland leading to hybridized lives. In order to comprehend the establishment of identity for long-established diasporic communities, notions of home need to be opened up to spatial explorations as identities are constructed through a complexity of social relations overlapping spaces and places. Linkages connecting diasporic communities do not necessarily need to be articulated predominately through a real or symbolic homeland, decentred connections may be as significant as those formed around notions of origin or return. At any moment in the diasporic trajectory tensions are released in different orders of home as well as different feelings of belonging. As such, the connections between 'home' and 'identity' need to be studied in a spatial context as it is an 'imaginary' construction which is continually undergoing transformation.

Clearly through the experience of long-established ABC, Chineseness is never an absolute or unitary culture as its meanings and constructions are ever-changing. The identities of 'Chinese' in diasporas are always intertwined with, and inseparable from, people, land, history and culture. As Ang (1998, p. 225) articulates:

> Chineseness is not a category with a fixed content – be it racial, cultural or geographical – but operates as an open and indeterminate signifier whose meanings are constantly renegotiated and rearticulated in different sections of the Chinese diaspora. Chineseness is a multi-layered and contested discourse which is continuously being formed and reformed in different sites of negotiation.

The 'Chinese' identity varies in different locations and there are myriad ways of being Chinese. Chineseness is not merely shaped by transnational forces but also intergeneration influence of memory and imagination in different parts of the world as people construct their identities. So one could ask, if memories are reconstructed, identity is fluid and home is imagined, why are they still significant in diasporic lives? Although these notions are constantly changing and are contextually activated, nevertheless they act as a source of stability and security. Diasporic communities are continually constructed, negotiated and imagined through the intersection of memories and identities. Lastly, how do history, articulations of travels, homes, memories and transnational connections appropriate and shift the discourse of Chineseness? The answer to this question lies in the particularity of feelings of home, belongingness and identification which are constructed not by fixing its location in space and defining it through distinctive positioning with a particular locality, but in interconnections porous and open. Such an approach will allow us to understand the process of identity formation in a world where identities are becoming increasingly pluralistic and malleable in orientation.

Notes

1 Within assimilation models of migrants two main patterns are emphasized: firstly, increasing acculturation leads to subsequent integration into the white middle class; secondly, unsuccessful acculturation leads to downward mobility and incorporation into the underclass (Alba and Nee 1999).
2 The term 'long-established Australians' was used in the 2001 Census data on ancestry to describe respondents as a particular generational group. Since the study focuses on the experience of the descendants of Chinese migrants, 'Australian' is replaced by 'ABC' to emphasize their ancestry. It needs to be noted that while the categorization according to birthplace is conceptually neat, the definition quickly proves problematic in the face of empirical realities; for example, it is not possible to differentiate between third and higher-order generations.
3 Traditional Chinese jacket made of silk floss, worn in winter for warmth.

References

Alba, R. and Nee, V. 1999, 'Rethinking Assimilation Theory for a New Era of Immigration', in C. Hischman, P. Kasinitz and J. Dewind (eds), *The Handbook of International Migration*, Russell Sage Foundation, New York.
Ang, I. 1998, 'Can One Say No to Chineseness? Pushing the Limits of the Diasporic Paradigm', *boundary 2*, vol. 25, no. 3, pp. 223–42.
Ang, I. 2001, *On Not Speaking Chinese: Living between Asia and the West*, Routledge, London.
Basch, L., Glick, S.N. and Blanc-Szanton, C. 1994, *Nations Unbound: Transnational Projects, Postcolonial Predicaments, and Deterritorialized Nation-States*, Gordon and Breach Publishers, Luxembourg.
Chan, H. 2001, 'Ears Attuned to Two Cultures', in J.M.T. Khu (ed.), *Cultural Curiosity: Thirteen Stories about the Search for Chinese Roots*, University of California Press, California.
Chu, R. 2001, 'Guilt Trip to China', in J.M.T. Khu (ed.), *Cultural Curiosity: Thirteen Stories about the Search for Chinese Roots*, University of California Press, California.
Clifford, J. 1994, 'Diasporas', *Cultural Anthropology*, vol. 9, no. 3, pp. 302–38.

Cook, P. 2005, *Screening the Past: Memory and Nostalgia in Cinema*, Routledge, London.
Cornell, S. and Hartmann, D. 1998, *Ethnicity and Race: Making Identities in a Changing World*, Pine Forge Press, Thousand Oaks, California.
Davidson, A. 2003, *Belongingness and Memories of Home*, Marshall Cavendish, Singapore, pp. 121–43.
Gans, H. 1979, 'Symbolic Ethnicity: the Future of Ethnic Groups and Cultures in America', *Ethnic and Racial Studies*, vol. 2, pp. 1–20.
Hall, S. 1996, 'Introduction: Who Needs Identity?' in S. Hall and P.D. Gay (eds), *Question of Cultural Identity*, Sage Publications, London.
Khu, J.M.T. 2001, *Cultural Curiosity: Thirteen Stories about the Search for Chinese Roots*, University of California Press, California.
Ma, L.J.C. 2003, 'Space, Place and Transnationalism in the Chinese Diaspora', in L.J.C. Ma and C. Cartier (eds), *Chinese Diaspora: Space, Place, Mobility and Identity*, Rowman and Littlefield, Lanham.
Mageo, J.M. (ed.) 2001, *Cultural Memory: Reconfiguring History and Identity in the Postcolonial Pacific*, University of Hawaii Press, Honolulu.
Nonini, D.M. and Ong, A. 1997, 'Towards a Cultural Politics of Diaspora and Transnationalism', in A. Ong and D.M. Nonini (eds), *Ungrounded Empires: the Cultural Politics of Modern Chinese Transnationalism*, Routledge, New York.
Ong, A. 1999, *Flexible Citizenship: the Cultural Logics of Transnationality*, Duke University Press, Durham.
Pe-pua, R., Mitchell, C., Iredale, R. and Castles, S. 1996, *Astronaut Families and Parachute Children: the Cycle of Migration between Hong Kong and Australia*, Australian Government Publishing Service, Canberra.
Phizacklea, A. 2000, 'Introduction: Transnationalism and the Politics of Belonging', in S. Westwood and A. Phizacklea (eds), *Transnationalism and the Politics of Belonging*, Routledge, London.
Rapport, N. and Dawson, A. 1998, 'The Topic of the Book', in N. Rapport and A. Dawson (eds), *Migrants of Identity: Perceptions of Home in a World of Movement*, Berg, Oxford, pp. 3–17.
Rouse, R. 1991, 'Mexican Migration and the Social Space of Postmodernism', *Diaspora*, vol. 1, pp. 8–23.
Ryan, J. 2002, 'Chinese Women as Transnational Migrants: Gender and Class in Global Migration Narratives', *International Migration*, vol. 40, pp. 93–116.
Said, E.W. 1978, reprinted 2003, *Orientalism*, New pref. edn, Penguin, London.
Tan, C. 2001, 'Chinese Families Down Under: the Role of the Family in the Construction of Identity amongst Chinese Australians, 1920–1960', in *International Conference 'Migrating Identities: Ethnic Minorities in Chinese Diaspora'*, Centre for the Study of Chinese Southern Diaspora, ANU.
Wang, J. 2002, 'Religious Identity and Ethnic Language: Correlation between Shifts of Chinese Canadian Religious Affiliation and Mother Tongue Retention, 1931–1961', *Canadian Ethnic Studies*, vol. 34, pp. 63–78.
Waters, J.L. 2002, 'Flexible Families? "Astronaut" Households and the Experiences of Lone Mothers in Vancouver, British Columbia', *Social & Cultural Geography*, vol. 3, pp. 117–33.
Wolf, D.L. 2002, 'There's No Place Like "Home": Emotional Transnationalism and the Struggles of Second Generation Filipinos', in P. Levitt and M.C. Waters (eds), *The Changing Face of Home*, Russell Sage Foundation, New York.

6

Moving through Memory: Chinese Migration to New Zealand in the 1990s

Andrew P. Davidson and Rosa Dai

Introduction

> But memory, whether individual or collective, is constructed and reconstructed by the dialects of remembering and forgetting, shaped by semantic and interpretive frames, and subject to a panoply of distortions. Such complexities are what make memory of such compelling interest to so many – that and the question Humpty Dumpty raises: who is to be the master of memory and, with it, the master of meaning? For the masters of memory and meaning also control much else.
>
> (Cattell and Climo 2002, pp. 1–2)

Memory typically refers to an individual's representation of what he or she has experienced. In this respect, memory is a continuous though fragmented process, from the initial encoding of an event to its recall, albeit through constant revision. Then too memory is a symbolic representation and value-laden emotive force that suggests that personal memory is not the sole expression of behaviour and the interpretation of self. Memory is social as well, 'transmitted and sustained through the conscious efforts and institutions of groups' (Yerushalmi 1982, p. xv). Social or collective memory thus provides 'a point of transit of unparalleled import, most significantly perhaps between the social and the personal' (Mageo 2001, p. 2). In tracing and interpreting memories, it is therefore necessary to observe both the personal and social expressions or repressions of memories as this has important implications for the kinds of inferences and nuances that go into identity formation and the nurturing of belonging. Such an approach can be particularly useful in exploring the identities of transnational migrants through the interplay of the individual and the collective.

Memory, as a site of transit, is the articulation and contestation of belonging and involves the 'selective remembering' and 'ideological forgetting' of symbols that link the past with the present and point to the future (Chang 2005). As memory entails its historical context, it also suggests that memory creates an understanding of the past and thus provides a foundation for present and future identities (Friedman 1992). Nevertheless, memories are filtered by hierarchies of power and privilege which contribute to shaping these processes, creating receptive and welcoming environments, while at other times instilling oppositional or indifferent surroundings (Code 1995). It is in this sense that memories are ineluctably social, including sites and contexts of transmission, 'among individuals, within groups and among groups' (Crumley 2002, p. 39) in this case, diasporic migrants.

Migration is inherently contradictory; it heightens social and economic dependence while necessitating independence; it binds families together while also pulling them apart, it forms new communities while weakening old (Wong 1998). Diasporic communities illustrate the importance of group characteristics and the uses of identity as a potential resource (in terms of networks and the social capital they generate). Moreover, migration also entails the manipulation of a myriad of identities: communal, regional, ethnic and nationalist identity (New Zealand and PRC as nation states), as well as past-oriented heritage identity ('Chineseness'). Besides developing and deploying these different identities to meet the demands arsing from specific situations, Chinese migrants also devise different identity strategies in their negotiations with the ever-changing politics and expectations in different host countries (Tu 1994). But as Chow (1995, p. 25) notes, it is never easy to 'unlearn that submission to ethnicity ... as the ultimate signifier'.

To explore these lines of questioning, this chapter builds on the work of the politics of memory. Memory, as it is used here, refers to the practice of memory work and entails how memory is objectified and contextualized in different social and cultural forms (Litzinger 1998). As such, it is a process of symbolic and mnemonic ordering that can reveal the construction of a collective identity under conditions where power relations are at play that involves the differential recognition and signification of identities. Memory work thus has a great deal to offer as a method of inquiry into identities and feelings of belonging or acceptance. It makes available the ideational forms through which identities are constructed from the stories or images which shape memories and the multiple ways that memories constitute the emerging selves through what was remembered to what was imagined and to what was forgotten

(Mageo 2001). It thus also reveals the centrality of memory to the processes of continuity and change, themselves at the heart of individual and collective identity, and to the concatenation of private and social experiences.

The purpose of this chapter is thus to develop an understanding of how migration conjoins with politics (historical context) and influences people's movements, but through the lens of memory work. It also investigates the strategies and transnational social networks of these Chinese migrants to New Zealand from the People's Republic of China (hereafter Chinese). This chapter thus aims to locate and assess the migration experiences of Chinese individuals and families by locating them in the personal, economic and social conditions that articulate the world(s) they have left with the world(s) they have entered. Nevertheless, we also acknowledge the need for caution 'in approaching certain transcultural contexts' and the inherent danger of overextending the concept of memory (Berliner 2005, p. 198). Information was obtained from in-depth interviews with 75 Chinese migrants (from the PRC) who moved to New Zealand between 1990 and 2001.

Transformation of memory: immigration policies and Chinese movements

> ... skilled immigrants earn more, pay higher taxes, and require fewer social services than less-skilled immigrants. Put differently, skilled immigration increases the after-tax income of natives, while the tax burden imposed by the immigration of less-skilled workers probably reduces the net wealth of native taxpayers. From a fiscal perspective, therefore, there is little doubt that skilled immigration is a good investment, particularly when compared to the immigration of less-skilled workers.
>
> (Borjas 1999, pp. 190–1)

There has been a large outflow of Chinese from the mainland over the past two centuries, as traders in Singapore, Indonesia, the Philippines and elsewhere, as well as a source of cheap labour in the tin-mines of Malaya, in the guano beds of Peru, and for railway construction in Canada and the United States (Greif 1976). Chinese first went to New Zealand in the 1860s when gold was discovered in the South Island. Many of them came over from Australia, some directly from China. As in Australia and elsewhere such as South Africa, the Chinese in the gold-fields were resented by white miners. Anti-Chinese actions, however, were primarily limited to individual assaults. In 1874, there were 4818 Chinese in New Zealand, but a series of Immigration Restriction Acts which ordered Chinese to pay a tax of 10 pounds reduced the number to 2673 by 1907. In 1908, Chinese were no longer allowed to become naturalized citizens and were required to be thumbprinted when entering or leaving New Zealand. This policy was not changed until 1952. In 1961, there were about 3100 Chinese in New Zealand (Yee 1974). From 1962 to 1971, Chinese refugees from Hong Kong and Indonesia arrived, and in 1975 the Indochinese refugees arrived from Cambodia, Laos and Vietnam. In this respect, the discrimination of the past gave way to the embrace of multiculturalism. In short, collective memory has given way to individual expressions of remembering as migrants find a home in their newly adoptive country.

Opportunities for Chinese to migrate to New Zealand prior to 1986 were limited. In the context of enhanced global competition for skilled migrants New Zealand removed the 'White New Zealand Policy' in 1986 by abolishing policies giving preference to migrants from 'traditional source countries', such as Britain, north-west Europe and North America (Bedford et al. 2002). Selection of immigrants since then has been based on a general policy of attracting skilled people or people with money to invest; a separate category in economic immigration provided for the admission of entrepreneurs and business people (Zodgekar 2005). As the qualifications of the migrants changed over the years, so too has their contribution to national economies. The present trajectories of international migration are now manifested in migration streams that operate on a global basis, operative in increased capital mobility, the activities of transnational corporations, and mobility of labour (Massey et al. 1998).

During the past two decades New Zealand's population has become significantly more culturally diversified as a result of substantial immigration from Asia and other non-traditional source countries (Bedford et al. 1996). A large number of recent migrants came from Asian countries such as the People's Republic of China (PRC), Taiwan, India, South Korea and Malaysia. With the establishment of the Business Investment Policy (BIP) in 1986 (Poot 1993), and its further refinement with the Point System in 1991 and 1995, the General Skills and Business Investor category requirements were adjusted allowing more and more skilled Chinese into New Zealand (Zodgekar 2005). For example, the total number of people approved for residency in 1998 was 29,334. China was one of the leading countries of origin then with 14 per cent of total migrants. From 1992 to 1998 some 22,775 Chinese moved to New Zealand (New Zealand Immigration Service 2000, data updated in November 2004) and have now become the principal migration source for New Zealand, surpassing migrants from the United Kingdom.

Immigration changes aimed to provide a mechanism for better management of immigrant numbers, to encourage a broader mix of skills, and, perhaps more importantly, to attract people with a genuine commitment to living in New Zealand, making it home. According to the then Minister of Migration, Hon. Tuariki Delamere:

> Quality immigration policy enables us to attract people to this country who will help to make New Zealand a better place for all of us to live in. The policies announced today are aimed at attracting highly skilled migrants to New Zealand by building on the relationships with people already associated with New Zealand and by simplifying processes to ensure that we don't miss out on the people we want here ... (Delamere 1998)

According to a New Zealand government report, the proportion of settler arrivals (i.e. permanent arrivals) from New Zealand that are foreign-born has not changed appreciably over the past four years. In 1994–95, the proportion was 23.4 per cent and in 1997–98 it was about 24.3 per cent. In absolute terms this was a change from 3180 out of 13,618 in 1994–95, to 4714 out of 19,393 settlers in 1997–98. The total number of people approved for residency in 1998 was 29,334. For this year, 40 per cent of the total numbers of approvals were for people applying under the Family category. A further 46 per cent were under the General Skills and General categories. The PRC is one of the top countries of origin, accounting for 14 per cent of migrants in 1998. Figure 6.1 shows applications approved for permanent residence from the PRC to New Zealand.

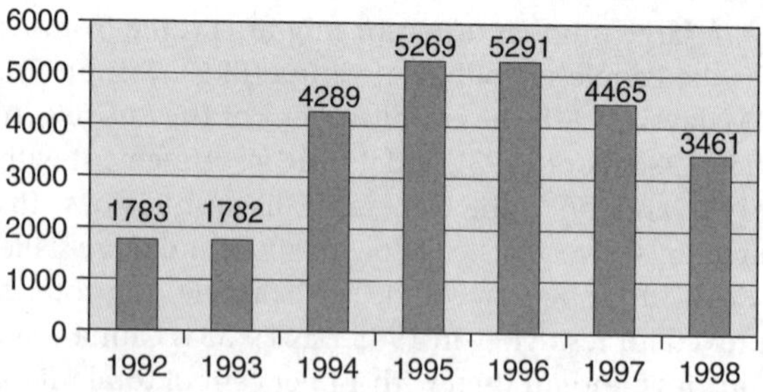

Figure 6.1 PRC Chinese migration to New Zealand in the 1990s
Source: New Zealand Immigration Service (2000)

The neoclassical model of migration claims that the economic success of immigrants – as measured by their average earnings – is determined by education, work experience and other elements of human capital. According to many of the people interviewed in this study, human capital in the case of Chinese, however, is frequently discounted as their 'skills' are of foreign origin (and thus deemed 'inferior'). Clearly education, knowledge of English, and work experience are important factors affecting newcomers' employment prospects, but they do not suffice to fully explain occupational mobility and earnings (Portes 1998). More importantly, although the causes of migration are typically individual economic motivation, once initiated migration patterns are sustained and perpetuated by well-established regional *networks* of trade, production, investment and communication.

Migration factors

Economics is such a dominant factor in the sociological studies of international migration that the very language of analysis tends to marginalize social or cultural factors. Migrant studies still tend to focus on single major factors and track the consequences of dominant structures rather than attend to obscure networks or subtle processes (Papastergiadis 2000, p. 33).

Memory work involves not only a technique, but the much wider and more problematic issues of knowledge and power such that memory is a relationship between pasts and a particular present (Radstone 2000). Radstone contends that memory is an energizing factor which makes it more likely that an individual will pay more attention to various kinds of information that might offer a solution to his/her situation. She further argues that memory provides direction to resolutions and leads ultimately to the choice of where the migrant will settle; in this case New Zealand. The reasons that Chinese migrants choose to migrate to New Zealand offer a contextualizing backdrop against the initial migration experiences of adjustment. Movement was particularized by pressure from spouses, family push and friends' suggestions. Whether the decision resulted in an actual move to New Zealand also depended in large measure on more macro-level influences such as immigration policies, securing a sponsor, applying for an assisted passage, and so on.

Unexpected opportunities factors

For most Chinese interviewed in this study, New Zealand was not the country of first choice. Most of the migrants interviewed had thought of Western countries as a place of emigration since their early childhood.

After many of them had graduated from university, a number of their colleagues, classmates and friends moved to the United States, Australia or Canada. This outflow helped fuel their desires and inspired their imaginations of life in a 'better place'. Fifteen per cent of informants were thinking about a move to the USA, Canada and Australia, while 57 per cent were undecided or felt they were not ready to move abroad. Another 20 per cent claimed they were following their spouse, 'no matter where he went'. Most notably, this included women who were pressed by their husbands to quit their jobs and move to New Zealand (attesting to the patriarchal strictures of China). There were also 8 per cent who had received a job offer in New Zealand prior to their migration. Then too, when asked the reasons why they chose to migrate to New Zealand, 59 per cent of the informants explained that they went to New Zealand because 'it was the easiest country to immigrate to at the time'. As one informant said, 'Before I came to New Zealand, I was crazy about the United States. For me, to get away from China was the most important goal of my life. But it was too hard, too many restrictions.' Nevertheless, before migrating, 79 per cent of them had imagined New Zealand as a better living environment than China, 4 per cent stated they were looking for new lifestyle and a new experience and 17 per cent believed they would earn more money in New Zealand.

Without changes in government immigration policy from 1986 onwards, opportunities to migrate to New Zealand were minimal for 'non-whites'. Most of the informants in this study (87 per cent) went to New Zealand after 1991 because of the changes in the skilled immigration policy loosening residency requirements. Needless to say, this easing of requirements provided a strong precipitating factor that influenced migrants' choice of where to migrate. An individual's personal circumstances, however, presented migrants with the necessary motivation to migrate. Final initiating events included social and economic pressures such as a tight domestic labour market, divorce and family pressures.

Personal circumstances initiating migration

The exploration of the connection between memory and the production of personal identity leads to interesting insights into spoken and visual forms of expression through which self-identity is actualized. It is in memory work that narrative is opened up as a means to encode and capture experience. Narrative constitutes part of the conflicts over the engendered, power-laden nature of specific forms of expression. Nevertheless, the centrality of this is in composing versions of the self in everyday social interaction. As Radstone (2000) notes, in order for a sequence of events to become a narrative they must be ordered and related from a particular and personalized point of view. Thus memories may be communal but they were also deeply personal. It is in this sense that people displayed different responses to similar circumstances by the way an individual, through memory, deconstructed and reconstructed social phenomena.

The respondents offered a variety of individual and personal reasons for migrating. Although their circumstances varied, the majority referred to non-economic factors that informed their decisions to migrate. Some of the migrants in this study left China because they were experiencing personal problems 'too awful to cope with'. For example, in the words of a 34-year-old female from Guangdong, 'I did not get along with my husband but did not want to get a divorce. I decided to go to New Zealand, I could avoid a fight.' Another related in a sad voice of being unable to secure a 'good job' in China because he was from the countryside. Memories of 'feeling inadequate' and 'humiliated' punctuated his story.

Traditionally, Chinese emigrated because they earned very little in their home country. With the easing of travel restrictions in China in 1990, many Chinese left to escape problems associated with a large population and to increase their children's educational opportunities. In this study, 23 per cent of informants believed that New Zealand would provide a significantly better education system than China. Human rights also comprised a powerful motive for some of the respondents, particularly with respect to China's one-child policy. According to one female, 'I love children, but the Chinese government only allowed us to have one. I needed to get away to have more babies.'

Chinese students who migrated in the early 1990s claimed New Zealand afforded opportunities for civil liberties and personal freedom. The respondents particularly enjoyed personal privacy which is a notion they claimed did not exist in Chinese culture and communist politics. They also stated the joy in being able to freely confide in friends without fearing that their conversations would be reported to governmental authorities. One respondent related an incident where a friend turned out to be an agent provocateur (see also Fung and Mackerras 1998). Since the mid-1990s (post Tiananmen Square), however, the purpose for Chinese migration to New Zealand seemed to have changed considerably, with more focus being placed on personal issues such as children's education, family reunion and employment.

What the stories of the migrants began to tell was the underlying relationship between action orientation and movement participation, and depending on their action orientation, movements triggered different aspects of the migrants' motivational dynamics. Participation-oriented behaviour emphasized the opportunities for individuals to engage in activities that were satisfying in and of themselves (Klandermans 1993). As a result, the value of the selective costs and benefits a person associated with migration played an important role in each individual's decision to depart China. Interestingly, only 11 per cent thought they would stay in New Zealand for ever.

Migration strategies and social networks

> The ensemble of social networks and intermediaries ... is a complex articulation of individuals, associations and organisations which extends the social action of and interaction between these agents and agencies across time and space.
>
> (Westwood and Phizacklea 2000, p. 129)

An actual decision to migrate largely depends upon an opportunity to migrate and of course on the personal circumstances of the migrant that enables recognition of that opportunity and motivation that initiates migration (Janis 1968). An additional element of migration theory suggests the creation of a momentum or ever-growing stream in which migrants are caught up. Social scientists have long understood the importance of networks to migrant communities or what Wilson (1998) describes as 'network-mediated migration'. Migrant networks are sets of 'interpersonal ties based on kinship, friendship and shared nationality that connect migrants, former migrants' (Grieco 1998, p. 704). Silvia Pedraza (1991) argues that social networks support and channel migration on a continuously widening scale; thus migration that was initially propelled by an external, structural dynamic and logic increasingly acquired an internal dynamic and logic of its own. She further states that migration comes to fuel itself as families make migration part of their survival strategies and deploy it during various stages of the life course; individual motivations, household strategies and community structures are consequently reshaped by migration, making further migration more likely. The communication revolution, which has intensified globalization, also supports the maintenance and expansion of transnational social networks created by migrants. In the case of Chinese migrating to New Zealand, a rational decision to leave one's homeland for New Zealand was insufficient in itself; it was existing networks that made migration possible.

Networks and immigration transitional bridges

> These ties and corresponding networks eventually crystallize as new transnational linkages. It is sort of a racheting effect because one of the prerequisites for migration is usually pre-existing linkages between emigration and immigration states.
>
> (Faist 2000, pp. 193–4)

What is the world of the migrant? How do we acknowledge their perceptions, motivations, values and attitudes? Migration is conceived of as a sociocultural process with some aspects located within the migrants' personal characteristics as well (Meadows 1980). The experiences of migrants revealed the importance of migrant networks and illustrated how identities and cultural allegiances extended far beyond specific geographical reference points (Brettell and Hollifield 2000). Migrants, as social groups, developed intricate patterns of decision-making that preceded migration. Of course there were broad predisposing factors encouraging migration. But in the end it was individuals and often families who made the decision to migrate (Brown and Foot 1994). The common pattern among Chinese moving to New Zealand is termed 'chain migration' which points to the importance of families, kinship and community relations in the process of devising a migration strategy. The new migration bridges, including migration agencies and friends, acted as transitional networks that facilitated their migration.

Migrant networks served many important functions for individual migrants such as reducing migration costs, minimizing disruptions to their lives and sense of self (culture shock), maintaining links between sending and receiving communities, serving as channels for information and resources, and influencing the rate of adaptation and integration into the destination society (Gurak and Caces 1992). As such, the sociocultural networks provided migrants with an important source of social capital.

Migration agencies

> OnArrival New Zealand – Here to help make your move to New Zealand as easy and stress free as possible. We specialise in helping people settle in New Zealand. With a presence in Auckland, Hamilton, Wellington, and Christchurch, no matter where in New Zealand you want to live we can work with you to ensure your relocation needs are met.
>
> (EscapeArtist.com since 1996)

Social mobility relates to the ability of groups to organize effectively in order to protect and promote communal interests. Chinese migrants in New Zealand quickly developed effective community organizations (see Lalich in this volume). The development of migration agencies was a sustaining network factor during the 1990s for Chinese. The strong demand for international migration creates a lucrative economic niche for entrepreneurs and institutions dedicated to promoting international movement for profit (Chin 1999). The migration of Chinese was supported by a large number of organizations, which ranged from migration agencies to networks. Without the support of these organizations and networks, as Table 6.1 shows, most Chinese could not have found a way by themselves to move to New Zealand. About 79 per cent of Chinese migrants who went to New Zealand were supported by migration agencies, while some 13 per cent were self-applied. Moreover, about 7 per cent received support from friends and relatives in China. The majority (76 per cent) of Chinese respondents, however, had saved money and supported themselves upon arrival in New Zealand.

In this study, migration agencies provided an important service when Chinese migrants first relocated. These agencies not only supplied information, they also offered assistance in filling out applications for residence visas. The agencies too benefited from this relation, charging about US$5000. An important element of memory work is the absence of positive public versions of the Other's memories of the migration experience. As many informants noted, popular opinion in New Zealand assumed that migration agencies provided everything for the migrants, giving them more benefits than the average (white) New Zealander enjoyed. It was in their memories which made this misconception so personal and concrete. Here memory foregrounds the production of

Table 6.1 Overview of migration chains

Migration chains	*CNNZ*	
	No.	*%*
Migration agency	59	78.8
Self-applied	10	13.3
Friends	1	1.3
Relatives	4	5.3
Job offer	1	1.3
Total	75	100

Source: Dai (unpublished, data collected in 2001–2).

identities under pressure; of remembering and asserting the self against the cultural grain. It reminded the Chinese migrants daily that the most publicly recognized forms of memory are often the most subordinating (Radstone 2000). Li, a 35-year-old female from Hunan, highlighted this point: 'How much the migration agency had helped me? Nothing, except ask us for US$5000 immigration fee.' Other informants claimed that after they migrated the agency gave them their passport and that was the last contact they had with them. As expressed by another migrant:

> After the airplane arrived in Auckland, the first thing my husband and I had to do was look for a motel by ourselves. The lucky thing was that we did not bring our 2 year old son; we left him with my parents in China, because we really didn't know what would happen after we arrived. Two day later, we found an accommodation in a Chinese newspaper. And then, we started our new life in the strange country without any support, our first arriving experience was a nightmare that I could never forget in my whole life.

Of course some agencies did provide assistance but most migrants felt they were insufficient in terms of the money paid.

Relative-assisted migration

An additional factor reinforcing migration was family members and relatives. Reunification with loved ones proved a recurrent factor in immigration. After the first wave of skilled Chinese immigrants or overseas students settled in New Zealand, their parents and siblings followed in their footsteps. It was important that a potential migrant be exposed to information concerning the main difficulties that their family could expect to meet prior to migrating. Other relatives in China provided financial assistance or kept young children until they could be sent to New Zealand. About 6 per cent of Chinese received some form of support from their relatives. In the words of Hun, a 40-year-old male from Zhuhai:

> My uncle went to New Zealand from Australia in 1987, when he knew immigration policy changed in the mid 1990s; he told me this news and filled some forms for me. He applied for New Zealand PR for me successfully in 1995. Without my uncle's help, I didn't know how to migrate. Actually, my uncle contacted us very often by mail after he left China, and my parents always asked him to find a way to move abroad. Finally he did.

This case provided insight into one element of Chinese migration; namely that migrants bring with them from China the generalized familial and interpersonal relationship norms associated with Confucianism. And these comprised a core memory which underpinned much of Chinese migrants' behaviour. These included, in familial terms, well-defined roles for individual members, family solidarity and family discipline. More generally, these social norms stressed the importance of personal networks and reciprocal assistance as the basis of action. For example, education in these terms was prized for its capacity for enhancing familial social and economic status (see also Brown and Foot 1994).

Engendered migration strategies

Migration decisions are generally reached within a context of socially recognized and mutually reinforcing expectations that reproduce asymmetrical gender relations. Family considerations, for example, created different migration risks for men and women. Men were usually regarded as economically motivated sojourners while women's participation was to later join husbands, the primary purpose being for family reunification rather than economic gain (Enchautegui and Malone 1997). When the wives in this study were asked reasons for migrating, a common response was in reference to their husband; for example, 'my husband wanted to come' or 'because of my husband's wishes' or 'better opportunities for husband'. One wife commented, 'I had to come because my husband was coming. The only reason really. I don't like a separate family.' Chinese women followed their husbands, forgoing old opportunities in China and taking up new burdens in New Zealand. Wang, a 31-year-old woman from Wuhan, stated:

> I followed my husband to New Zealand when I was 24. I had a diploma in accounting in China and had worked in a bank for about two years. My husband was a computer programmer in China. His brother is working in USA, he really wanted to move overseas, but for me, I did not think about moving.

With the assistance of a migration agency they found in the local newspaper, Wang and her husband moved to New Zealand in 1995. In New Zealand they met another family from the same province in China. They decided to pool resources and shared a motel initially and later rented a unit together. Wang's husband secured a computer job a few months later. Her husband found a language school from a Chinese newspaper and Wang immediately enrolled, despite the expensive fees.

Aside from English lessons, Wang enjoyed the student community and friends she made there.

> In the language school, almost all the classmates were in the same difficult position. We shared information, had barbeques and fished together. Our friendships stayed very strong. [Wang later attended a university in New Zealand to study accounting, and at that time had a daughter.] It is easier to find a job as an accountant. And even though I worked in a bank [in China], I still needed retraining. Although when we are in New Zealand, my husband wanted to go to USA or Australia, I do not know where is my home? It is still dependent upon my husband.

This example shows that the migration of female migrants in this study was defined mainly in terms of their sponsoring males rather than in terms of the women's qualities. There were two main reasons why many skilled women migrate as dependants rather than principal applicants; one is a woman's position within the family unit, the other is the status of women in the countries of origin, that of a subordinate (Castles et al. 1994). Although different in New Zealand, women's status was reproduced within the diasporic communities in New Zealand; this was changing, however.

Conclusion

> We live by a series of encounters – with friends, lovers, books, places – but every encounter, as Jacques Derrida says, is 'separation', a 'contradiction of logic' in that it signals an encounter with something other than ourselves, a long-felt absence, that element of difference than breaks the illusory unity of the self. For the story ... is always already about the foreigner in ourselves.
>
> (Kamboureli 1993, p. 143)

The construction and configuration of identities have significant import for migrants, for their feeling of belonging and in their adjustment process in their new 'homes'. Unquestionably, social networks – clusters of obligations, reciprocity and solidarity – provide an important means of connecting a migrant's life worlds, not only linking them to visas, jobs, information and other resources, but in dealing with homesickness, insecurity, social dissonance and cultural dislocation. Once the number of network connections in an origin area reaches a certain threshold, migration becomes self-perpetuating as migration itself creates the social structure needed to sustain it. Every new migrant reduces the costs of subsequent migration for a set of friends and relatives, and some of these people are thereby induced to migrate, which further expands the set of people with ties abroad and, in turn, reduces costs for a new set of people, causing some of them to migrate, and so on (Tanton et al. 1996).

The role of social networks becomes clearer when we stop thinking about migration as a single homogeneous experience, and start recognizing its sharply contrasting forms. Tilly (1990) offers a useful typology distinguishes colonizing, coerced, circular, chain and career migration. In this study, chain and career migration were of particular importance. Chain migration involves sets of related individuals or households who migrate through a set of social arrangements in which people at the destination provide aid, information and encouragement to the newcomers. Career migration characterizes individuals and households that migrate in response to opportunities to change their position within large structures such as corporations and professional labour markets. A study finding further suggests that quality of participation in social and economic life in China and then New Zealand affects the migration experience.

Memory work reveals the confluence of memory and identity on the social processes of recognition and misrecognition, whether embedded in intimate relations and small groups, or mirrored in larger political discourses. Migration was (and is) neither about individuals nor households but sets of people linked by acquaintance, kinship and work experience who somehow incorporated the destinations into the mobility alternatives they considered. Overall, the data in this study supported the conclusion that effective participation in the social networks facilitated movement to New Zealand, concomitant with the political backdrop of immigration laws. The data also suggested the additional burden migration places on women, with cultural memories of Chinese refixing them into social roles and expectations. In the end, variations in movement were inevitably linked with the ebb and flow of personal and collective memories.

References

Bedford, R., Bedford, C., Ho, E. and Lidgard, J. 2002, 'The Globalisation of International Migration in New Zealand: Contribution to a Debate', *New Zealand Population Review*, vol. 28, no. 1, pp. 69–97.

Bedford, R., Lidgard, J. and Young, J. 1996, 'Globalisation and Population Change in New Zealand, 1986–1994', *New Zealand Geographical Society*, University of Waikato, Hamilton.

Berliner, R. 2005, 'The Abuses of Memory: Reflections of the Memory Boom in Anthropology', *Anthropological Quarterly*, vol. 78, no. 1, pp. 187–211.

Borjas, G. 1999, *Heaven's Door: Immigration Policy and the American Economy*, Princeton University Press, Princeton.

Brettell, C. and Hollifield, J. (eds) 2000, *Migration Theory: Talking across Disciplines*, Routledge, London.

Brown, J.M. and Foot, R. 1994, *Migration: the Asian Experience*, St. Martin's Press, Oxford.

Castles, S., Iredale, R. and Vasta, E. 1994, 'Australian Immigration between Globalisation and Recession', *International Migration Review*, vol. 28, no. 2, pp. 370–83.

Cattell, M. and Climo, J. 2002, 'Introduction: Meaning in Social Memory: Anthropological Perspectives', in J. Climo and M. Cattell (eds), *Social Memory and History: Anthropological Perspectives*, AltaMira Press, Walnut Creek, pp. 1–38.

Chang, T.C. 2005, 'Place, Memory and Identity: Imagining "New Asia" ', *Asia Pacific Viewpoint*, vol. 46, no. 3, pp. 247–53.

Chin, K.L. 1999, *Smuggled Chinese: Clandestine Immigration to the United States*, Temple University Press, Philadelphia.

Chow, R. 1995, *Writing Diaspora: Tactics of Intervention in Contemporary Cultural Studies*, Indiana University Press, Bloomington.

Code, L. 1995, *Rhetorical Spaces*, Routledge, New York.

Crumley, C.L. 2002, 'Exploring Venues of Social Memory', in J. Climo and M. Cattell (eds), *Social Memory and History: Anthropological Perspectives*, Bergin & Garvey, New York, pp. 39–52.

Dai, R. unpublished, 'Survey Data for "Examination of PRC Chinese Immigration Experience in Sydney, Australia" collected in 2001–2002', PhD Candidate thesis, University of New South Wales, Sydney.

Delamere, T. 1998, *Making New Zealand a More Attractive Destination*, Executive Government – for the current Administration, viewed 3 January 2007 <http://www.executive.govt.nz/96-99/progress/immigration/destination.htm>.

Enchautegui, M. and Malone, N. 1997, 'Female Immigrants: a Socio-economic Portrait', *Migration World*, no. 25, pp. 18–23.

EscapeArtist.com since 1996, *About Moving to New Zealand: Resources to help you move to New Zealand*, EscapeArtist Inc., viewed 10 January 2007 <http://www.escapeartist.com/nz/nz.htm>.

Faist, T. 2000, *The Volume and Dynamics of International Migration and Transnational Social Places*, Clarendon Press, Oxford.

Friedman, J. 1992, 'The Past in the Future: History and the Politics of Identity', *American Anthropologist*, vol. 94, no. 4, pp. 837–59.

Fung, E. and Mackerras, C. 1998, 'Chinese Students in Australia: an Attitudinal Study', in A. Milner and M. Quilty (eds), *Australia in Asia: Episodes*, vol. 3, Oxford University Press, Melbourne.

Greif, S. 1976, 'The Overseas Chinese in New Zealand', *Pacific Affairs*, vol. 49, no. 2, pp. 382–5.

Grieco, E. 1998, 'The Effects of Migration on the Establishment of Networks', *International Migration Review*, vol. 32, no. 3, pp. 704–37.

Gurak, D. and Caces, F. 1992, 'Migration Networks and the Shaping of Migration Systems', in M. Kritz, L. Lim and H. Zlotnik (eds), *International Migration Systems: a Global Approach*, Oxford University Press, New York.

Janis, I.L. 1968, 'Stages in the Decision Making Process', in R.P. Abelson, E. Aronson, W.J. McGuire, T.M. Newcomb, M.J. Rosenberg and P.H. Tannenbaum (eds), *Theories of Cognitive Consistency: a Source Book*, Rand-McNally, Chicago.

Kamboureli, S. 1993, 'Of Black Angels and Melancholy Lovers: Ethnicity and Writing in Canada', in S. Gunew and A. Yeatman (eds), *Feminism and the Politics of Difference*, Allen and Unwin, Sydney, p. 143.

Klandermans, B. 1993, 'A Theoretical Framework for Comparisons of Social Movement Participation', *Sociological Forum*, vol. 8, no. 3, pp. 383–402.

Litzinger, R. 1998, 'Memory Work: Reconstituting the Ethnic in Post-Mao China', *Cultural Anthropology*, vol.13, no. 2, pp. 224–55.

Mageo, J.M. (ed.) 2001, *Cultural Memory: Reconfiguring History and Identity in the Postcolonial Pacific*, University of Hawaii Press, Honolulu.

Massey, D., Arango, J., Hugo, G., Kouaouci, A., Pellegrino, A. and Taylor, J. 1998, *World in Motion*, Clarendon Press, Oxford.

Meadows, P. 1980, 'Immigration Theory: a Review of Thematic Strategies', in R. Bryce-Laporte (ed.), *Source Book on the New Immigration*, Transaction Books, New Brunswick.

New Zealand Immigration Service 2000, *Tourism and Migration 2000 – Table 11.01: Residence Approvals by Nationality*, Statistics New Zealand, viewed 10 January 2007 <http://www.stats.govt.nz/NR/rdonlyres/247F6F1F-C24A-48BE-AB98-29621218628E/0/TM2001Table1101.xls>.

Papastergiadis, N. 2000, *The Turbulence of Migration*, Polity Press, Cambridge.

Pedraza, S. 1991, 'Women and Migration: the Social Consequences of Gender', *Annual Review of Sociology*, vol. 17, pp. 303–25.

Poot, J. 1993, 'Adaptation of Migrants in the New Zealand Labor Market', *International Migration Review*, vol. 27, no. 1, pp. 121–39.

Portes, A. 1998, 'Divergent Destinies: Immigration, the Second Generation, and the Rise of Transnational Communities', in P. Schuck and R. Münz (eds), *Paths to Inclusion*, Berghahn Books, New York, pp. 33–57.

Radstone, S. 2000, 'Working with Memory: an Introduction', in S. Radstone (ed.), *Memory and Methodology*, Oxford International Publishers, Berg, pp. 1–22.

Tanton, J., McCormack, D. and Wayne, W. 1996, *Immigration and the Social Contract: the Implosion of Western Societies*, Ashgate, Avebury.

Tilly, C. 1990, 'Transplanted Networks', in V. Yans-McLaughlin (ed.), *Immigration Reconsidered. History, Sociology and Politics*, Oxford University Press, New York, pp. 79–95.

Tu, W.M. 1994, *The Living Tree: Changing Meanings of Being Chinese Today*, Stanford University Press, Stanford.

Westwood, S. and Phizacklea, A. 2000, *Trans-Nationalism and the Politics of Belonging*, Routledge, London.

Wilson, T. 1998, 'Weak Ties, Strong Ties: Network Principles in Mexican Migration', *Human Organization*, vol. 57, no. 4, p. 394.

Wong, B. 1998, *Ethnicity and Entrepreneurs: the New Chinese Immigrants in the San Francisco Bay Area*, Allen and Unwin, Boston.

Yee, S. 1974, *The Chinese in the Pacific*, The South Pacific Social Sciences Association, Suva, Fiji.

Yerushalmi, Y. 1982, *Zakhor: Jewish History and Jewish Family*, University of Washington Press, Seattle.

Zodgekar, A. 2005, 'The Changing Face of New Zealand's Population and National Identity', in *The XXV International Population Conference*, Tours, France.

7
Collective Memories as Cultural Capital: from Chinese Diaspora to Emigrant Hometowns

Kuah-Pearce Khun Eng

Introduction

As a group of people migrated from one region to another and settled down in a new environment, they brought along their cultures and memories of the distant land that used to be their home. As they seek to reproduce their social values, customs and values in their new diasporic community, the process of reproduction is often governed by what they remember and the selective process of what they want to remember and reproduce for their new home. At the same time, through the recall of their collective memories, these migrants also re-explore their relationship with their home of ancestral origin, and establish transnational kinship ties and networks. The latter process was especially rapid after the 1978 Open Door Policy which allowed ease of movement of people between the Chinese diasporic communities and mainland China.

This chapter will explore the role of collective memories as cultural capital that propelled the Singapore Anxi Chinese migrants to revisit their ancestral home, and rekindled transnational kinship ties and networks with their village kin. The Singapore Chinese through this journey re-established and revitalize their transnational kinship networks and in this process of transnationalizing their kinship ties, they helped revitalize a moral economy that aided in the reconstruction and development of their ancestral village.

Social construction of collective memory

There are many types of memories that people use in their attempt to build identity. Usually a crisis situation brought about a definitive set of memories that become deeply etched into the psyche of the individuals and the community at large. War is one big crisis situation that is deeply entrenched into the memory of those people and communities affected by it. Pre-migration, migration and post-migration traumas too are periodic interstices that forced their way into the memory of those affected by these movements. As individuals are exposed to different types of experiences that shaped that memory, memory as a thought process is therefore necessarily subjective. Personal memories are therefore highly contextualized and experience driven, as individuals often chose to remember in a selective way that best helped them to preserve those that they want to remember and dismissed others that are either too painful or too embarrassing to reveal. Likewise, the community as a whole is also selective as to what they wanted to incorporate into the genre of their collective memory and what they have chosen to leave out. It is therefore interesting not only to understand how and why individuals and collectives remember those that they remembered, but also to understand why they choose to leave out others. For the latter, it is often the case that unrecorded memories could be permanently lost with little hope of recovery unless they are recorded or housed by individuals and thus enable those memories to find their way into the open, into the collective conscious.

These memories are often transmitted in a variety of ways. The common methods of personal memory are through diary entries, personal memoirs, letters sent to kin members and friends. Collective and social memories are often transmitted through storytelling and oral transmission and become the oral history of the community. Thus, Halbwachs argues that 'while the collective memory endures and draws strength from its base in a coherent body of people, it is individuals as group members who remember' (Halbwachs 1992, p. 22). In all communities, one or more sets of collective memories are in circulation and represent the various voices of the population (Halbwachs 1992, p. 22).

The production of memory is neither a systematic nor logical process and is often a fragmented account of what people could or choose to remember. In this sense, it represented important slices of oral and social history of the individual, social group or community concerned. This is now becoming increasingly important for people scattered through the diasporic community in their search for a lost past and a sense of identity in a condensed globalized world. It also allowed individuals and communities to chart the socio-historical trajectories of their shared past and of the movement towards their present state of affairs, however wealthy, prosperous and comfortable they presently are. It allowed them to compose a mental map and build a social tapestry of how their forebears and ancestors, their society or nation, were in the past, and to empathize with the lifestyle, living conditions, political turmoil, etc. that their forebears experienced at different historical conjunctures.

Thus, while historical events were often narrated by individuals and appeared in bits and pieces as snapshots, they should not be conceived as such, for each constitutes a piece of mosaic in the broad jigsaw puzzle, ultimately building the tradition of that society. The centrality and focus of such snapshots are constantly evolving and changing according to the availability of recently found information on the one hand and the changing emphasis of members of that community on the other. In short, subjective interpretations need to be contextualized according to the needs of those who narrate them. Thus what were considered significant then could be considered insignificant now, and the reverse was often the case when reinterpretations took place among a group of people or a community who embarked on the rewriting of their history.

In this way, individuals and the community as a whole would experience a sense of historical and social continuity cemented by their memory flow. This is essential in providing a society with a tradition. It might not be an overstatement to claim that the invention or reinvention of a tradition starts with the flow of memory in each society and it is this flow of memory that helps to spell out the unique characteristics of that society.

Collective memories as cultural capital

Among the Singapore Anxi Chinese, along with migration, they too brought along individualized as well as collective memories of their home villages. One key area of the individual and collective memories of this group of Chinese migrants is the shared understanding of life experiences in their ancestral village: their childhood in a rural environment, severe poverty, material deprivation, bitter winter cold with insufficient warm clothing, lack of food, lack of education, working as farmhands and collecting firewood in the hills for cooking and warmth during the winter months. A second area of their individual and collective memories concerns their migration experiences and early life as migrants: of their decision to migrate, where to go, their sea passage and arrival at their destination, of the initial contact and feelings as new migrants in a foreign land, their interaction with fellow migrants, their working experience. A third area involves life as fully fledged migrants in a diasporic community: settling down in a new environment, their adaptation process, sinking their roots in a new environment, *luodi shenggen*, how they became citizens of the new country, their social experiences, cultural and religious reproduction, their economic and political success, a new government and lifestyle and how they view their present world, the rapid transformations that they faced and their social security in the new home and their national, cultural and ethnic identity.

These three sets of memories serve as comparative forces in helping the Chinese to make sense of their social existence in the diasporic community. At one level, the collective memories allow for comparison of life then and now – thereby allowing them to formulate their life universes according to their understanding of their life destiny and fate, *ming-yun*. According to the Chinese cosmological world view, these migrants were destined to escape poverty, material deprivation and hardship as they embarked on a life-transforming journey to South East Asia. Indeed, many have made their life comfortable and good in the diaspora in comparison with their village counterparts. The elevation of social status and its transformation in an urban cosmopolitan dweller have also served to contrast them with their village kin.

At another level, it has also served to widen the gap between these Singapore Chinese and their village in terms of global knowledge and wealth attainment. This attainment of wealth, which is necessarily relative in nature, together with their collective memory of poverty that was deeply etched into their mental faculty, serves to create a feeling of guilt that propelled them to extend a helping hand to their ancestral village and ultimately how such actions help them to define their own identity in the village parlance and an overseas diasporic home.

To this group of Singapore Chinese from Anxi County in Fujian Province, their recollection of the events, people and actions etched in their memory are bittersweet experiences that gave rise to intense emotions and sentiments towards their ancestral home and tugged at their hearts, propelling them to return to their ancestral village and contribute much to the sociocultural and economic life there. On the other hand, such memories also acted as a resistance force against their return, especially for those who did not make it in the overseas environment and were thus 'failures' in the eyes of their village kin. This rollercoaster of emotions was expressed in the things, events and social experiences they choose to remember and are finally embedded into their individual and collective memories.

Using the methodologies of participant observation as well as narrating oral and social histories, this chapter will endeavour to present some of the emotions, dilemmas, thoughts and feelings of this group of Chinese encapsulated in their voices in order that we might empathize with how such traumatic experiences of migration distilled into their memorial psyche and actions and to understand how collective memories are transformed into significant cultural capital that could be tapped for sociocultural and economic developments in the ancestral hometowns.

Embedding social experiences into the collective memories

Among the Chinese migrants, collective memories inform the community of their shared history, shared ideology and shared culture and tradition. At the same time, collective memories also inform and remind individuals and the community as a whole of their social and moral obligation to preserve their shared history, ideology and cultural tradition. In our context here, it refers to revitalizing the ancestral villages and helping with development in order that they too become prosperous, since in the Confucian tradition, migrants have a moral obligation as their attainment of wealth in an overseas environment cannot be divorced from their ancestors. Thus, the following saying that is firmly etched into their psyche, *fugui bu lizu*, serves as a moral parameter to push these migrants into their proper Confucian role befitting the loyal and patriotic descendants of the lineage that they belong to, hence their collective identity both within the home village and in the diasporic community.

As argued, collective memories are distilled from a wide repertoire of social experiences encountered by the migrants. Among the early migrants, their memories consist of a vast store of social experiences that included an intense and prolonged period of social suffering in the social, economic as well as political arenas. In the early years of migration, migration itself was a disruptive move and many migrants suffered from social dislocation and incomplete adaptation processes. The latter was a big challenge to both the men and the women, often wives with young children. As with all migration processes, existing social networks were often left behind and these migrants had to start with a new set of social networks. For many Chinese, the immediate family network that they left behind was fortunately substituted by the existence of other forms of social networks in the forms of voluntary clan and territorial based associations. Women had to form their own social groups and networks to help them with all aspects of life, including the daily routine of family life, reproduction and maternity needs as well as children and their education.

(a) The collective memories of social suffering

Social suffering among the early migrants was related primarily to poverty although political persecution also played a role. Poverty was the single most important reason for migration. The push factor together with the hope of a better future had many villagers moving out of the home village to a completely alien environment in the hope of a better future not only for themselves, but for their family and future generations.

This is how poverty was described by Pei, an 85-year-old male migrant who migrated to Singapore in 1947:

> In the village that I came from, life was very hard. We had very little agricultural land and we had to work long hours for little reward. Insufficiency of food was one of the major problems that we faced all the time. We also suffered much at the hands of the landlords. However, in the late 1930s and 1940s, we also feared communism. Because we had some relatives who had migrated to Nanyang, we therefore decided to follow them to Nanyang as they promised that they would help us to find a job there.

Having lived in Singapore for over five decades, Pei has become a Singapore citizen and has also become a relatively successful businessman accumulating sizeable wealth. Today, he is considered to be well-off by Singapore standards and of middle-class status. His children have also become reasonably successful in their professions.

During his five decades of life in Singapore, he has constantly maintained relationships with his village kin in the ancestral village. His social experiences centred around two sets of social relationship. The first is his pre- and post-migration relationship with his ancestral village. The second is his post-migration relationship with his co-ethnics and other ethnic groups in the diasporic community and host society.

In the early years of migration, there were many economic opportunities for the migrants to kick-start family businesses and Pei was one of those who started a small family business; living frugally, he was able to accumulate sizeable wealth and provide some education for his children in Singapore. Much of his time, energy and wealth were expended on his immediate Singapore family. Prior to communism, he, like other migrants, would send remittances at regular intervals to his village kin. However, after communism, especially from 1966 until the 1978 Open Door Policy, there was little communication between the two factions of the family and lineage.

Pei recalled those early days from the mid-1960s to the 1970s:

> Our village kin only wrote two letters a year to me. Usually they paid a small sum to the village letter writer and asked him to write the letters

> as almost all the elderly kin were illiterate. In the letter, they would inform us of their health and general well-being. This was followed by a modest request for some material products, usually medicinal products. However, we knew at that time that village life was harsh and there was insufficient food and clothing to go round everybody. In our reply letter, my wife generally enclosed a parcel of medicinal products as well as some used and new clothing for the family. However, we were also very careful about what to send in the parcel to them as we did not want them to get into trouble with the authorities. So, it broke my heart to see them suffering from cold during winter time because of lack of clothing or insufficient food because of food rationing that was common at that time. But we could not do much for them. This was probably the most difficult period in their life and I often felt guilty that I was unable to do more.

(b) Embedding responsibility and guilt in collective psyche

Another issue here is the proliferation of a guilt complex among these migrants. As the Chinese migrants have become members of the growing Chinese community in the diaspora and citizens of their adopted home, they have benefited socially, economically and politically from the changes and progress of these communities. Along with this, we witnessed the accumulation of wealth and social status and the growth of a changed sociopolitical ideology. The feeling of being the 'lucky ones' who have benefited from migration has resulted in many migrants feeling contented with their own success and comfort. At the same time, such a sense of contentment was complemented by a deep sense of guilt for they had left behind other loved ones to suffer in a poverty-stricken village under harsh communist rule, as narrated by Pei.

As the diasporic Chinese community in Singapore matured, these migrants became more confident and there was a general feeling of urgency that they needed to help develop their ancestral village. This sense of urgency was reinforced by the fact that many of the migrants who have become economically successful are approaching old-age status. Furthermore, from the mid-1970s onwards, more information on rural village life became available to the diaporic Chinese community as some Singapore Chinese managed to visit their home village. As narrated by Siew:

> I have been to my ancestral village many times, sometimes two times a year. I am now over eighty years old and have only a few more years to

> live. I like to see the village develop and prosper as we have in Singapore. I think with the opening up of China, this is a window of opportunity and they could benefit from a little help from us. We should try to understand from their point of view and not only from ours. I am able to empathize with them more, maybe because I was born here. But the younger generation of Singaporeans do not look at things the way we older generations do. So, they tend to find faults with the villagers. We often hear them complaining about the villagers being lazy, unhygienic and adopt a 'cannot be bothered' kind of attitude. This is not true. We must understand that under Communism, they cannot pursue a capitalist style of trading and doing business, they cannot even dress nicely and brightly. It is not their fault. Having said this, I think given our better economic conditions in Singapore, we should try to help them. I certainly have been doing this or I will feel guilty for the rest of my life and not rest in peace.

It was this guilt that propelled her to convince her husband to actively contribute to rebuilding their old home that was dilapidated and in ruins. Since the late 1980s, they have rebuilt and extended their old house into a grand house with many rooms to accommodate the extended family members. However, today the grand house has only several elderly occupants as the young members of the extended family have chosen to leave for the bright city lights. They have also helped with small retail businesses and to renovate village temples. At the same time, they have also helped some of the younger-generation village kin to find employment beyond the village boundaries.

Such empathy contrasted starkly with the viewpoints of younger generations of Singapore Chinese who regarded their village kin with a sense of disdain and inferiority. One of the younger-generation diasporic Chinese, Kwang, provides the following narration which was widely circulated among the Anxi diasporic community in Singapore:

> These village people were very pragmatic. They looked at you and sized you up. If they know that they can get things out of you, they will be very friendly and will hang around you like a 'lap dog'. Otherwise, they will simply ignore you. This is why they are often seen crowding around the wealthy elderly overseas Chinese. While some might be their relatives, many are at most distant relatives but they nevertheless hovered around them in the hope that the wealthy overseas Chinese will give them some money. It is understandable among the older villagers. But this is also the same for the younger villagers who are often

> economically not so productive. They tend to sit around, drinking tea and engaged in idle talks. But to be fair, with the changing economic situation in China, some have started small businesses and others have gone to the towns and cities to look for jobs. But still, whenever the overseas kin arrived, they continue to hover around. Such an attitude makes it really unpleasant for me and the other younger Singapore Chinese.
>
> Besides, we don't really know them and it is really difficult to socialise and make small talk with them without feeling that they are expecting something from us. I prefer my non kinship based friends in Singapore to them for at least we share common interests and speak the same *lingo*.

These negative imageries of the villagers in Anxi as being 'greedy', 'bandit-like', 'demanding' and 'inconsiderate' become an important part of the negative memories etched into the psyche of the younger generations of Singapore Chinese (Kuah 2000, p. 86). Today, they continue to be circulated with the Chinese diasporic community in Singapore and South East Asia. As a consequence of this, negative feelings for their village kin persuaded many not to venture into their ancestral village for fear of being 'bled to death' or 'fleeced by the villagers', thereby creating the following stereotypical images of the villagers and the ancestral village as thus:

> ... the archetypal village kinsperson is utilitarian: his or her friendliness is measured by the amount of gifts and money given to him/her. He/she is demanding and greedy, and thinks that the *qiao-qing* [young overseas Chinese] owes him/her a living. He/she may be subtle, but is outright in demanding material goods and money from the *qiao-qing*. He/she is lazy and does not bother to work for a living, but sits around and does nothing except talk with other villagers, drink tea and smoke. He or she expects the *guanxi* network to work to his or her favour and that the world should revolve around them.
>
> The archetypal village is one with an undeveloped road system and limited accessibility. There are few or no modern amenities, such as piped water, air conditioning, or electricity. There is also no proper sanitation. The village is very undeveloped – with few schools, bridges, roads, or hospitals to cater for the local needs. There are also no entertainment facilities such as cinemas, karaoke bars and skating rinks. There is also a lack of economic facilities – few factories and shops, the main activity being farming. (Kuah 2000, p. 86)

(c) Memorizing ritual obligation

A third set of collective memories revolved around the inability of the diasporic Chinese, especially the sons and male descendants, to discharge their filial duties to their forebears and ancestors. Under the Confucian tradition, the male descendants are required to look after their parents, conduct the last rites for their deceased parents and conduct ancestor worship. For many male migrants, migration overseas meant that they were unable to discharge their moral duties to their parents who remained behind in the village and their dead ancestors. While in an overseas environment, many Chinese households set up a domestic altar with ancestral tablets to worship their ancestors and some lineages also have a memorial hall, *ci-tang,* but many felt that ancestor worship was incomplete without re-establishing an ancestral house, *zu-wu,* in their ancestral village (Kuah 2000, pp. 139–72). Such sentiments are narrated by many as echoed here by Ann:

> If there are branches and leaves, there must be a tree. Likewise, if there is water, we must also know the source. We are an offshoot from the parent tree, so we should not forget who our parents are and where we come from. Otherwise, we are no better than orphans who have no clue of who they are and where they come from. This is why when you have a house, you must have an owner. This is the same for us, a group of Singapore Anxi Chinese. We must know our roots and we must acknowledge them. It is only by acknowledging our roots that we can fully come to understand our origin and identity. This is why when we drink the water, we must search for the fountain. It is also important for us to understand that our success and failure are closely tied to our ancestors for it is our ancestors that blessed us with good fengshui and good fortune. Thus, we should always remember that 'wealth should not be divorced from our ancestors' (*fu-gui-bu-li-zu*). It is only by coming to Anxi and to acknowledge our ancestors that we become full again, knowing that we have a root and a source to go back to. Otherwise, we would be running around but not having a home to go. Otherwise, we will be like the refugees that wander aimlessly without a home to go to.

Thus, among the Singaporean Chinese, this set of collective memories propels them to return to the ancestral village to rebuild an ancestral house, resulting in a revival of ancestor worship as well as various religious rituals and rites since the 1978 reform.

While the Chinese in the diasporic community have consciously developed their version of collective memories to cater for their needs, the village kin in the emigrant hometowns also wrestle with their own version of memories. Apart from sharing with their diasporic counterparts memories of poverty, material deprivation and social suffering, they too have selectively chosen to remember their social encounters with their diasporic counterparts and passed down this memory to their descendants. The village version of collective memories concerned more of their feelings and relationship with their diasporic kin and circulated widely within the village precinct. Villager Peng narrated his feelings that are echoed by the elderly village kin:

> I am an old man now and I have seen the great disasters that had befallen our village and life used to be very difficult in the 1950s to 1970s. Today, things have changed and it is much easier for us although there is still poverty all around us. But as you can see, things have improved. We have better housing, better food and even some social enjoyment. The village also has some economic life injected into it. Previously it was agricultural and there was not even enough land for us to till. Today, many have moved out of farming and started their little shops and the land is even rented out to outsiders for cultivation. Some of our relatives simply let the landless kin till their land for free. Many of these new developments are possible because of our Singapore relatives. They, and especially the older ones, have been very generous. Some of the younger ones are not so, but they nevertheless are very respectful of their parents' wishes and they also helped a lot. This is also why you often see them accompanying their elderly parents to visit the village.

Another village elder and an official cadre remembered:

> In the early days, life was very hard and we had very little in terms of food or material possessions. Many villagers were fortunate to have some supplements from their Diasporic kin on either a regular or intermittent basis which went a long way to help with our lack of resources. This contribution became even more valuable under the Communist rule where everything was rationed and an individual could not have more than his or her quota of needs. And the quota of needs was barely sufficient for a child or an adult. So, an overseas contribution, in however small way, was the only supplement that we could have.
>
> From the 1970s, when the Communist government relaxed its rule on overseas Chinese visiting their home village, a small number of them came and visited us. Some of the elderly Diasporic Chinese have a great heart. When they started visiting the ancestral village

> and discovered that the village lacked basic infrastructure such as roads, bridges and schools, they would contribute much money to help build these infrastructures, in addition to building houses for their own kin. Often, there are several leaders and they organised fund raising within the Diasporic community to help with other infrastructure development. Without them, our emigrant village, *qiaoxiang* would not be what it is today.

The various sets of memories circulated within the diasporic community in Singapore and the villagers' outlook on overseas Chinese were often less than flattering. On the one hand, among the diasporic Chinese, the collective memories created a sense of suspicion and distrust of their village counterparts. On the other hand, the villagers looked upon their diasporic kin as being snobbish and selfish. These negative collective memories were often translated into negative sentiments that resulted in tensions and uneasy relationships between the diasporic Chinese and their village kin. Such tensions often intensified when the two groups of Chinese met face to face.

Transforming collective memories into diasporic community capital

Today, the social experiences, social sufferings and guilt feelings of these migrants have become an important part of the collective memories of the Chinese diasporic community. They have been narrated in many different forms and translated for co-ethnics as well as other ethnic groups to consume. At the same time, they are considered as important cultural and community capital that would propel its members to contribute to the well-being of the diasporic community and the host society in general.

Within the Singapore community, the migration history of the early migrants, stories of the migrants and their social experiences, social sufferings and guilt feelings have been popularized as such memories are captured and made into movies and soap operas for popular consumption. Movies on early migrant life experiences such as the *Nanyang Story* and the *Hakka Story*, the *Story of the Chaozhouese* are some examples. Popular books on life histories of successful Chinese migrant entrepreneurs and professionals have also been written for the general public, in addition to a proliferation of academic books and articles on the subject.

By presenting and reinventing social experiences, social sufferings and guilt feelings in a simplified and popular form, catering for mass consumption, these collective memories have become an imperative and integral part of the social history of the migrant society to be shared by all Chinese within the diaspora. Along with this shared history is a sense of shared ideology and above all a shared culture not for the early Chinese migrants to witness, but more significantly for the descendants of the Chinese migrants and the future generations to come. They become testimonies of early generations of pioneers who have braved all odds to make their story a successful one and who have created a new path to benefit their future generations.

In the Chinese diaspora, ethnic community capital has been used to arouse the sentiments of all Chinese from different generations for the construction of the community. In the early years, ethnic community capital was converted into economic and financial capital to help with the formation of voluntary Chinese organizations such as the clan associations, territorial-based associations, temples and various charity organizations for the benefit of groups of Chinese or the general Chinese population (Kuah-Pearce and Hu-Dehart 2006). It was also used for infrastructural development especially in the areas of education where Chinese vernacular schools first started in the 1930s as well as welfare institutions for the migrants. Chinese temples were also constructed to cater for the beliefs of the Chinese and allowed for both individual and communal worshipping of gods, goddesses and deities, thereby facilitating the reproduction of Chinese customs, behaviour and culture. This, together with the development of a Chinese philanthropic culture, enabled the society to establish various social and welfare infrastructures for its own diasporic community in the early years. It thus enabled the community to become independent with little reliance on the colonial government during the nineteenth and early half of the twentieth centuries. After independence, the community continued its own self-reliance policy. In post-industrialized Singapore, ethnic community capital, accumulated with the Chinese community, is now extended to non-ethnic-based organizations and caters to the needs of a multiethnic Singapore society. Chinese philanthropy has increasingly been tapped for the construction and development of non-ethnic-based kinds of infrastructure and facilities.

Flow of cultural capital to the ancestral home village

These social and cultural experiences, social sufferings and guilt feelings were transformed into important moral–cultural capital, resulting in a moral economy used for the benefit of the emigrant ancestral hometown, *qiaoxiang*. As moral–cultural capital, collective memories became, in part, a guiding principle for the migrants in establishing a framework for the reconstruction of their ancestral villages. Reconstruction projects, large and small, proliferated and cater for the immediate family members, the lineage, the local society, the county and province. The operation of the moral economy in the emigrant villages was also facilitated by the friendly official Chinese policy towards the overseas Chinese and the official cadres who adopted a friendly and supportive disposition towards the diasporic Chinese and the projects that they embarked upon. Indeed, there were attempts by the official cadres to establish strong *guanxi* networks with the diasporic Chinese.

Since the Open Door Policy of 1978, the Bureau of the Overseas Chinese Affairs, Qiaolianban, has consciously cultivated *guanxi* networks with the Chinese in the diasporic communities. At the initial stage of Chinese economic reforms, the Qiaolianban was instrumental in encouraging diasporic Chinese capital into China. Its friendly policy and preferential treatment, including land acquisition and tax rebates, towards the overseas Chinese have facilitated the entry of Chinese capital into China. Likewise, its policy of encouraging the Chinese to help with the development of emigrant villages has also met with a measure of success. One of the policies was to treat the emigrant villages as growth nodes that would filter down development to the surrounding districts. This was especially pertinent for the interior regions where there were limited development opportunities. To further facilitate the operation of the moral economy, the official policy of viewing ancestor worship as an integral part of Chinese culture and permitting the revival of ancestor worship and religious activities have made it more attractive for the diasporic Chinese to visit and contribute to the development of their ancestral villages.

The moral economy operates at three levels. The first operates within the immediate family where financial resources were channelled to help with the rebuilding of the existing houses where the family kin continued to live. This was one of the most immediate tasks of the diasporic Chinese when they made their first visit to the emigrant village after four decades of separation. Most of the houses that they occupied as a child or young adult were in extremely bad condition, with some parts having collapsed in ruins. So there was much reconstruction going on from the late 1970s up to today, fuelling a booming construction industry in rural China. The second concerns a demand for modern-style housing fuelled by the emergence of nuclear families among the younger generation within the village. Thus, construction of modern-style three- to four-storey housing became fashionable within the village environment, which is now a ubiquitous sight. The third concerns employment opportunities for the family members and kin. It is not uncommon for the diasporic Chinese to provide start-up capital to help members of their immediate and extended family to start small businesses or factories either within the village setting, local society or even in the county towns.

Within the family, there was a revival of domestic ancestor worship where the diasporic Chinese discharge their filial obligations by performing the necessary rituals and rites for their deceased parents and ancestors. Thus, *Gong-de* rites, after-death rites, were performed long after their parents had passed away in order to make up for the inability to discharge their duties as sons and daughters (Kuah 2000, pp. 148–58). Such rites are significant for they allowed the diasporic sons and daughters to grieve for the loss of their parents and ancestors in a public fashion. They also provide them with a sense of emotional closure.

The second level operates at local society level, *xiang* level. In the first years of the Open Door Policy, the ancestral districts continued to be poor and lacked many facilities. There was a lack of good roads both within the district and from the big cities such as Xiamen to regional cities that connect to the village. Thus, many financial resources were channelled to the building of roads that would halve the travelling time from Xiamen city to the ancestral village. More importantly, it enables the development of a viable economy in the rural region. Besides this, resources were also put into the construction of bridges to facilitate movement of people and transport in the region as the district is cut in two by the River Xi. Apart from transportation, the district also lacked medical and school facilities which the diasporic Chinese have contributed much to. Today, modern medical facilities, a new hospital and new school premises stand as testimony of the reach of the moral economy into this region.

On the cultural front, there was a revival of ancestor worship, together with the rebuilding of lineage and sub-lineage ancestral houses and various religious festivals that attracted the participation of the villagers as well as a sizeable number of diasporic Chinese. These cultural and religious activities were organized on a large-scale level and created much noise and energy on a regular basis, thereby enlivening the previously sedate and monotonous village landscape. Today, various religious activities take place on certain occasions such as the Lunar New Year, and the birthdays of various gods and deities have become standard religious events in the village environment. To the official cadres, ancestor worship is seen as cultural capital, given as a concession to the diasporic Chinese in order to bind them to the moral economy. To the diasporic Chinese, the cultural capital of ancestor worship is a motivating factor to engage in the moral economy.

On the economic front, an agrarian economy leaves few opportunities for the young villagers who prefer to leave for the bright city lights. Thus, it falls upon the diasporic Chinese to help with providing employment opportunities for the villagers. Small-scale factories were set up in the villages and in the county towns. However, because of its interior location, they were not as successful as those found in the Pearl River Delta. For the diasporic Chinese, setting up a factory in the *qiaoxiang* was never meant for profit but more out of moral duty to help the ancestral village.

At the county and provincial level and beyond, for the diasporic Chinese entrepreneurs, some have set up medium-sized factories in the county towns or the big cities, thereby tapping into the preferential policies accorded to the overseas Chinese in an attempt to tap into the vast Chinese economy. For them, the moral economy has a double edge where they too tapped into it for their own financial benefit.

Conclusion

The social experiences embedded in the collective memories have become important events of nostalgic and sentimental value, for they play an important role in luring first-generation migrants into visiting their home villages. They helped the early migrants to continue to have a strong sense of belonging and identity to the ancestral village. This is imperative for their socio-psychological well-being, for it allows them to locate themselves within a known and manageable social framework, which, grounded in kinship ties, facilitates the revival of relationships and lost primordial kinship ties. It has also allowed them to measure their self-worth and to fulfil their moral duties, which include providing a bridge to link the younger Singapore Chinese to their ancestral home.

Memories of the past and present, of the ancestral home, transmitted orally or in written form, are important for keeping alive images of home villages and the people's social experiences, which can then be related to children, grandchildren and other kin in routine conversation. By doing this, the older members have had some success in making the younger Singapore Chinese more aware of the plight of their ancestral village. These memories are kept alive and circulated within the kinship circle.

In keeping alive the memories of their home villages, the Singapore Chinese are reminded of ritual obligations and of their initial failure to carry them out both in Singapore and also in their ancestral villages, at a time when the communist regime prevented even their village kin from carrying out religious rituals and ancestor worship on their behalf. As the political pressure has now eased, the Singapore Chinese hope once again to re-establish links with their Anxi kin and revive and reproduce these rituals for communal ancestor worship and religious ceremonies. Confucian teachings have dictated that a son continues perform ancestor worship to the dead ancestors and look after living parents. However, migrating to the Nanyang has meant that sons were indeed contradicting this teaching. Having made it good in the Nanyang, many of these migrants have made trips back to their ancestral home since the 1970s. From the 1970s, trips made to the ancestral village were infrequent but from the 1980s onwards, there has been an increased traffic from the diaspora to the ancestral village as a result of the Open Door Policy and the encouragement by the Chinese government to visit emigrant villages. The Chinese government gave various types of incentives and concessions to lure in the Chinese from the diaspora to visit their home villages.

Collective memories, as we have witnessed, are not static, they are subjected to change through time where revision often takes place as individuals or a group of people have chosen to highlight certain social experiences and downplay others in order to use them to explain certain actions or for various purposes. Collective memories exist not only for altruistic purposes which inform us of our culture, history and identity. They are also used in an instrumental way as a form of social and ethnic community capital to help with the progress and development of the ancestral villages. To this end, the ability to tap into guilt feelings embedded in collective memories, as illustrated by the Chinese villagers, have enabled the emigrant villages to prosper and develop into economically and socially vibrant communities in modern-day China.

References

Halbwachs, M. 1992, *On Collective Memory*, Chicago University Press, Chicago.

Kuah, Khun Eng, 2000, *Rebuilding the Ancestral Village: Singaporeans in China*, Ashgate Publishing Ltd, Aldershot, England and Brookfield, Vermont.

Kuah-Pearce, K.E. and Hu-Dehart, E. (eds) 2006, *Voluntary Associations in the Chinese Diaspora*, University of Hong Kong Press, Hong Kong.

8

Politics, Commerce and Construction of Chinese 'Otherness' in Korea: Open Port Period (1876–1910)

Sheena Choi

There is a growing body of literature on the role that colonial Japan had on the Korean national imagination or memory.[1] While Japan's role is fundamental, this chapter will suggest that China's influence on the Korean 'imagined community' in its national memory (1983), albeit very different, is equally irrefutable. This account explores the restructuring process of the Sino-Korean relationship (Choson Korea 1392–1910; Qing China 1644–1911) in Korea during the Open Port Period (1876–1910), a period marked by internal disorder and external calamities for both countries, as each was in the midst of dynastic decline. This meant a reorientation of the two nations' relationship to each other and, more broadly, to the world order. In a historical irony, through the process of restructuring the Sino-Korean relationship, China became an 'informal empire' (Schmid 2002), an imitation of a modern form of imperialism to which China was subjected by Western imperial powers.

An examination of political, economic and social interactions between the two countries in transition illuminates the process of identity formation and, by extension, national memory. What emerges from this exploration is a powerful link between international power politics and identity formation. The unequal relationship between China and Korea was discernible in social relationships during the time of nascent Korean national consciousness. The power disparity that the Koreans felt in the new world order provides the basis for construction of self which is set out in an ultranationalistic legal framework in the post-independence Koreas (1945–present), a break from the traditionally transnational culturalism of East Asia rooted in Confucian values. Examination of the Sino-Korean social relationship in Korea during the modern Korean nation-building process provides a foundation for consideration of Chinese identity in contemporary Korea.

Background

Korea, with a very small minority population, is known as one of the most homogeneous societies in the world. The ethnic Chinese who arrived in Korea at the turn of the twentieth century represent the single largest ethnic minority group, yet they comprise less than 0.5 per cent of the total Korean population. According to the Korean Ministry of Justice's *Annual Report of Statistics on Legal Migration* (2000), there are 23,282 ethnic Chinese residing in Korea as legal aliens. Moreover, many ethnic Chinese estimate that about 7000–8000 of their own are floating members, residing elsewhere while keeping resident alien status in Korea. Thus, the actual number of ethnic Chinese is approximately 15,000 (Do Rosario 2000), with some estimates as low as 10,000. A study by Poston et al. (1994) indicates that Korea saw the greatest loss of its ethnic Chinese population – 7 per cent annually – during the 1980s. This study revealed that Korea is one of the few countries experiencing decline in Chinese population.

This leads to a question – why in peacetime with high economic growth and an apparent absence of ethnic hostility, would there be such an exodus of Chinese? Some recent studies identify inhospitable laws and policies regarding Chinese in Korea. Citizenship laws that excluded them from Korean citizenship as well as subsequent economic discrimination, such as prohibition of landownership, had been cited as major causes of Chinese emigration (Choi 2001a, b, c; Kim 1995; Kuk 1991; Park 1986; Yang 2002). While the literature provides understanding of the current state of ethnic Chinese in Korea, it lacks historical context. This study will examine the historical framework of the Chinese diaspora to Korea and social formations of identity with a focus on the Open Port Period (1876–1910). This chapter will construct inferences from scholarly and popular articles, personal interviews and oral histories in order to clarify and augment the historical data and to amplify the cumulative patterns and mechanisms of the historical development of Chinese identity in Korea. As renowned historian Eric Hobsbawm (1983) emphasized, the importance of knowing the history to supplement the data can provide a link between the past and the present. History can thus serve as a guide for future directions.

Theoretical framework

It is well acknowledged that 'the process of state building affects the norms of citizenship' (Brubaker 1996; Hobsbawm 1990; Li 1998, p. 7), by extension, ethnic relations. National boundaries and norms of citizenship alter as political changes occur. In discussing the requirement for citizenship, Galstone noted that 'sense of the community' and 'loyalty' is associated with a 'communitarian view of rights and obligation in the democratic state'. This suggests that 'belonging requires the consent of the community' (Galstone 1993; quoted in Klausen 1995, p. 250). Elaborating on Galstone's view, Klausen contends that the modern 'welfare state has in effect intensified the importance of belonging to these communities' as a result of the elevated level of state obligation toward its citizens (Klausen 1995, p. 250).

Within the frame of citizenship and nation-building, a nation is composed of two mutually inclusive memories: the institutional memory and the cultural memory. According to Li (1998, p. 7) the institutional memory, such as the juridical and territorial boundaries, is defined by politics, while the cultural memory, such as people's affiliation and belonging, is defined by the norms and values of the in-group. In other words, cultural memory is as powerful a force as an institutional memory. Within this 'memory', 'cultural wars' (Graff 1992) are waged over the origin and goal/direction of a nation, and within this cultural memory lies the construction of the national identity and ethnic identity in response to this national identity.

Korean nationality law since 1949 can be characterized as ascriptive citizenship based on *jus sanguineness*, specifically the patrilineal principle. While such a framework is modelled on traditional conventions of East Asia that were framed by Confucian values, this essay suggests that circumstances during the nation-building process at the close of the nineteenth century and beginning of the twentieth reinforced a narrow interpretation of 'imagined community', legitimizing ethnic and cultural homogeneity.

With the above in mind, there is a paucity of academic discourse on the ethnic Chinese in Korea and their role in the nation-building process. It is imperative to understand the particular historical context of the social condition and process of nation-building, which forms national self-image, because the context furnishes a pertinent rationale for institutional and cultural imaging of the nation. This historical (re)formulation of modern Korea demonstrates the centrality of Korea's national memory and formation of the Chinese 'Other' in Korea, thus enabling the locating of ethnic Chinese in Korea from a more holistic perspective. As Etienne Balibar informs us, 'imaginary unity' takes part in 'real [historical] time *against* other possible unities' (Balibar quoted in Wallerstein 1991, pp. 46, 49). In that sense, the preclusion of Chinese from citizenship in independent Korea is a historical reciprocity – a manifestation of

Korean apprehensions about their destiny in the global system during the inception of modern Korea.

Sino-Korean relationship: tradition and transition

Throughout the Choson period, Korea participated in the Sinocentric world order where China was positioned as the 'Middle Kingdom' in the transnational Confucian cultural sphere. However, Korean scholars felt they were more faithful to authentic Confucianism than were Chinese scholars. Authentic Confucianism, the basis for East Asian civilization, was considered intellectually and morally superior to its Chinese counterpart (Haboush 1999, p. 69). Korean orthodoxy, according to Haboush and Deuchler (1999, p. 3), 'received its institutional underpinnings when, in 1610, five Korean scholars were enshrined in the Shrine of Confucius (Munmyo) in Seoul'. This act, which was a major assertion of Confucian orthodoxy in itself, had not only 'symbolic significance for the history of Korean Confucianism' but also significance in the shaping of the Korean psyche in relation to the Middle Kingdom (Haboush and Deuchler 1999, p. 3).

Through attaining an eternal and eminent position within the broader framework of Confucian civilization, Korean Confucians crowned themselves on the same level as their intellectual forebears of Sung China. At times, Koreans even asserted that they were more faithful guardians of Confucian orthodoxy than were the Ming Chinese. Therefore, to the Koreans, enshrinement was an affirmation of the supremacy of Korean Confucian tradition and the neo-Confucian world (Haboush and Deuchler 1999, p. 3). Such pride among Koreans in their intellectual and moral supremacy over the Chinese reached its height when Manchus invaded China (Deuchler 1999). Koreans viewed the rise of Qing as a 'barbarian' usurpation of the centre of civilization.

While Korea's military weakness necessitated their political subordination to Qing China for its security and survival (Korea is about one-fortieth the size of China), Koreans harboured cultural contempt toward the barbaric force of its more powerful neighbour. The status–power disequilibrium with Qing China was a constant source of anxiety to Korean intellectuals throughout the Choson dynasty, which led Koreans to feel that they were 'responsible for upholding Confucian civilization in the face of barbarian rule in China' (Deuchler 1999, p. 92). Drawing from *Sukchong sillok* (King Sukchong's Memorial), Haboush (1999) notes that the Choson court routinely referred to Qing envoys as 'barbarian messengers (*hoch'a*)', and King Sukchong referred to the K'ang-hsi Emperor as 'that northerner (*pugin*)'.

The Qing–Korea relationship was informed by the two basic principles of hierarchy and strict non-interference in political matters, domestic or foreign (Larson 2000, p. 11). The hierarchical relations predicated by Confucian principle regarded China as the elder brother with more prestige and Korea as the younger brother. The Korean court dispatched annual missions to the Chinese Imperial Court to pay tribute in expression of its subordinate position, and in turn, as suzerain, China was to assist its vassals in times of crisis and grant investiture to Korean kings. Thus a strange but effective relationship was maintained, summarized by Zongli Geguo Shiwu Yamen (shortened to Zongli Yamen, the Office for the Management of the Business of all Foreign Countries): 'Korea, though a dependency of China, is completely autonomous in her politics, religion, prohibitions and orders. China has never interfered into it' (Chien 1967, p. 16).

The complex ritual exchanges of 'Chinese expressions of benevolent concern, and Korean prostrate declarations of vassalage' (Larson 2000, p. 15) provided stability in the relations between the two countries '[a]s long as [the] Korean court declared fealty to China, it was virtually left alone to do as it please[d]' (Clark 1983, p. 15; Larson 2000). Elite participation in the Sinocentric world order and tributary system was later criticized as *Sadae* (literal meaning 'serving the great') and became synonymous with toadyism or flunkeyism (Larson 2000, p. 19), while others saw the ritual as a pragmatic way to secure 'peace and autonomy' (Clark 1983, pp. 77–89) with minimum commitment. Aside from such rituals and politics at the state level, all other forms of contact between the two countries were stringently guarded or entirely proscribed by mutual agreement.[2]

The nineteenth century saw even greater trepidation in Korea as the state was facing *naeu oehwan*: internal crisis and external calamities. The decline of China and ascendancy of Japan resulted in historic changes in regional power formations that had important consequences for the ways in which Koreans viewed the world and themselves.

In particular, events in both countries during the 1870s and 1880s seriously challenged the established order; and Qing eventually abandoned its principle of non-interference in Korean affairs while maintaining its suzerainty (Larson 2000), a situation some scholars termed as 'informal empire'. Only the dramatic Qing defeat in the Sino-Japanese War of 1894–95 ended the formal suzerain–vassal relationship and Qing's influence over Korea.[3]

Externally, such a shift in relationship was a manifestation of the diffusion of Western imperialism to which China was subjected (Larson 2000);

internally, the Soldiers' Riot of 1882 (*Imo Kullan*), in which the old Korean military protested its displacement by the formation of a modern Japanese-style army (Lew 1990, p. 205), provided the opportunity for Chinese military intervention in Korea – a departure from traditional non-interference. Japan, harbouring imperial ambitions towards Korea, sent in its military under the pretext that it was protecting Japanese subjects in Korea. The Qing government, understanding Korea's geopolitical importance, immediately responded by sending 4500 soldiers under the command of General Wu Ch'ang-ch'ing to counterbalance Japanese influence in Korea – a pattern to be repeated in the Tonghak Peasant Uprising of 1894 (Eckert et al. 1990).[4]

In a traditional sense, the dispatch of Chinese troops in aid to a vassal state in distress could be viewed as a legitimate practice. However, the continued presence of Chinese troops on Korean soil was a break from traditional 'non-intervention', and the beginning of Qing's disastrous attempt at 'informal empire' in Korea (Larson 2000; Schmid 2002). Japanese and Chinese soldiers were eventually withdrawn by 1885; however, the traditional hierarchical relationship, in addition to Qing military presence during this time, provided a psychological and practical advantage to China and played a crucial role in the reformation of Sino-Korean relations.

The Qing government's intrusion was broad in both the political (domestic and international) and economic arenas (Ch'en 1972; Fairbank 1989; Larson 2000; Lew 1990; Schmid 2002). The most common venue of Qing control of Choson Korea was through various small but influential numbers of Qing officials sent to operate the Qing *yamen* (magistracy) in Seoul and other Qing-sponsored enterprises such as the telegraph line to China, Korean Maritime Customs Service, and loan schemes in which Qing and its sponsored foreign advisors served the Qing interest (Kim 1971; Larson 2000, p. 77; Lee 1992,1993b, p. 171; Lew 1984, pp. 93–7; Sigel 1980, p. 93; Yi 1984). The interventions were most audacious during the Residency of Yuan Shikai (1885–94), who frequently abused his position to advance Qing commercial interests in Korea (Peng 1992).[5] Such Chinese efforts bore significant fruit; and Sino-Korean trade showed stunning growth, following that of Japan, which had increasing influence in Korea (see Table 8.1).

The majority of Chinese in Korea during this period were merchants, whose far-flung networks extended to China, Japan, Hong Kong/Macao and beyond. They made maximum use of these connections, supplying wealthy Koreans with Chinese silk, textiles and European goods. Goods imported from and through China increased year after year and were distributed throughout Korea (Park 1986). Naturally, 'Clashes between

Table 8.1 Korea's total trade (by country), 1877–1910

Year	*Japan*	%	*China*	%	*Russia*	%	*Other*	%	*Total*	%
1877	439	100.0	0	0.0	0	0.0	0	0.0	439	100.0
1878	426	100.0	0	0.0	0	0.0	0	0.0	426	100.0
1879	1,179	100.0	0	0.0	0	0.0	0	0.0	1,179	100.0
1880	2,548	100.0	0	0.0	0	0.0	0	0.0	2,548	100.0
1881	3,826	87.7	538	12.3	0	0.0	0	0.0	4,364	100.0
1882	4,441	90.7	454	9.3	0	0.0	0	0.0	4,895	100.0
1883	3,153	100.0	0	0.0	0	0.0	0	0.0	3,153	100.0
1884	2,409	100.0	0	0.0	0	0.0	0	0.0	2,409	100.0
1885	2,002	83.5	395	16.5	2	0.1	0	0.0	2,399	100.0
1886	3,421	83.3	674	16.4	14	0.3	0	0.0	4,109	100.0
1887	4,034	80.5	962	19.2	13	0.3	0	0.0	5,009	100.0
1888	3,990	75.4	1,269	24.0	30	0.6	0	0.0	5,289	100.0
1889	4,016	71.8	1,569	28.0	9	0.2	0	0.0	5,594	100.0
1890	6,821	75.6	2,198	24.3	9	0.1	0	0.0	9,028	100.0
1891	6,697	71.9	2,596	27.9	18	0.2	0	0.0	9,311	100.0
1892	5,181	65.6	2,687	34.0	26	0.3	0	0.0	7,894	100.0
1893	3,917	60.3	2,534	39.0	46	0.7	0	0.0	6,497	100.0
1894	6,337	69.8	2,522	27.8	218	2.4	0	0.0	9,077	100.0
1895	9,158	76.8	2,612	21.9	154	1.3	0	0.0	11,924	100.0
1896	9,493	75.0	3,010	23.8	147	1.2	0	0.0	12,650	100.0
1897	15,470	73.4	5,359	25.4	248	1.2	0	0.0	21,077	100.0
1898	12,493	62.8	7,242	36.4	167	0.8	0	0.0	19,902	100.0
1899	12,912	71.1	5,041	27.8	205	1.1	0	0.0	18,158	100.0
1900	18,538	77.2	5,119	21.3	356	1.5	0	0.0	24,013	100.0
1901	21,311	75.7	6,554	23.3	287	1.0	0	0.0	28,152	100.0
1902	20,243	75.2	6,428	23.9	251	0.9	0	0.0	26,922	100.0
1903	24,611	74.2	6,908	20.8	456	1.4	1,178	3.6	33,153	100.0
1904	29,703	76.7	6,297	16.3	92	0.2	2,656	6.9	38,748	100.0
1905	34,157	77.5	7,448	16.9	114	0.3	2,352	5.3	44,071	100.0
1906	34,433	81.1	4,869	11.5	539	1.3	2,612	6.2	42,453	100.0
1907	44,396	71.2	7,646	12.3	658	1.1	9,617	15.4	62,317	100.0
1908	39,775	66.4	7,129	11.9	818	1.4	12,188	20.3	59,910	100.0
1909	40,046	68.6	7,676	13.1	230	0.4	10,458	17.9	58,410	100.0
1910	49,347	72.2	6,871	10.1	1,173	1.7	10,926	16.0	68,317	100.0

(unit = 1,000 yen, %)

Notes: 1881–82 figures for China include only the northern border trade at Chunggang/Zhongjinang; other figures for China do not include the northern border trade. Above data are quoted from Larson (2000, p. 354).

Sources: Kang, Tok-sang. 'Rishi Chosen kaiko chokugo ni okeru boeki no tenkai' 1–18; Chosen Boeki Kyokai (ed.).

Chosen boekishi, 48–52; *TSIS; HGP; CSR; YHWN; KKKK; KKSC; KKSR; British Consular Reports*.

Korean and Chinese merchants and repeated protests and boycotts by merchants were frequent' (Larson 2000, p. 165).[6]

Some Chinese behaved insolently towards Koreans. Reports were made of Chinese nationals assaulting and even killing Koreans. A high-profile case known as the Yi Pomjin incident occurred in 1884, in which Qing merchants mauled a son of a high-ranking Korean official for his refusal to sell his inherited property (Jin 1976). Such incidents caused a 'firestorm of controversy and criticism' (Larson 2000, p. 157) resulting in a strained relationship between the two governments.[7] In spite of these incidents, Chinese merchants continued to reside and even thrive (Larson 2000, p. 165).[8] Economic specialization occurred: while Korean society was divided between the scholar/gentry class and the peasant majority, the Chinese began to form a mercantile class.[9]

However, internal disorders such as the Boxer Rebellion (1900) and natural disasters of famine in China brought different groups into Korea, predominantly the Chinese peasant class. Furthermore, the political instability of the weakened Qing government during the late 1900s made leaders unable to control bandits, mobs and other undesirable elements; social unrest became a threat to daily living (Jin 1976). For the Chinese populace from Shandong Province, where the turbulence was greatest, who were afraid to live in this state of anarchy without protection, Korea was the nearest place and thus a natural destination.

These Chinese refugee labourers who migrated to Korea began to compete with Koreans for jobs such as construction and often caused labour unrest in Korea because these Chinese migrant workers caused displacement of Korean labourers.[10] The Chinese migrant labourers, most of whom were single males, competed unfairly with Korean labourers with lowered wages, causing labour conflicts. Chinese migrant workers usually came to Korea in the early spring and returned to their homes in China in late autumn (Jin 1976). These migrants saved their wages to send home by living in crowded shacks and subsisting on a few dumplings per day. Small numbers of Chinese farmers participated in market agriculture and supplied produce to an increasingly urbanized population (Jin 1976). Because of such economic success, the Chinese population multiplied (see Table 8.2).

Resentment bred by unequal power relationships, particularly on the part of China whose prestige was declining, was articulated through national discourse, often through the newly established newspapers. At the top, Yuan was criticized for his brash and overbearing personality, meddling in Korean affairs, and conducting himself as if a royal commissioner (Larson 2000; Lee 2002; Lew 1984).[11] However, the behaviour

Table 8.2 Chinese population in Korea, 1883–1910

Year	*Population*
1883	209
1884	354
1885	700
1906	3,661
1907	7,902
1908	9,978
1909	6,568
1910	11,818

Source: Park (1986, p. 47).

that brought scorn from many scholars was his hampering and even thwarting most of Korea's modernization efforts in diplomatic, economic and military spheres (Lee 1988, p. 171). The powerful Yuan, through plots and intrigues, achieved this by removing anyone who opposed him, regardless of their nationality (Larson 2000, p. 72). Other Chinese conduct, such as Chinese officials' use of Chinese gunboats in smuggling and officials' lack of effort in dealing with people involved in smuggling activities, was 'highly visible to observers of the day' and fuelled Korean concerns (Larson 2000, pp. 200–8).

Korean rage over lopsided power relations began a public discourse on the nation's future. In such discourse, China was in general portrayed as an uncivilized, backward nation. They scorned China, calling it 'the laughing stock of the world' (*Independence News* 20 June 1896). *Cheguk Shinmon* [Cheguk News] cautioned, 'We [Korea] hope we do not become like [China]' (5 July 1900 quoted in Schmid 2002). In Koreans' views, the 'Middle Kingdom' no longer occupied the centre of civilization and thus was unequivocally demoted to the periphery, both globally and regionally. And as peripheral, China was 'anything but civilized' (Schmid 2002, p. 11).

The comparisons between 'backward' China and the 'enlightened' West and Japan were often a topic of editorial discussion. Comparing Chinatown in the US, the editor of *Independence News* noted that even when Chinese lived in a civilized nation, they were unable to reform their 'savage' customs. An editorial in the *Tongnip Shinmun* [Independence News] declared that, 'As merchants they sold silks and velvets and clocks to fat-pursed officials or else they peddle thread, matches and pipe mouthpieces on the street'. However, the same editorial concluded that,

> We are sorry to see a tendency on the part of the Chinese to come in here[,] for their coming will have the same influence[,] only in less

> degree[,] that it did in America. He will underbid the Korean laborer and drive him to the wall. The reason is evident. He will wear clothes, the ordinary Chinese coolie, which no Korean would wear even though he had to go naked. For abject and irremediable filth commend us to the Chinese coolie. He will eat anything that any creature will eat and grow fat on absolute garbage. Some people call this economy, frugality, and commend the Chinese for it, but we believe this condition is the result of a lapse toward barbarity rather than an evolution toward enlightenment. (21 May 1896, in Kim 1999)

The editor further criticizes the Chinese for their introduction of opium to Koreans and making Korea's already dirty streets even filthier, in sum, '[t]here are not even the slightest benefits that accrue in their coming to Korea' but 'many harms'. Considering Chinese merchants as leeches who sucked the blood of Koreans, the editor lambasted them for greedily making profits without engaging in civilizing endeavours (in contrast to Americans and other Westerners, who engaged in civilizing enterprises in Korea such as setting up schools and hospitals, teaching skills, etc.) and declared, 'We don't want such people coming to Korea' (21 May 1896, in Kim 1999).

Other incidents fanned such sentiment, such as tax exemptions for foreigners and their doing business in Korea while Koreans, especially commoners, bore the burdens (*Independence News* 11 June 1896, in Kim 1999). Koreans in general at that time saw the Chinese as a moral and economic threat – boorish moneybags without honour. An editorial in *Independence News* declared,

> It was a happy day for Korea when the Chinese merchants and coolies decided that things were getting too hot for them here and 'folded their tents like the Arabs and as silently stole away'. It is safe to say that Korea never missed them; that neither the commercial, social nor moral interest of the country suffered a bit because of their departure. (21 May 1896, in Kim 1999)[12]

Some Korean merchants shared this contempt for China. 'The spate of arson attacks on Chinese business in the late 1880s, various "strikes" of Seoul shopkeepers protesting Chinese (and Japanese) competition, and numerous "incidents"– physical altercations between Chinese merchants and Koreans – all attest to the fact that many Koreans resented the Chinese presence in Korea' (Larson 2000, p. 233).

Therefore, complex images of the Chinese during this period ranged from moneybags to coolies, deviants, and a peril to Korean civilization.

The moneybag image was that of Chinese merchants conducting business unscrupulously devoid of civilization. The coolie image was that of the servile Chinese workers who were willing to work endless hours at low wages, accepting substandard living conditions that posed a threat to the Korean working-class family's standard of living. The deviant image was that of the Chinese use of opium that may bring menace to the morality of the Koreans. The coolie peril was a panic about Chinese overrunning Korea.

However, to be sure, the Sinophobia and general resentment apparently were limited to some political elites, merchants and labourers. The average Korean consumers preferred doing business with the Chinese due to practical advantages such as price, quality and trust. In comparison to the Japanese, who were concerned with short-term profits and 'often cold and brutal in their dealings with the Koreans', the Chinese were 'cordial and ingratiating, cultivating their customers and doing their best to accommodate' their Korean customers (Duus 1995). Further, Chinese business networks that enabled them to travel to and do business in the interior contributed to their success (Park 1986). One 1893 report noted that Chinese could be found in every place that showed commercial potential and concluded that unless measures were taken the Chinese would likely dominate the interior trade throughout Korea (Yi 1985).

Other evidence also indicates 'many Koreans thought more of the Chinese than they did for other foreigners' (Larson 2000, p. 233). For example, China and Chinese merchants in Korea were rarely if ever the target of the popular anti-foreign sentiment chain of disorder that followed the 1882 *Imo Kullan* and the 1882 Kapsin coup attempt to the Tonghak Rebellion (Eastern Learning Peasant Uprising) of the early 1890s (Larson 2000). In 1888, during the so-called 'baby riots', Chinese were exempted from being targeted when rumours circulated about Seoul accusing all 'foreigners' in Korea – Japanese, Germans, Americans, French and British – of participating in the vile deed of stealing and devouring Korean infants (Larson 2000).

However, politically, Qing's defeat in the Sino-Japanese War reaffirmed Qing's backwardness and advanced the process of 'decentering the Middle Kingdom' (Schmid 2002). China was demoted from its previously privileged position and became an example of self-destruction that 'Koreans should avoid' (*Hwangsong Shinmun* 25 January 1900 and *Independence News* 10 January 1899, in Kim 1999; Schmid 2002). The decentring process began with Korean recognition of its isolation and the limitations of the Sinocentric world view of the past.

> It would be bad enough for a highly advanced and prosperous country to impose its will on a technologically and politically weak nation without any regard whatsoever to the welfare and interest of that nation; and ... it would be even worse for a degenerated country such as nineteenth-century China, unable even to take care of itself, to try to impose its will on a tiny neighbor (Korea) trying to improve itself. (Lee 1988, p. 7)

An *Independence News* editorial remarked that Koreans had lived in 'one corner of the Eastern Sea' without knowing anything about the larger world and continued,

> The only thing [Koreans] knew was to revere China as the central plain [*chungwon*], scorn Japan as the country of *wae,* and call all other countries barbarians [*orangk'ae*]. Now, for more than ten years, our doors have been open, and we have welcomed guests coming from all places. With our ears we can hear and with our eyes we can see the customs and laws of Western countries. We can generally judge which countries are the civilized ones and which countries are the barbarous ones. (5 June 1899, in Kim 1999)

The process of 'decentring of the Middle Kingdom' had several elements: resisting and expurging Chinese culture from Korea; rediscovering authentic Korean culture; and making pure Korean identity, language and rituals popular topics in public discourse.

The unequal power relationship imposed upon Korea by China, at the time when it was experiencing its own decline and humiliation by the West and rising Japan, became the basis for new Korean national memory. Such a memory is clearly identifiable in the new laws, regulations and policies concerning the foreign population[13] (i.e. nationality law, property ownership) which were made when Korea became independent from the Japanese colonial yoke (1945).

Conclusion

Knowledge about self is relational, laden with cultural, political, economic and historical bearings and nuances. The historical context of the Sino-Korean relationship shaped Korean self-perception and the resultant construction of the Chinese 'Other'. At the close of the nineteenth century and opening of the twentieth, Qing China was a victim of Western imperialism domestically, while internationally it became a practitioner of modern imperialism through its relations with Korea. While the most significant and lasting aspects of Qing imperialism in Korea are in politics and the economy, this chapter argues that Qing's doomed attempt to restore its suzerainty in Korea during the historical moments of the 1880s and early 1890s backfired. Upon Qing's defeat in the Sino-Japanese War, Korean intellectual discourse identified China as a symbol of the backward 'Other', a fate that Korea should avoid (Larson 2000, p. 74; Schmid 2000). In its place, Korean elites encouraged 'counter' identity through the process of 'decentring the Middle Kingdom' in the modern Korean memory.

Such attempts in the face of China's own decline encouraged formation of the model that uniquely shaped the Sino-Korean relationship, especially the construction of the Korean national self and Chinese 'Other'. More importantly, the shift in relationship from traditional non-interference to modern imperialism at the critical juncture of Korean national memory no doubt influenced the construction of the Korean identity and, consequently, Chinese diaspora 'Otherness'. This reminds us that history is a long arm of memory.

Postscript

The integration of foreign 'Other' is a major concern in modern states. While integration policies are an outcome of historical interpretation and the current political and social consideration of each nation state, primarily they represent the national trajectory on 'belonging'. Recent news about South Korea granting voting rights to foreigners who have lived in the country for three or more years (a first in Asian countries) is a departure from past Korean exclusiveness and a promising development towards a more inclusive future. South Korea's recent economic development and vibrant democracy afford South Koreans confidence in their place within the increasingly globalizing world. While the new law is framed in a broader context, the immediate and significant beneficiaries are nevertheless the ethnic Chinese, the only ethnic minority group in Korea which has resided for generations as foreign nationals. It signals Korea's imagined community as more cosmopolitan, heralding a brighter chapter in the history of ethnic Chinese in Korea. It is reported that since the 1990s there has been a reverse migration back to Korea of ethnic Chinese who emigrated during the 1960s and 1970s.

Notes

1 The following may be considered to be the most exemplary writings on this subject: Shin Gi-Wook and Michael Robinson (1999) and Pai Hyung Il and Timothy Tangherlini (1999).

2 Recently, scholars noted the significance of the tributary trade system on economic spheres of both centre and periphery states. For example, see Hamashita (2006).
3 Larson (2000) argues that while 1895 marks the formal ending of the suzerain relationship, the traditional Sino-Korean relationship actually ended in 1882 when the Qing Empire began to impose modern imperialism.
4 This intervention constituted the first instance of Chinese military involvement in Korea since the Manchu attacks in 1627 and 1637. There are different accounts of how many troops were sent by the Qing government. Lew Yong Ick (1990) claims that 4500 soldiers were dispatched under the command of General Wu Ch'ang-ch'ing. However, other sources, including a biography of Yuan Shikai written by Jerome Ch'en (1972), note 3000 troops were sent. Kirk Larson (2000) notes six battalions were sent (p. 39), and subsequently 3000 troops were stationed in Korea (p. 41). Korean sources also differ in their accounts. Sohn Jung Mok (1982) notes 4000, while Dham Young Seong [Chinese: Tan Yingshing] (1976) cites 3000.

It is said that Queen Min of Korea built the monument in commemoration of General Wu Ch'ang-ch'ing, the commanding general of the Qing troops, at the current site of Dongdaemoon Woondongcha'ng [East Gate Stadium], where the Qing troops were stationed at that time. It was outside the East Gate, one of the four gates of the old city. However, with expansion of the city, this temple was neglected. During the 1970s, leaders of the ethnic Chinese community moved this temple to the backyard of the Seoul Overseas Chinese High School, Yonhee Dong, Seoul.
5 Jerome Ch'en (1972, pp. 33–4) notes Yuan's title in Korea as 'Commissioner of Trade of the Third Rank', while on his English-language calling cards, he described himself as 'His Imperial Chinese Majesty's Resident, Seoul'.
6 For details of Chinese commercial activities in Korea, see Larson (2000, Chapter 5). Chinese at that time were visible, as they dressed in traditional Chinese clothes and spoke only rudimentary Korean. Ethnic Chinese in Korea during the end of Choson period were *Huashang* – Chinese traders (Wang 1981), who were mainly sojourners. Therefore, Chinese migration to Korea during this period can be characterized as a 'trader' diaspora. However, while the majority of Chinese in Korea during this period (1882–1910) were merchants, there was considerable variation among their ranks. While some were intrepid peddlers with little more than the bag of thread on their backs, others were businessmen who controlled far-flung networks that extended to China, Japan, Hong Kong and beyond. In addition, there were numbers of labourers (*Huagong*) as well as farmers, barbers, servants to resident Westerners, etc., even in this early period. In addition, there were small but influential numbers of Qing officials sent to man the Qing yamen in Seoul, the offices of the 'Commissioners of Trade' in the treaty ports, or the various Qing-sponsored enterprises such as the telegraph line to China and the Korean Maritime Customs Service.
7 One can deem that such callous Chinese behaviour resulted in precarious legal status for ethnic Chinese in Korea in later years when Korea gained independence. The Korean leaders, who grew up during this troubled historic moment of declining national power and were subsequently oppressed by foreign powers on their own soil following the brutal colonial experience by

Japan, became fervent nationalists and deliberately designed laws to protect Korean interests from other nations and prevent foreign encroachments.

8 In spite of an agreement restricting Chinese residence and business to new settlement areas, Chinese acquired land through illegal means (Larson 2000). Also, see the *Independence News* 6 October 1896 report that 'The rumor of opening Jinnampo in the near future aroused the speculative spirit among the enterprising Chinamen in Chemulpo [present Inchon]. Several of them have gone to Jinnampo for the purpose of buying up real estate in that locality.'

For studies on Chinese settlement, see Moon Enjoeng (2001), Nam Gisook (1987), Lee Jaejoeng (1993a) and Cho Heejoeng (1986).

For studies on Chinese business, see Chae Heenam (1982), Park Inho (2001), Park Jaesoo (1998) and Kim Byungha (1974).

9 Tongshuntai, founded by Tan Jiesheng (also known as Tan Yishi), could be considered as the premier Chinese firm in Korea during the Open Port Period. Tan Jiesheng economically was equal with Yuan Shikai in politics and acted as financer for many of the Chinese-sponsored enterprises in Korea. According to the family tales, Tan moved to Korea in 1874 as a 20-year-old. While it is not verified, Chinese in Korea enjoy recollecting tales of Tan, 50-odd years later, becoming the highest taxpayer in Seoul. See Larson (2000, pp. 241–9) for further details.

10 In his memoir, Jin Yookwang (Chinese Qin Yuguang) used the term 'coolie' (meaning toil) in referring to these Chinese migrant workers – the term that was generally used at that time.

11 There are many criticisms of Yuan's political and diplomatic activities in Seoul. They include: Denny (1888), Lew Young Ick (1984), Swartout (1980), Lee Yur-Bok (1988,1994), Peng Hongzhi (1992) and Yi Yangja (1981).

12 The same day *Independence News* also reports a Chinese found dead. It explains cause of death as 'over-indulgence in the use of opium'.

13 The general term 'foreign population' is directed toward the Chinese, as they constitute the majority of the foreign population residing in Korea. Laws on citizenship and regulations on property ownership by foreign populations are good examples of articulating this sentiment.

References

Brubaker, R. 1996, *Nationalism Reframed: Nationhood and National Question in the New Europe*, Cambridge University Press, Cambridge.

Chae, H. 1982, 'Naraui Hwakyo Kyungche e Kwanhan Yongu [A Study on Korean Chinese's Economy]', Master's thesis, Chonnam University.

Ch'en, J. 1972, *Yuan Shih-k'ai*, 2nd edn, Stanford University Press, Stanford.

Chien, F.F. 1967, *The Opening of Korea: a Study of Chinese Diplomacy*, Shoe String Press, Hamden, Conn.

Cho, H. 1986, 'Jeahan Huakyo e kwanhan jirihakjok yongu', Master's thesis, Sookmyung Women's University.

Choi, S. 2001a, 'Disclosing Ethnic Identity: Ethnic Chinese Youths in South Korea', *American Journal of Chinese Studies*, vol. 8, no. 1, pp. 41–55.

Choi, S. 2001b, 'The Effects of Citizenship on Educational Choices: Observations of Ethnic Chinese in Korea', *International Journal of Educational Reform*, vol. 10, no. 3, pp. 200–14.

Choi, S. 2001c, *Gender, Ethnicity, Market Forces on College Choices: Observations of Ethnic Chinese in Korea*, Routledge, New York.
Clark, D.N. 1983, 'The Ming Connection: Notes on Korea's Experience in the Chinese Tributary System'. *Transactions of the Korea Branch of the Royal Asiatic Society*, no. 58, pp. 77–89.
Denny, O.N. 1888, *China and Korea*, Kelley and Walsh, Shanghai.
Deuchler, M. 1999, 'Despoilers of the Way–Insulters of the Sages: Controversies over the Classics in Seventeenth-century Korea', in J.K. Haboush and M. Deuchler (eds), *Culture and the State in Late Choson Korea*, Harvard University Asia Center, Cambridge/London, pp. 91–133.
Do Rosario, L. 2000, 'Seoul's Invisible Chinese Rise Up', *The Straits Times*, 22 October 2000, p. 4.
Duus, P. 1995, *The Abacus and the Sword: the Japanese Penetration of Korea, 1895–1910*, University of California Press, Berkeley.
Eckert, C., Lee, K.-b., Lew, Y.I., Robinson, M. and Wagner, E. (eds) 1990, *Korea Old and New: a History*, Harvard University Press, Cambridge.
Fairbank, J. 1989, 'Imperialist Encroachments on China, Vietnam, and Korea', in J. Fairbank, E. Reischauer and A. Craig (eds), *East Asia: Tradition and Transformation*, Houghton Mifflin, Boston.
Galstone, W. 1993, 'The Promise of Communitarianism', *National Civic Review*, no. 82.
Graff, G. 1992, *Beyond the Cultural Wars: How Teaching Conflicts Can Revitalize American Education*, Norton, New York.
Haboush, J. 1999, 'Constructing the Center: the Ritual Controversy and the Search for a New Identity in Seventeenth-century Korea', in J.K. Haboush and M. Deuchler (eds), *Culture and the State in Late Choson Korea*, Harvard University Asia Center, Cambridge, London, pp. 46–90.
Haboush, J. and Deuchler, M. 1999, 'Introduction', in J.K. Haboush and M. Deuchler (eds), *Culture and the State in Late Choson Korea*, Harvard University Asia Center, Cambridge, London, pp. 1–14.
Hamashita, T. 2006, 'Historical Transformation of Coastal Urban City Networks in East China Sea Zone'. Paper presented in 'Towards the Construction of Urban Cultural Theories', International Symposium for COE Program at Urban-Culture Research Center, Osaka City University, viewed 3 January 2007 <http://ucrc.lit.osaka-cu.ac.jp/200603sympo/20060319pdf/hamashita_e.pdf>.
Hobsbawm, E. 1983, 'The New Threat to History', *New York Review of Books*, no. 9, pp. 62–4.
Hobsbawm, E. 1990, *Nations and Nationalism since 1780: Programme, Myth, Reality*, Cambridge University Press, Cambridge.
Jin, Y. 1976, 'Huakyo [Overseas Chinese in Korea]', *Joongang Ilbo [Joongang Daily]*, 17 September–17 December.
Kim, B. 1974, *Jaehan Huakyo e Kyungchesa jok gochal [Economic History of Overseas Chinese in Korea]*, Department of Management, Kyunghee University.
Kim, D.-C. 1971, 'Korea's Quest for Reform and Diplomacy', PhD thesis, Fletcher School of Diplomacy, Tufts University, Medford, Mass.
Kim, K.-H. 1995, 'Cha-Han Hawgyo ui Ethnicity e Kwanhan Yon'gu [Study on Ethnicity of Ethnic Chinese in Korea]', Master's thesis, Koryo [Korea] University.
Kim, Y. 1999, *100 Kyonduie Dashiignun Dongnip Shinmoon [Collections of Independence News]*, KyungIn Moonhwasa, Seoul.

Klausen, J. 1995, 'Social Rights Advocacy and State Building: T.H. Marshall in the Hands of Social Reformers', *World Politics*, vol. 47, no. 2, pp. 244–67.

Kuk, P. 1991, *Uri-nun Wae Jajangmyon Changsa'pakke Halsu'opnunga? [Why Are We (Ethnic Chinese in Korea) Condemned to Do Chinese Restaurants Only?].* Han'guk Hwakyo Munje Yonguso, Seoul.

Larson, K.W. 2000, 'From Suzerainty to Commerce: Sino-Korean Economic and Business Relations during the Open Port Period (1876–1910)'. PhD thesis, Harvard University, Boston.

Lee, J.-J. 1993a, 'Hankukui Hwakyo Keojoo ui Yongu: Inchon Jiyok ul Chongshim uro [A Study of Korean Huakyo's Settlement: Inchon Area]', Master's thesis, Kyunghee University.

Lee, Y. 2002, *Choson esoui Wonsegae [Yuan Shih-k'ai in Korea]*, Shinji Seowon, Seoul.

Lee, Y.-B. 1988, *West Goes East: Paul Georg von Mollendorff and Great Power Imperialism in Late Yi Korea*, University of Hawaii, Honolulu.

Lee, Y.-B. 1992, 'Politics over Economics: China's Domination of Korea through Extension of Financial Loans, 1882–1894', in Han'guk Sahak Nonch'ong (ed.), *Such'on Pak Yongsok Gyosu Hawgap Kinyom Nonch'ong Kanhaeng Wiwonhoe, 81–94*, Sudun Pak Yongsok Gyosu Hawgap Kinyom nonch'ong Kanhaeng Wiwonhoe, Seoul.

Lee, Y.-B. 1993, 'Robert Hart and China's Domination of Korea: a Study of Misguided Imperialism'. *Papers of the British Association for Korean Studies*, no. 4.

Lee, Y.-B. 1994, 'The Sino-Japanese Economic Warfare over Korea, 1876–1894', *Russia and the Pacific*, vol. 1, no. 5, pp. 122–32.

Lew, Y.I. 1984, 'Yuan Shih-K'ai's Residency and the Korean Enlightenment Movement', *Journal of Korean Studies*, vol. 5, pp. 64–107.

Lew, Y.I. 1990, 'Growth of the Forces of Enlightenment', in C. Eckert, K.-b. Lee, Y.I. Lew, M. Robinson and E. Wagner (eds), *Korea Old and New: a History*, Harvard University Press, Cambridge, pp. 199–230.

Li, D.L. 1998, *Imagining the Nation: Asian American Literature and Cultural Consent*, Stanford University Press, Stanford.

Ministry of Justice 2000, *Annual Report of Statistics on Legal Migration*, Ministry of Justice, Seoul.

Moon, E. 2001, 'Masan Jiyok Huakyoui Hyungsongkwa k Kujo [The Formation and Structure of Overseas in Modern Masan Region]', Kyungnam University.

Nam, G. 1987, 'Seoulsi Huakyoui Girihakjuk Gochal:1882–1987 [Examination of Seoul Huakyo's (Overseas Chinese) Settlement Pattern: 1882–1987]', Master's thesis, Yihwa Women's University.

Pai, H.I. and Tangherlini, T.R. (eds) 1999, *Nationalism and Construction of Korean Identity*, Institute of East Asian Studies, Center for Korean Studies, University of California, Berkeley.

Park, E. 1986, *Hanguk Hwakyo ui Chongcheseong [The Ethnic Identity of Ethnic Chinese in Korea]*, Korea Research Centre, Seoul.

Park, I. 2001, 'Hwakyo kiupui songjangkwa kyongjangryuk e kwanhan yongu [Korea's Huakyo Business: Expansion and Competitiveness]', Master's thesis, Donga University.

Park, J. 1998, 'Hanguk Hwakyo Kiupui Kyungyoung T'uksong e Kwanhan Yongu [A Study on the Management Character of Overseas Enterprises in Korea]', Hannam Graduate School.

Peng, H. 1992, '13 nyongan Choson eso ui Won Segae sohaeng [13 Years of Yuan Shik-kai's Deeds in Korea]', in Han'guk sahak nonch'ong (ed.), *Such'on Pak Yongsok gyosu hwagap kinyom nomch'ong kanhaeng wiwonhoe*, Sudun Pak Yongsok Gyosu Hawgap Kinyom nonch'ong Kanhaeng Wiwonhoe, Seoul, pp. 95–105.

Poston, J.D., Mao, M.X. and Yu, M.Y. 1994, 'The Global Distribution of the Overseas Chinese around 1990', *Population and Development Review*, vol. 20, no. 3, pp. 631–45.

Schmid, A. 2000, 'Decentering the "Middle Kingdom": the Problem of China in Korean Nationalist Thought, 1895–1910', in T. Brook and A. Schmid (eds), *Nation Work: Asian Elites and National Identities*, University of Michigan Press, Ann Arbor, pp. 83–107.

Schmid, A. 2002, *Korea between Empires: 1895–1919*, Studies of the East Asian Institute, Columbia University Press, New York.

Shin, G.-W. and Robinson, M. 1999, *Colonial Modernity in Korea*, Asia Center, Harvard University, Cambridge/London.

Sigel, L.T. 1980, 'The Role of Korea in Late Qing Foreign Policy', *Papers on Far Eastern History [Australia]*, vol. 21, pp. 75–98.

Sohn, J. 1982, *Hangug Gaehanggi Doshibyonhuaguajong Yongu [Korea's Urban Changes during the Open Port Period]*, Ilchisa, Seoul.

Swartout, R.R. 1980, *Mandarins, Gunboats, and Power Politics: Owen Nickerson Denny and the International Rivalries in Korea*, Asian Studies Program, University of Hawaii, Honolulu.

Wallerstein, I. 1991, *Geopolitics and Geoculture: Essays on the Changing World-System*, Cambridge University Press, Cambridge.

Wang, G. 1981, *Community and Nation: Essays on Southeast Asia and the Chinese*, Heinmann Educational Books, Kuala Lumpur/Hong Kong.

Yang, P. 2002, *Globalization and Human Rights: the Establishment of Permanent Resident Status*, Seoul Chinese Studies, Seoul.

Yi, P.-C. 1985, 'Kawhanggi oeguksangin ui ch'imip kwa Han'guksangin ui taeung [Invasion of Foreign Merchants and Korean Merchants' Self-Protection: Confrontation during the Open Port Period]', PhD thesis, Seoul National University, Seoul.

Yi, Y. 1981, 'Ch'ong ui tae Choson Kyongje Chongch'I wa Won Segi [Qing's Economic Policy on Korea and Yuan Shih-k'ai]', *Pusan Sahak*, vol. 5, no. 2.

Yi, Y. 1984, 'Ch'ong ui tae-Choson kyongje chongch'aek kwa Won Segi [Qing's Economic Policy on Choson and Yuan Shikai]', *Pusan Sahak*, no. 8, pp. 113–53.

9

Imagination, Memory and Misunderstanding: the Chinese in Japan and Japanese Perceptions of China

John Clammer

China has always loomed large in the Japanese imaginary. The source of its primary written script, much of its religious culture, its tradition of tea, many of its features of architecture and aesthetics, Confucian ethics and concepts of government, China is in a sense the great continental 'mother culture' for Japan (Pollack 1986). And like children everywhere, Japan has reacted to this in complex ways – a deep appreciation of the language and culture of China, combined with the need to separate itself from the maternal bonds and to establish a distinct identity. More recent historical events beginning with Japan's colonial involvement in Manchuria that spread into full-scale war, the establishment of the People's Republic and the political separation of Taiwan from the mainland, the penetration of the postwar Japanese economy into China and post-Cold War political and commercial rivalries between the country with the world's largest population and the one with the world's second largest economy, have ensured and will continue to ensure an intimate bonding between China and Japan.

On the other hand, China's perception of Japan has taken a rather different route. From being regarded as a peripheral country on the outer boundaries of the Chinese world, Japan has passed through successive stages of the model of Asian modernity to which many Chinese flocked for education and experience of a new industrial economy, colonial invader, opponent in one of the twentieth century's bitterest wars marked by atrocities such as the Nanjing Massacre which still scar the Chinese collective psyche, to trading partner and major source of foreign direct investment. The asymmetrical nature of the relationship still shows in many ways, at the pragmatic level in the perception from Japanese business of China as a potentially huge market, and the perception of many individual Chinese of Japan as a rich country in which they are happy to study or work, even if illegally, for wages far higher than could be obtained at home. But beneath this practicality much older tensions remain – the anti-Japanese riots that broke out in Beijing in August 2004 following China's defeat on its home ground by Japan in the Asian Cup football tournament, and the growing awareness in Japan that many of the escalating violent crimes that have occurred in that hitherto remarkably safe society have been the work of Chinese from the PRC, shows how beneath the surface tranquillity the two major East Asian powers still keep a cautious distance in their political and economic minuet.

It is in the midst of this complex and many layered historical context that the contemporary Chinese community in Japan must live. A simple sociological description of their demographics and economic status will not suffice if justice is to be done to the fullness of their actual life situation. Rather the Chinese community in Japan must be situated at the intersection of competing imaginaries – Chinese/Japanese, People's Republic/Taiwan, older migrants now long settled/recent newcomers, China's growing perception of itself as the major political (and potentially military) power in East Asia/Japan's perception of itself as the major economic power in Asia, but still tied in security terms to US military hegemony and interests. It is out of these complex intersections that memory and belongingness are forged, and where notions of space, place and time converge.

In order to demonstrate these intersections and their outcomes in terms of the current situation socially, politically and economically, of the Chinese community, we will move through three phases – a brief history of Chinese migration to Japan in the context of larger historical events, the development of the post-1945 Chinese community against the background of Japan's changing relationships with the PRC and Taiwan, and finally and most importantly, the detailed psychology of the relations between the contemporary Chinese communities and the Japanese out of which have emerged or been constructed both memories and narratives of exile and belonging, the gendered aspects of Chinese settlement in Japan and the ways in which this influences social memory and the new negotiations of identity now taking place between the older established Chinese and the very recent newcomers, mostly from the PRC, whose relationship to Japan is very different from that of the long-resident communities. All of this must finally be placed in the context of changes in Japanese society and culture. Neither Chinese nor Japanese identity are fixed – both evolve and mutate as both China and Japan re-evaluate their roles in the world order, as the unprecedented effects of globalization penetrate Japan and as Japanese popular culture spreads in East Asia and internationally and as the Japanese themselves struggle with their twenty-first-century identity and possible futures against the backdrop of the collapse of the high-growth 'bubble economy' and the progressive internationalization of their own once secluded culture and society.

Chinese settlement in Japan

In a survey of Chinese settlement in Japan, Andrea Vasishth suggests that the contemporary perception of the Chinese as being a 'model minority' – reasonably affluent, peaceful and not directly competing with Japanese in the labour market – in fact conceals a record of exclusion and exploitation (Vasishth 1997, p. 108). Although Chinese emigration to Japan was on a much smaller scale than the massive movements to South East Asia and North America, Chinese have been moving to and settling in Japan for a very long time – as Buddhist monks, expatriate scholars, temple craftsmen and traders. It was, however, after the opening of Japan to the larger world following the Meiji Restoration that Chinese moved there in larger numbers, partly as the result of the new political order in Japan, and partly to escape poverty and political chaos in China. The arrival of real Chinese people from the actually impoverished and disorderly *Zhongguo* ('Middle Kingdom') or *Zhonghua* ('Civilized Centre') further convinced Japanese who, despite their assimilation of Confucianism, had already begun in the late Tokugawa period to question the centrality of China (and by implication their own categorization as outer barbarians), to re-evaluate their intellectual and cultural debt to China. Indeed a major intellectual trend in Japan even before the late nineteenth-century opening of Japan was the 'nativism' of renowned scholars such as Motoori Norinaga and their rejection of Chinese influence which they believed had in fact corrupted the pure Japanese spirit.

It was into this complex debate about Japan's relationship to China, that the new migrants came. Despite Ming (1368–1644) prohibitions on trade with Japan, commercial contacts between the two countries had been going on unabated, and trading settlements and Chinese artisans flourished. Even during the closure of Japan during the Tokugawa era of isolationism, much weaker restrictions were applied to Chinese merchants and residents than to the Dutch, the only other foreign community to maintain a trading base in Nagasaki, despite the official designation of the Chinese as barbarians (Vasishth 1997, pp. 116–17). After the conclusion of the Sino-Japanese treaty in 1871 large numbers of Chinese began to appear as sailors, servants, stevedores, shopkeepers, restaurant owners, tailors, hairdressers, and in many other capacities, especially in the foreign concession areas such as Yokohama, Kobe and Nagasaki, where even today large numbers of Chinese are still concentrated, the first two cities having large and flourishing Chinatowns. As a more settled community began to be established, the familiar pattern of establishing guilds and regional associations began to appear and dialect as in South East Asia formed a major internal division in the Chinese community, with occupational specialization being structured along these lines, the Cantonese for example dominating the restaurant business, the Shanghainese the tailoring business and the Fujian speakers the barbershop sector (Yamashita 1979).

But with this increasing visibility came anti-Chinese sentiment and from the 1870s on, Japanese newspapers contained numerous articles on the criminality, slyness, materialism, unsociable behaviour and even personal hygiene of the Chinese living in Japan, a tendency accelerated by Japan's rapid victory in the Sino-Japanese War of 1894–95. An Imperial ordinance of 1899, while it allowed the Chinese to reside among Japanese (outside of the treaty ports in other words), also banned the further immigration of labourers and led to the emergence of a settled Chinese community of merchants and skilled workers. After the Japanese colonization of Taiwan in 1895 large numbers of students from the new colony came to Japan for study, and indeed Japan became a base for anti-Qing radicalism (Sun Yat-sen for example having made Japan his base for a time). With Japan's increasing industrialization in practice many labourers did enter the country, from Taiwan and also from the mainland, but after the Manchurian Incident in 1931 many students studying in Japan returned to China and increasing controls and surveillance were imposed on the resident Chinese community, the members of which became enemy aliens on the outbreak of war. During the war itself large numbers of Chinese labourers were brought in to work in harsh conditions in mines, construction and cargo-handling, together with prisoners of war. While almost all the survivors were repatriated at the end of the war, many Taiwanese chose to stay in Japan as they were still Japanese subjects, a situation terminated in 1947 with the passing of the Alien Registration Law which reclassified both Chinese and Koreans (the real target of the legislation) as aliens, thus excluding them from Japanese citizenship and access to employment in the public sector and many other benefits. The sociological result of this was to force Chinese residents back on their own networks of ethnic and occupational associations and the 'Chinatownization' of residential and educational patterns. These wartime experiences and the harsh and often brutal treatment of

Chinese forced labourers and the lack of recognition of Chinese (and Korean) victims of the firebombings of Tokyo and the two atomic bomb attacks on Hiroshima and Nagasaki have continued to scar memories and with them ongoing relationships between the Chinese community and the Japanese host society.

The outcome of this has been a fluctuating and far from smooth relationship between Chinese and Japanese in Japan. Particularly from the Chinese side, deep memories of exclusion, uncertainty, persecution and prejudice have been formed, although these operate rather differently depending on location within the contemporary Chinese community, within which numerous subdivisions, many originating from these past patterns of migration and inclusion/exclusion, can be found. While some scholars have attempted to divide Chinese migration to Japan into simply early, middle and recent periods, in fact the periodization and its underlying sociological patterns are considerably more complex. One of the most significant differences is between Taiwanese and mainlanders among older-generation migrants. Up until their loss of Japanese colonial citizenship, Taiwanese were not subject to restrictions on movement, residence or occupation and usually had a fair command of the Japanese language (something still true in Taiwan amongst older-generation residents), many having come to Japan to study. As a result few of them lived in the old Chinatown areas, unlike mainland migrants who did. As a result social contact between the Taiwanese and mainlanders was quite limited although both congregated in the major urban areas, and Taiwanese did not belong to the network of associations that facilitated economic networking among those of mainland origin. Similarly there are substantial differences in social networks between those Chinese aligned with Taiwan, those also aligned with Taiwan but in favour of Taiwanese independence, and those aligned with the PRC, the different groups maintaining separate Chinese schools for example, and having different economic patterns, the Taiwanese having expanded their range to coffee shops, cinemas, food manufacturing, medicine, dentistry, pachinko parlours (a form of Japanese pinball arcade) and other activities outside of the usual Chinese occupations and in some cases closer to those of the Korean minority.

In turn the older-settled Chinese (almost 70,000 in 1975) are very different in culture and attitudes from the newly arrived PRC citizens, mostly in Japan for study of language or in universities or working illegally in a wide range of unskilled or semi-skilled occupations, entering on short-term visas and then overstaying or in some cases being smuggled in by boat. The result again has been little contact and even some social distancing between the established and newcomer communities, and while the former have become the beneficiaries of something of a 'China boom' subsequent on Japan's recognition of the PRC in 1972 leading to large numbers of domestic tourists visiting Chinatowns and the spread of Chinese restaurants outside of the traditional areas, and indeed the huge expansion of Japanese tourism to China, the latter remain in a somewhat ambiguous position, being like their predecessors of a century earlier, blamed for rising crime and violation of immigration rules. Today's Chinese community then needs to be situated at the intersection of several forces – the long-term outcomes of historical fluctuations in the relationships between China and Japan, domestic fads in consumption, fashion and culture, the tensions between an already diverse established community and newcomers from the PRC (and to a lesser extent also from Taiwan, Malaysia, Singapore and from overseas Chinese communities even further abroad) who bring with them a new set of cultural practices and political attitudes (Nonini 1997).

Today then we see a Chinese population of 234,264 in a Japanese total population of 125 million (less than 0.19 per cent of the total) of whom only a little over 30,000 have permanent resident status (Kyo 1998). While an increasing number of Chinese residents are seeking Japanese citizenship, as a minority it is clearly still one deprived for the most part of the full benefits to be derived from possessing that status. Many of the arriving highly skilled Chinese who come legally to Japan under the *kensui* or trainee scheme (over 10,000 at any one time) find themselves not learning the latest Japanese technology, but actually working in low-grade jobs in remote factories. Others have arrived as brides for Japanese farmers who find it very difficult to attract young Japanese women to the hard lifestyle that their profession entails. An increasing number are coming to study in Japanese universities, some on scholarships but others on borrowed money or supporting themselves through working (often illegally) out of class hours. And so the constant dialectic of the political, social and cultural relationships between Japan and China goes on. It is out of this complex soil that social memories are made, and it is to these that we will now turn.

Constructing memories

There has been a tendency in many studies of the Chinese overseas to adopt a homogenizing position – the assumption that there is one kind of experience more or less common to the entire community in a given place. The history of Chinese migration to Japan suggests that this is a dubious assumption. Even within a small community like that in Japan there prove to be not only the expected variations in speech-group affiliation, but also of time of arrival and depth of residence, political identity, class, gender and occupation. The effect of the Imperial Ordinance 352 shortly after the conclusion of the Sino-Japanese War was to create a settled Chinese community of merchants and the propertied and to exclude or relegate to the margins labourers and unskilled workers, who found themselves not only excluded from Japan (although as we have seen this was reversed twice with the necessity of workers to staff Japan's expanding industries, and later with the demands of war production), but also excluded from the Chinese community itself, as many wealthier Chinese in Japan actually welcomed the ban on unskilled and rural migrants as their presence in large numbers diminished their own status (Ito 1995). Yet certain groups, like Hokchia petty traders and pedlars, managed to evade these restrictions and were exempt from the immigration ban, and because of their mobile lifestyle spread all over Japan, even as far north as the Hokkaido city of Hakodate. And while certainly until recently the vast majority of migrants were male, the story of the Chinese women has never been told, their experiences, rather like those of their Korean sisters, being very different from those of the men, especially those commercially visible men who appear prominently in the histories of Chinese associations in Japan. Social memory itself is stratified and generational.

Social scientists have recently and in increasing numbers turned their attention to the question of social memory (for example Connerton 1995; Freeman 1993; Rubin 1996), and with it the methodologies for collecting those memories (Tonkin 1992). This interest signals, among other things, a recognition of the ways in which the past shapes the present, the re-emergence of the idea of nostalgia as an operative notion in shaping social experience, and also perhaps of the ways in which memory is political and shapes not only images, but also practical strategies in the present. All of these factors and more are present in the ways in which the contemporary Chinese community in Japan manages both its own narratives of becoming and belonging, and its ever-shifting relationships with the Japanese community within which it is encapsulated.

History from this perspective is not merely the past – it is the past drawn into the present in order to construct narratives of meaning, a making sense of experience and a means to shape contemporary relations with the present. In the specific case of the Chinese community in Japan, I will suggest that social memory is shaped by a number of factors, and then itself becomes one of the primary mechanisms through which the community (or actually communities) structure their relationship to the contemporary Japanese host society in which they find themselves. In brief I will suggest that these mechanisms of memory construction are of five main kinds: socio-psychological, institutional, political, narrative and romantic.

In a classic early paper, Barbara Ward wrote of the ways in which the 'Tanka' boat people of Hong Kong, perceived as only marginally Chinese by the land-dwelling Cantonese, asserted a Chinese identity through the appropriation of the symbols of literati culture (Ward 1969). The Tanka of course were living in Chinese waters; the Chinese of Japan quite definitely in another country, but one physically very close to China (it is only two and a half hours from Tokyo to Shanghai or three to Beijing) and tied to it culturally and historically. Travel between the two countries is easy, and for some people frequent (Chinese students returning to China for Chinese New Year for example). The creation of an imaginary China of the kind that existed for many overseas Chinese in South East Asia for example, especially in the decades when local governments proscibed travel to mainland China for other than very restricted official purposes, has never been a necessity for most Japanese Chinese (Clammer 2002, pp. 183–213). The social construction of memory/the construction of social memory has consequently taken a rather different path in Japan than it did in, say, Singapore, since in the latter case actual contact with China was limited and ties to ancestral villages were effectively severed, people born before 1965 grew up in a British colonial context and the host society had none of the deep cultural ties with China that Japan has always had. In short, if in South East Asia the need was to invent an imaginary China, in Japan the looming presence of an actual China has always been the issue, and the fluctuating fortunes of the Japanese Chinese has very much been a function of the evolving relationship between Japan and especially the mainland (many of these factors being less applicable to Japanese-Chinese of Taiwanese origin).

As we have noted, during the Sino-Japanese War the status and security of the Chinese fell to an all-time low, whereas after the recognition of the PRC in 1972 the 'China boom' ensured that the Chinese suddenly became, as it were, 'cool'. The relationship between Japan and China in other words has always been the factor that has most dynamically structured the position of the Chinese community in Japan, and so internal developments in China have always been crucial to the Japanese-Chinese, in a way not true for the Singaporean Chinese. While certainly events in China and Chinese policies towards their overseas compatriots have had significant influence on the status of overseas Chinese communities, these have mostly been so from the perspective of Chinese policy, rather than actual effects on the ground. Attempts to attract overseas Chinese back to China in the years preceding the Cultural Revolution and to establish special schools and universities for returnees and their children, to recognize the citizenship in their new homes of overseas Chinese and so on, have of course influenced those communities, but in relatively indirect ways. Singaporean Chinese, for example, lived untouched through the Cultural Revolution and while that event shaped intergovernmental relations, it had virtually no impact on the everyday life on any but the most left-leaning Singaporeans (Fitzgerald 1972). For the Japanese-Chinese on the other hand, every tremor on the Chinese political seismograph registered virtually instantly and this continues to be the case. A permanent sense of insecurity, intensified by the lack of Japanese citizenship on the part of most Japanese-Chinese, is the psychological result.

This insecurity has been managed, as in other overseas Chinese communities, by the building of the typical network of institutions – regional and dialect associations, occupational guilds, temples and recreational, educational and cultural organizations. But these of course are not community wide and in a sense act to divide the Chinese community rather than unify it as a specific 'ethnic' group. Many of the Taiwanese are excluded from these groupings and form their own rival ones, and the newcomers are for the most part entirely unassociated and form groups around residential or professional interests – for example student networks, in which they might in fact have more contact with other foreign students such as Koreans than they do with the older-established Chinese community (Tanaka 1991).

Linked to the institutional framework – the belonging to a nested hierarchy of associations specifically Chinese in membership and linking contemporary Japanese-Chinese at least symbolically and sometimes materially to China (and in some instances to a China no longer recognizable) – is political affiliation. As was noted above, the older Chinese community is split, rather like its larger counterpart the Korean community, into those who support or identify with the PRC, and those who continue to support Taiwan. After the recognition by Japan of the PRC, the Yokohama Chinese Association, the biggest of the few community-wide groups, split along political lines. The dramatic political developments in Taiwan with its democratization process, the rise of a strong independence movement and the decline of the old Guomindang in the last decade, have further confused the picture for the pro-Taiwan group. Each group maintains its own Chinese schools, and the presence of large numbers of mainland students and Taiwanese students often studying together in the same Japanese universities or language schools, has introduced an interesting new dynamic into both the mutual perceptions of PRC and ROC students, and the spillover effects of this on the older Chinese community who see the grounds on which they have attempted to build their identity shifting once again.

It is out of this material that the narratives of Chinese identity have been built. Here it is necessary to listen to the stories that Japanese-Chinese tell, and while there are a wide variety of narratives, reflecting the classed and gendered as well as political dimensions of identity, several elements predominate (and here we are speaking of the old-established communities, not the post-1990s and often short-term newcomers). These elements are those of belonging, nostalgia, insecurity, suffering, marginality and ambiguity. For the Japanese-Chinese community does have a rich and complex set of relationships with its host society. The ties of history and culture are undeniable, and for older-established Chinese, Japan has been their home for generations, they speak Japanese, their children in many cases go to Japanese schools, date Japanese and in some cases marry them, and indeed for younger Japanese-Chinese Japan is their homeland, much as it is for their Korean counterparts, who, while still discriminated against and in many cases without citizenship, nevertheless form an essential and permanent element in the social make-up of Japan (Lee and DeVos 1981).

So in one sense this feeling of belonging, of having been assimilated into the Japanese social landscape, is real. But it is of necessity moderated by other factors: a nostalgia for a China that no longer exists and probably never existed, the insecurity inseparable from being a small minority with very little control over the international forces that constantly reshape the host society's attitudes and expectations and a long history of suffering at the hands of the Japanese – persecution during the Sino-Japanese War, destruction of life and property following the great Kanto earthquake of 1923, forced labour during the Pacific War, lack of recognition of Chinese (and Korean) victims of the atomic bombings of Nagasaki and Hiroshima, rumours of statelessness and property sequestration or forced repatriation after the recognition of the PRC in 1972 together with the historical memories of Japan's violent and colonialist involvement in China from the 1920s on.

The marginality of the Chinese as a small, but today in Vasishth's terms 'model minority' is built on layers of history and ambiguities. Even today this 'model' status is not uncontested: by extreme right-wing activists, by the vagaries of a consumer economy in which one month things Chinese are 'in', but the next they may well be 'out', and by the sudden presence of large numbers of both mainland and Taiwan students and, more threateningly, of illegal workers in large numbers and even pseudo-refugees. The 'romantic' image of China held by many members of the Japanese-Chinese community is really that of belonging to an ancient and once great civilization, a cultural pride in the society that is not only seen as 'older' than that of Japan, but as the fountainhead of Japanese culture itself, especially of its written language and its Buddhist heritage. This has been abetted in the very recent past by the widespread popularity in Japan of films from or about China, and usually a very romanticized version of the ancient civilization wrapped up in a modern hi-tech package (such as the box office hit *House of Flying Daggers* in which the male lead – Kaneshiro Takeshi – is a Japanese born and educated in Taiwan, speaks Mandarin and Cantonese, or the Hong Kong production *Peony Pavilion* about the decadent lifestyles of upper-class Chinese in 1930s China which stars the well-known Japanese actress Miyazawa Rie). At the moment then it is popular culture that is making China cool in the eyes of especially younger Japanese, a fad that may or may not last, although it probably will for some time to come with the Olympic Games scheduled for 2008 in Beijing.

The cultural politics of being Chinese in Japan involve a complex and never settled interplay between actual belonging and effective biculturalism on the part of the Chinese, political events in China, the economic relationships between Japan and China, the depiction of China in Japanese popular culture and the media and fads in foods and fashion – not something to be sniffed at in intensely consumer-oriented Japan (Clammer 1997). Layered into this are of course the gendered nature of many of these experiences, an essential feature that has only belatedly been recognized in the study of Chinese communities outside of China (Jaschok and Miers 1994). Memory is political, classed and gendered and of course generational. Diverse cultural experiences, alternative cultural identities and very different subjectivities shape narratives of belonging and exile. While the Taiwanese Chinese in Japan are in a very real sense 'postcolonial', the newcomers are instead 'post-revolutionary', while the current established mainland-roots community is caught up in new forces of globalization, cultural hybridity, consumerism and the media-shaped nature of identities all filtered both through narratives of past suffering and contemporary racism. It is to this specific issue of race that we will now turn.

Japanese nationalism and the racialization of identity

It is widely accepted that national identity in Japan has long been racialized (Yoshino 1996). That is to say the Japanese think of themselves in racial terms, as a distinct people, largely homogeneous in language and culture and with clear phenotypical markers, such that one can neither join nor leave the race. Foreigners, especially of non-Asian stock, who possess Japanese citizenship or mixed race children of Japanese nationality, are looked upon as distinctly odd. Despite the empirical evidence of diversity, linguistic variation and the evidence of continental influences, the myth of homogeneity is still strong. The results of this racialization of identity are many, ranging from the national preoccupation with the distinctiveness of Japanese culture reflected in the large literature collectively known as *Nihonjinron* or the 'theory of being Japanese', through the great difficulties in assimilating refugees, even those of Indochinese origin who attempted to settle in Japan in the aftermath of the Vietnam War (Nakano 1995), to the constant difficulties of managing relationships with the resident minorities, both those of foreign origin (especially the Koreans at a little over 80 per cent of resident foreigners, and the Chinese at 7.4 per cent), and those wholly indigenous, such as the Ainu people of Hokkaido and the Okinawans, or the excluded Buraku people (Weiner 1997). The Chinese community, although a tiny minority, find themselves caught up in this racialization. They are not Japanese, but are nevertheless Asian, not that that helps. Interestingly the linguistically and ethnically closest group to the Japanese are the Koreans, who are among the most excluded.

This racialization moreover, as it applies in particular to both the Chinese and the Koreans, has a history, both of internal Japanese attempts to define the concept of race, and of racial purity (Weiner 1996), of debates about both Japan's cultural debt to China centring on arguments about whether to continue in the early 1900s the study of *kanbun* or Chinese classics and classical writing that had been the cornerstone of Tokugawa education as Japanese colonialism on the continent began to require a theory of Japanese racial superiority over the 'inferior' Chinese. The developing attitude of superiority could no longer support the older idea of *dobun doshu* – 'same language, same race' that had previously provided an ideological basis for unity among the 'yellow' races as opposed to the 'white' ones, an idea popularized in Japan at the time of the First World War, but which did not survive long into the era of rising nationalism that began in the 1920s (Sato 1996). Space does not allow a detailed discussion of the evolution of Japanese racial discourse, especially as a result of Japan's colonial enterprises and particular in Manchukuo (Manchuria) which Japan had wrested from the Chinese and where, in Louise Young's terms, the exploitative and appropriative relations between the Japanese colonizers and the indigenous

Chinese (and large Korean population) 'breathed new life into old cultural stereotypes and generated new ones, in the process accelerating the growth of racist attitudes' (Young 1996, p. 289). But suffice it to say that the Chinese in Japan have been at the centre of this progressive racialization, one which furthermore, at least in Japanese intellectual circles, began as a theory of racial unity, but rapidly became one of racial differences, a move greatly accelerated by colonialism and then war which as in other contexts (Germany for example) produced the 'necessity' to present the enemy in the worst possible light and colonialism and war as a kind of civilizing project.

The contemporary Japanese-Chinese community live with the legacy of this history, in a society where national identity continues to be deeply racialized and where, even in the context of globalization, the problem of the 'Other' looms large in the national conciousness, today intensified not by war, but by the presence of visible numbers of foreign workers and by forms of globalization that are penetrating Japan in ways much less controllable than the largely cosmetic 'internationalization' of a decade ago (Clammer 2001). The paradoxical situation is of course that the Chinese themselves tend to a very racialized notion of identity. In Japan the two racializations are brought into head-on collision.

Transnationalism and new Chinese hybridities

It is not enough, however, to explore Chinese identity in Japan solely in terms of internal dynamics. The globalizing context provides an additional and essential frame for exploring both the evolving nature of identity of Japanese and of Chinese, in China and in Japan, and of their interaction with each other in this shifting social and cultural environment. Here two levels meet and intersect – the postcolonial and the global. Oddly in overseas Chinese studies, little attention has been paid to postcolonial studies, although in Singapore, Malaysia, Hong Kong and throughout much of the diaspora, that is exactly the situation that the Chinese communities find themselves in. The complexity of such relationships – with China, with the colonial past and with the new legal and political framework of the present – creates complex dynamics in which current life is lived, in all its indeterminacy.

Speaking of one of their contributors, in a recent volume on the intersection of law and colonialism, Sally Engle Merry and Donald Brenneis comment that 'Miyazaki does so, in large part, by examining the hopeful practices – new genres, new textual strategies, and the refiguring of imagined archival resources ... His materials and analysis point dramatically to the indeterminacy inherent within legal frameworks, indeed within any cultural practice' (Merry and Brenneis 2003, p. 23). What they draw attention to is indeed this 'indeterminacy' and the ability of a community to reinvent their own sources, even if these are largely imaginary.

The recent interest in China triggered by highly popular movies is an example of this – the Japanese becoming interested again in China through the medium of popular culture, which mostly depicts a China that never existed – of heroes, martial arts, amazing Taoist magic, but which has given the local Chinese community a new status, one which judging from the shops in Yokohama's Chinatown, they are all too ready to exploit.

Indeed a recent newspaper report (*Japan Times*, 14 August 2004) revealed that the Yokohama Overseas Chinese School, itself physically on the edge of Yokohama Chinatown, is receiving many applications from the parents of Japanese children who want them to seriously study Chinese and that already more than 20 per cent of the elementary pupils in the school are Japanese. The Chinese community then is very ready to draw on the advantages that accrue from these shifts in fashion and popular culture. The downside is of course that if the shift is in a negative direction, as it has so often been in the past, then they become the victims of these fads. But in fact at the moment the prognosis is good – China is a popular tourist destination, books about China sell well, the language is being studied again by an increasing proportion of young people, films with Chinese themes are box office successes, economic ties are strong and with active diplomatic cooperation between Japan and the PRC over the issue of North Korea's nuclear programme, seen as a potential threat to both countries. The result is a cautious rapprochement which has substantial effects on Chinese identities, which are shifting and adapting again, to the globalization of Japan and the rising transnational sentiment within Chinese communities scattered across the globe.

Some recent studies of the Chinese of the diaspora talk of a unilinear transition from trading minorities, through 'residual Chinese' to triumphal moderns (Nonini and Ong 1997, p. 5), a model in which ' "being Chinese" is an inscribed relation of persons and groups to forces and processes associated with global capitalism and its modernities' (Nonini and Ong 1997, p. 4). Our study of the Japanese-Chinese, however, suggests a more nuanced view, as while the local Chinese community can take some pride in being an outpost of the great 'ungrounded empire' of the Chinese diaspora, it is certainly not a community marked by any mood of triumphalism. Nor could it be, since any overt display of such triumphalism would only trigger a negative reaction within Japan, where a low profile is by far the better strategy. Furthermore, while the Japanese-Chinese represent a kind of petty to middle capitalism within Japan and in relation to Chinese trading networks outside of the country to Taiwan, the PRC, Singapore and Hong Kong in particular, they are themselves inscribed within Japanese modernity and with the massive international expansion of Japanese capital. And this is to some extent their central problem. Unable in fact to represent themselves as an 'alternative modernity', the Chinese community in Japan has had in shifting ways to situate itself within the alternative modernity model of Japan as a whole, a model that has stressed Japan's difference, rather than its continuity, with the rest of the world (Clammer 1995).

The new Chinese subjectivities and transnationalism alleged by Ong and Nonini to characterize Chinese diasporic communities at the turn of the century are at best only very selectively available to Japanese-Chinese, who must rather play the subtle interface between being a tiny minority with a history of exclusion, and their symbolic role as representatives not of the greater diasporic community, but of the great civilization of China. In this sense while physically and politically separated from China, the Japanese-Chinese are the most symbolically attached of all the diaspora communities, a symbolic attachment that paradoxically keeps them separate from the Japanese, but ensures their status as in some sense representatives of the great continental culture. The notion of 'being Chinese' itself then, while attributed through citizenship and legal status, is also a constructed category and one in constant discursive interplay with events in Japan, in China and elsewhere in the diaspora. Indeed the diasporic connections again initiated by the arrival of labour migrants from the mainland, Taiwan and South East Asia, if anything muddy the waters for the Japanese-Chinese, rather than connect them organically to a wider transnational Chinese community.

The social logic of Japanese particularism has filtered into the Chinese community, that has, partly unconsciously and partly for survival strategy, taken on the colouring of the host society. The social imaginaries of Japanese-Chinese are in consequence linked less to the deterritorialized images of a transnational Chinese business network than to the deterritorialized structures and practices of Japanese capitalism, a location that paradoxically requires rootedness in a location – Japan itself, and not in some virtual transnational space. The imaginaries of the established Japanese-Chinese community then are located at the complex and shifting intersection of a long history of exclusion, fluctuating perceptions of the cultural coolness of China, international relations focused on the

Japan–China–Taiwan triangle, growing pressures from the triumphalist diaspora theorists who are pressuring the community to move in a direction in which it cannot easily go, and its location within a much larger Japanese project of alternative modernity and capitalist expansion. Memories in this context are not simply the reproduction of the past, but the mechanism through which a narrative of meaning is constructed that allows the present to be shaped, and in Japan the trope of mobility ascribed to the consciousness of diasporic Chinese communities is displaced by one of belonging, but of belonging in the spaces allowed or created by a much bigger state and cultural project in which the Chinese provide the necessary Other within as representatives of the great Other without against which Japan has traditionally defined itself and continues to do so despite its entangled love–hate relationship with the West since the seventeenth century.

While the Chinese then are engaged in an evolving attempt to define themselves within Japanese society, the Japanese are engaged in the parallel and reciprocal enterprise of understanding the place of the Chinese not just within Japan, but as a defining feature of their own failed imperial project and the racialization of identities that it entailed. While statistically a small minority within Japan, the Chinese are symbolically a large one, the Other through which, far more so than the distant West, Japan attempts to define itself. In this sense the Chinese are a privileged minority and are at the centre of the debates that rage among Japanese intellectuals about Japanese war guilt and the place of Japan in Asia and the modern world in general. In that literature the place of memory looms large (for example Kato 1997), and in particular the concept of mourning – mourning on the part of the Japanese for a deeply blemished record especially in relation to the Chinese, and mourning on the part of the victims of Japanese aggression. It is very significant that debates about Japan's responsibility for the past are linked to its place in the world of the future, refracted in large part through Japan's relationship to the Chinese, and the perception that, despite the triumphalism of Japanese capital, Japan will never be a 'normal' country or one at peace with itself until it comes to terms with that past, a process that requires, among other things, the correlation of its memories with those of its victims (Morris-Suzuki 1998). The subjectivities of the Japanese and the Chinese are intimately linked and this fact alone sets the situation of the Japanese-Chinese apart from the situation of other diaspora communities and locates them in a unique relationship to the emerging scholarly debates on Chinese transnationalism.

References

Clammer, J. 1995, *Difference and Modernity: Social Theory and Contemporary Japanese Society*, Kegan Paul International, London and New York.

Clammer, J. 1997, *Contemporary Urban Japan: a Sociology of Consumption*, Blackwell, Oxford.

Clammer, J. 2001, *Japan and Its Others: Globalization, Difference and the Critique of Modernity*, Trans Pacific Press, Melbourne.

Clammer, J. 2002, *Diaspora and Identity: the Sociology of Culture in Southeast Asia*, Pelanduk Publications, Petaling Jaya.

Connerton, P. 1995, *How Societies Remember*, Cambridge University Press, Cambridge.

Fitzgerald, S. 1972, *China and the Overseas Chinese*, Cambridge University Press, Cambridge.

Freeman, M. 1993, *Rewriting the Self: History, Memory, Narrative*, Routledge, London and New York.

Ito, I. 1995, 'Yokohama ni okeru Chugokujin Shogyo Kaigijo no setsuritsu wo megutte', in *Yokohama to Shanhai – Kindai Toshi Keiseishi Hakaku Kenkyu*, Yokohama Shiryo Kaikan, Yokohama.

Japan Times 2004, 'Yokohama Chinese School Woos More Japanese Kids', *Japan Times*, 14 August, p. 2.

Jaschok, M. and Miers, S. (eds) 1994, *Women and Chinese Patriarchy: Submission, Servitude and Escape*, Zed Books and Hong Kong University Press, London and Hong Kong.

Kato, N. 1997, *Haisengoron*, Kodansha, Tokyo.

Kyo, S. 1998, 'Japan', in L. Pann (ed.), *The Encyclopedia of the Chinese Overseas*, Curzon Press, Richmond, pp. 332–40.

Lee, C. and DeVos, G. 1981, *Koreans in Japan: Ethnic Conflict and Accommodation*, University of California Press, Berkeley.

Merry, S.E. and Brenneis, D. (eds) 2003, *Law and Empire in the Pacific*, School of American Research Press and James Currey, Santa Fe/Oxford.

Morris-Suzuki, T. 1998, 'Unquiet Graves: Kato Norihiro and the Politics of Mourning', *Japanese Studies*, vol. 8, no. 1, pp. 21–30.

Nakano, H. 1995, 'The Sociology of Ethnocentrism in Japan', in J.C. Maher and G. Macdonald (eds), *Diversity in Japanese Culture and Language*, Kegan Paul International, London and New York, pp. 49–72.

Nonini, D.M. 1997, 'Shifting Identities, Positioned Imaginaries: Transnational Traversals and Reversals by Malaysian Chinese', in A. Ong and D.M. Nonini (eds), *Ungrounded Empires: the Cultural Politics of Modern Chinese Transnationalism*, Routledge, New York, pp. 203–27.

Nonini, D.M. and Ong, A. 1997, 'Chinese Transnationalism as an Alternative Modernity', in A. Ong and D.M. Nonini (eds), *Ungrounded Empires: the Cultural Politics of Modern Chinese Transnationalism*, Routledge, New York, pp. 3–33.

Pollack, D. 1986, *The Fracture of Meaning: Japan's Synthesis of China from the Eighth through the Eighteenth Centuries*, Princeton University Press, Princeton.

Rubin, D.C. 1996, *Remembering Our Past: Studies in Autobiographical Memory*, Cambridge University Press, Cambridge.

Sato, K. 1996, 'Same Language, Same Race': the Dilemmas of Kanbun in the Early 1900s', in B. Sautman (ed.), *Racial Identities in East Asia*, Hong Kong University of Science and Technology Press, Hong Kong, pp. 278–86.

Tanaka, H. 1991, *Zainichi Gaikokujin*, Iwanami Shinsho, Tokyo.

Tonkin, E. 1992, *Narrating Our Pasts: the Social Construction of Oral History*, Cambridge University Press, Cambridge.

Vasishth, A. 1997, 'A Model Minority: the Chinese Community in Japan', in M. Weiner (ed.), *Japan's Minorities: the Illusion of Homogeneity*, Routledge, London and New York, pp. 108–39.

Ward, B. 1969, 'Varieties of the Conscious Model: the Fishermen of South China', in M. Banton (ed.), *The Relevance of Models for Social Anthropology*, Tavistock, London, pp. 113–37.

Weiner, M. 1996, 'The Racialization of National Identity in Japan', in B. Sautman (ed.), *Racial Identities in East Asia*, Hong Kong University of Science and Technology Press, Hong Kong, pp. 251–66.

Weiner, M.A. (ed.) 1997, *Japan's Minorities: the Illusion of Homogeneity*, Routledge, London and New York.

Yamashita, K. 1979, 'Yokohama Chukakkai Zairyu Chugokujin no seikatsu Yoshiki', *Jinbun Chiri*, vol. 31, no. 4, pp. 33–50.

Yoshino, K. 1996, 'The Racialisation of National Identity in Japan', in B. Sautman (ed.), *Racial Identities in East Asia*, Hong Kong University of Science and Technology Press, Hong Kong, pp. 374–81.

Young, L. 1996, 'Rethinking Race for Manchukuo: Self and the Other in the Colonial Context', in B. Sautman (ed.), *Racial Identities in East Asia*, Hong Kong University of Science and Technology Press, Hong Kong, pp. 287–310.

10

Memories, Belonging and Homemaking: Chinese Migrants in Germany[1]

Maggi W.H. Leung

Migrants, more often than those who are rooted, have to juggle their memories in the process of moving across geographic and cultural boundaries, making new homes, both in psychological and material ways. Memories of diverse nature, anchored in experiences and imaginings from various times and different places, shape migrants' perceptions, identities and sense of belonging. As Fortier (2000, p. 157) states, 'memory becomes a primary ground of identity formation in the context of migration, where "territory" is decentred and exploded into multiple settings'. In essence, memories are influencing factors in migrants' lifelong projects in homemaking. 'Homemaking' is conceptualized here as a process made up of efforts undergone by an individual or community in economic, social, psychological and political spheres to create a habitable domestic environment. These projects can include an involvement in a network of co-ethnics to create a sense of home away from home, or putting children in Chinese schools to acquaint them with 'home' culture, or the establishment of a business in the new homeland to provide the basis of a livelihood. In the following, I shall explore how memories are shaped in these various aspects of homemaking among Chinese migrants in contemporary German society.

This chapter draws upon a broader study of the ethnic Chinese migrant communities in contemporary Germany (Leung 2004). A total of 68 in-depth interviews conducted between 1999 and 2002 formed the core of the data collection.[2] The informants were mainly ethnic Chinese women and men, drawn from diverse national, class, linguistic and age/generation backgrounds, who were, in one way or another, participants in the Chinese social network. During the interviews, attempts were made to steer the conversation to points relevant to the research interest: migration biography, motivations for moving, reasons for their choice of place to resettle, meanings they attached to 'home', the nature and roles of ethnic networks at different geographical scales, and their adaptation strategies. Shaped by their diverse socio-economic and migration biographies, informants embodied multiple memories, sense of home and future aspirations. It would therefore be erroneous to expect a particular set of 'Chinese memories' or 'Chinese migrant experience' in diaspora. This study conceives diaspora as a dynamic patchwork, a fluid collage made up of multiple, diverse, sometimes diverging while at other times overlapping, journeys embarked upon by individuals of a dispersed community, sharing a homeland, sometimes mythical or imagined, based on some shared memories (again, sometimes mythical or imagined) and a collective sense of belonging.

Memories and personal narratives were tapped extensively to examine migrant subjectivities, identities and behaviour in this research. Memories and personal narratives should not be perceived as a simplistic recorder of the past. Rather, they are mediated messages. They represent the moving 'reality' of those remembering after voluntary and involuntary processes of creating and forgetting, imagining and silencing. What is being remembered and forgotten, narrated and hidden results from complex negotiations performed by individuals in interaction with their social environment. This body of rich material still remains, however, outside the 'regular scientific tool kit' for studying migration (Chamberlain and Leydesdorff 2004, p. 228). Digging into memories is particularly important in the case of Chinese migration as it has generally been poorly documented (Wang 2003). This chapter represents an effort to explore the power of memories by connecting them to other important elements of diaspora, namely home and sense of belonging.

Chinese in Germany: an overview

Chinese sojourners arrived in Germany in the first half of the eighteenth century. Significant Chinese settlement in Germany, however, only began in the 1870s. These early settlers were mostly men, ranging from pedlars, labourers, seamen at one end of the social ladder, to diplomats and students at the other. Before the First World War, there were only a few hundred Chinese settlers. Between the two world wars, there were a few thousand Chinese in Germany, concentrated in Hamburg and Berlin. The Second World War disrupted the Chinese populations in Germany, and most of them left. The current geography of Chinese settlement can be traced back to the end of the 1950s when larger numbers came from

Hong Kong and Taiwan, most of whom went into the catering and restaurant business. In the 1960s and 1970s, a considerable number of ethnic Chinese from South East Asia arrived largely due to the anti-Chinese sentiment in their countries. Since the late 1970s, there has been a sharp increase in the number of students and business people coming from the PRC and Taiwan. Official census data stated that 78,239 individuals with Chinese or Taiwanese nationalities were living in Germany by the end of 2005 (Statistisches Bundesamt 2006). Community leaders estimate, however, that there are as many as 150,000 ethnic Chinese residing in Germany.

As Giese (2003) observes, new Chinese migration to Germany is a highly varied process, forming a, if at all, loosely connected migration system. The PRC has become the dominant source of new Chinese migration. This group of migrants is again highly heterogeneous. The new migration flow has also contained an increasing proportion of business, professional and skilled migrants, many of whom arrived first as students. As the demographic, socio-economic and political structure of this migrant group diversifies, an increasingly higher level of fragmentation and polarization is apparent.

The development of the ethnic Chinese migrant groups in Germany is not well documented. A small body of literature captures the life situation of Chinese migrants in different periods (Eberstein 1988; Giese 2003; Gütinger 2004; Harnisch 1999; Knödel 1995; Rübner 1997; Yao 1988; Yü-Dembski 1987, 1997). Another section of the literature is semi-biographical work by Chinese migrants (Hu 1995; Wang 1998; Zhu 1995). In addition, newsletters from Chinese community organizations, such as the *Chinesische Allgemeine Zeitung, Chinesische Zeitung, The-Kuo-Ciao-Bao* and *Chinesische Handelszeitung*, are also sources of shorter journalistic and expressive documents by Chinese migrants. Expressive documents are particularly telling as they allow readers to feel the pain and delight, agonies and joy experienced by migrants. Despite the existence of this small but slowly growing literature, I have observed that knowledge about the development of the community among contemporary Chinese migrants is not widespread, especially among the young German-born and new migrants who arrived after the 1980s. This echoes Wang's (2003) observation that Chinese overseas have rather imperfect knowledge about their past. While narratives by and about earlier Chinese settlers do not seem to play a very active role in framing the identities of contemporary migrants in Germany, illustrations in the following will demonstrate that memories of other kinds can exert an impact on the lived experiences of the migrants.

How the host society remembers

How the host society perceives and remembers a migrant group is crucial in determining whether the latter can feel at home in their new life world. The so-called 'Chinese Quarter' that existed between the two world wars in St Pauli, Hamburg, has continuously inspired journalistic efforts. In these, the Chinese are for the most part described as being exotic, often involved in drug trafficking. This series of work offers insight into the mental images associated with Chinese people during the early period of their settlement (Ardnt et al. 1995; Barth 1999; Ebeling 1980; Hücking and Launer 1988; Jürgens 1930; Morgenstern 1932). In Jürgens's (1930) eyes, the Chinese people were monolithic members of the 'yellow race' (p. 14), and on their faces 'two lacquer-dark slit-eyes flashing like a puzzle' (p. 17). The author encapsulates his awe with his following choice of words (p. 18):

> Schmuckstraße in the Chinese Quarter of St Pauli is as mysterious and puzzling as the large motherland in the Far East. No European is able to lift the veil which hides the Chinese soul. The eternal, friendly smile of the Chinese evades any European curiosity. It is always the same, whether one visits one of the many Chinese laundries: Mr Wu or Sung, Tschai or Schan is polite, obliging, with cheap prices and – smiling. (Translation)

The above quote vividly illustrates that the Chinese were perceived to be strange, exotic creatures, who smiled all the time. They were in this way rendered faceless as individuals, all appearing, sounding and acting exactly alike. It is baffling that, after decades have passed, even contemporary writers still reproduce these exotic Orientalist images and narratives uncritically. Even more so than the content, the titles of these recent writings reflect how the writers choose to remember the early Chinese settlers. Opium persists as a popular image. For instance, Barth (1999) entitled her article ' "Tschin Tschang" und die Opiumhöhlen' (' "Chin chang" and the Opium Caves'). Similarly, Ardnt et al. (1995) inscribe the Chinese characters for opium (*yapian*) in large font above the title 'Lächelnd überleben – Das "Chinesenviertel" in der Schmuckstraße der dreißiger Jahre' ('Survive smilingly – The "Chinese Quarter" in Schmuck Street in the 1930s') in their article. While the consumption and dealing of opium was common among Chinese in that period, reducing the Chinese migrant communities to a gang of smiling opium-smokers is simplistic.

The uncritical recycling of exotic images can be seen as a parallel to other acts of identifying the Chinese in the contemporary media. Exoticism of the Chinese and Asians in general is common in the popular media. Two images from *Stern* (23 May 2001), a popular German magazine, help to illustrate this kind of exoticism and Orientalism. A naked Asian-looking woman with long straight black hair and acupuncture needles in her back is portrayed on the cover as a prelude to a special report on 'the healing art from Asia' (Figure 10.1).

Turning the pages, one is again confronted with an exotically 'Chinese' image. In a frozen meal advertisement two men are dressed in 'traditional'

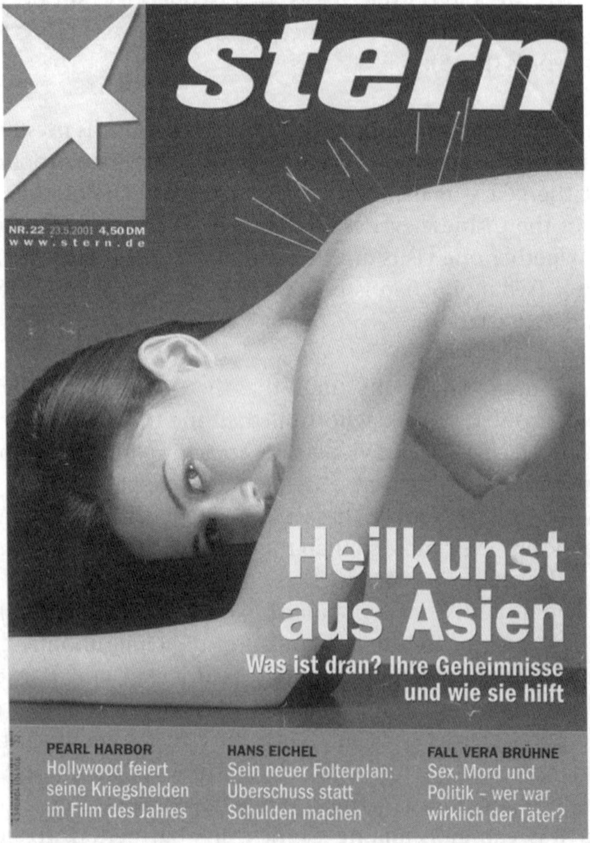

Figure 10.1 How Chinese arts of healing are perceived (cover of *Stern* magazine, 23 May 2001)

Oriental attire (red with a dragon print), one pulling the other's eyes into *Schlitzaugen,* both smiling merrily holding a plate of chop suey (Figure 10.2). While these images can be considered merely comic, eye-catching advertising tactics, they can also be interpreted as employing racist stereotypes that depersonalize or objectify people from different cultural backgrounds as being exotic oddities.

Weyrauch (1995), citing another example, contrary to what is suggested by the title of his book *Fluchtziel Deutschland: Migranten aus der Volksrepublik China; Hintergrund, Determination und Motive* (Refugees' Destination Germany: Migrants from the People's Republic of China: Background, Determination and Motives), devotes only a negligible portion of his writing to actual Chinese experiences in Germany. In that

Figure 10.2 Fashion of eating Chinese – frozen chop suey with slit eyes (*Stern* magazine, 23 May 2001)

short coverage, he includes a detailed description of the Chinese triads and various police arrests of these gangsters. Such economic activities are perceived to pervade Chinese society, echoing the images evoked by earlier authors like Jürgens (1930).[3]

The (re)production of memories filled with exotic imageries limits the social space available in Germany for Chinese migrants to claim a home where they are at times reduced to 'strange', 'exotic' and 'mysterious' beings. As argued by Brah (1996) in *Cartographies of Diaspora,* 'diaspora space' is a conceptual space inhabited by both those constructed as native *and* those as migrant. Marginalization, stereotyping and exotification are powerful forces that act to confine migrants' efforts to claim home.

Early Chinese migrants in private memories

Oral narratives of migrants reveal that the documentary evidence mentioned in the above section is only partial, exotifying and even misleading. Chau (in his eighties), who came from Guangdong to Hamburg in 1932, confirmed the presence of gambling places and opium dealing in the area. He described the 'Chinese Quarter' (Interview, 3 Mar. 2000):[4]

> What Chinatown? There was not much going on there. Just eight or nine shops and a few of these opium dealers. The sailors at that time brought opium in from Hamburg, Amsterdam or Rotterdam and sold it there. There were also gambling places. The Japanese like to gamble with us. They came to the port and played with us ... There were never a lot of Chinese anyway.

Bowles's (1992) personal communications with Ms Gao, a German woman who married a Chinese migrant, ran a laundry and lived near the Chinese Quarter in the late 1940s and early 1950s, reveal what living conditions were like in the early post-Second World War period:

> Her descriptions of the Chinese community in the late 40's and early 50's suggest neither mystery nor criminality. She described instead how hard people had to work to earn a living and the prejudice German-Chinese couples encountered. Social life evolved primarily around family gatherings, such as birthday parties (where she met her first husband) and two of the Chinese restaurants. (p. 68)
>
> Frau Gao was very vehement about German xenophobia, describing vividly the ostracism of the Chinese and Chinese-German community.

> When walking down the street she and her husband, 'had to hear a lot', and she felt herself shut out of German society. Gradually she let some of her friendships with other German women fade as they remained or became more xenophobic. When her first husband died, she received a lot of material and emotional support from the Chinese community. (p. 69)

Narratives of eyewitnesses as those above make a valuable contribution to the limited discourse, available from previously published and recycled accounts, which are predominantly ripe with exoticism.

Memories of the homeland(s)

Safran (1991) considers memories of the homeland as one of the six key characteristics of a diaspora. Indeed an attachment to, and memories of, the homeland are important markers of sojourners. But where exactly is *the* 'homeland'? Among diaspora Chinese, and even for each individual, homeland can assume different geopolitical entities in different historical eras. For the old sojourners, homeland means most likely the China before 1911; while for the newer migrants, homeland can be the PRC, Taiwan, Hong Kong, Vietnam, etc. Thus, when one follows Safran's categorization strictly, that is, judging whether the migration of Chinese peoples qualifies to be a diaspora by the presence of memories of *the* homeland (in singular form), the answer would not be absolute. As Chinese migrants identify themselves with different homelands, one could then argue that a series of Chinese diasporas exist (Skeldon 2003).

Communication with my informants reveals that memories of the homeland(s) undeniably play an important role in migrants' identities and life plans. The power of memories ranges from acting as an incentive for migrants to create and maintain social networks with each other, to feel the duty to lend a helping hand when disasters such as flooding occur in the homeland far away, to exclaim with joy when Beijing succeeded in its bid to host the 2008 Olympic Games, or to dream or plan for a return to the homeland.

Shared memories of the homeland act as a potent pulling force among migrants. Chinese migrants in Germany meet occasionally at communal events such as Chinese New Year or Mid-Autumn festivals. Regular meetings such as weekend Chinese language schools, women's associations, religious or business associations are more common in larger urban areas with more concentrated Chinese population. As in many other communities in the diaspora, communal organizations play an important role in (re)producing collective memories and thus keeping them alive. Articles about the history of the early settlers can occasionally be found in publications from these organizations. Activities by these associations are also settings when community history and identities are remembered and reinforced. During Chinese New Year parties, for instance, the lion dance on stage and traditional Chinese festive dishes on the tables evoke memories for the participants, creating a sense of being home away from home. Nevertheless, regarding communal associations and their activities as time-space where *only* shared cultural heritage is celebrated and friendly memories are recalled and created is too simplistic. A careful study of communal activities reminds observers that the Chinese 'community' does not share only one body of collective memories, identities and diasporic consciousness. Chinese migrants in Germany, similar to other overseas Chinese communities (or any other social groups in fact), are embedded in complex communal relationships, constructed along divisions of birthplace, language, gender, generation, professional background, political and religious affiliation. While communal organizations serve in general as an important source of support, entertainment and sense of belonging for migrants, they do not work to offer the same kind and level of support to all members in the diaspora. At a Chinese New Year celebration organized by the Hamburg Chinese Association, an organization with affiliation to the Taiwanese Overseas Chinese Affairs Commission, famous Taiwanese performance artists were invited to sing, as was expected, songs that aroused nostalgia for the homeland in the audience. All songs were popular items in Taiwan, a number of the songs were also in the Taiwanese language. As participants with Taiwanese background reminisced about the good old times in their homeland, members from other places could not avoid feeling somewhat out of place and excluded in this supposedly bonding experience.

In September 1999, the association organized a fund-raising dinner for the victims of the earthquake in Taiwan in place of their usual annual Mid-Autumn Festival. The master of ceremonies asserted the 'Taiwanese nature' of the event by opening the fund-raising auction with the following words: 'Tonight we are all here because *we are all Taiwanese* who care about what happened in Taiwan. Or, because *we are friends of the Taiwanese* in Hamburg. Please be generous and give a price for ...' The organizers further reinforced their Taiwanese identities by passing round copies of a news clipping, headed: 'Beijing, Please Shut Up!' This rebutted the mainland Chinese for their 'arrogant gratitude' in accepting international donations in the name of the 'Taiwan Province' and asserting that further donations should be made through the China Red Cross in the PRC. These leaflets provoked a round of whispered comments and an exchange of looks among the women from Hong Kong, with whom I was sitting. Being a Hong Kong Chinese, I felt somewhat out of place.

Indeed, among the many divisions transcending the migrant community, one's geographical background can be considered a particularly powerful one. 'Where are you from?' thus often functions as a powerful tool for delineation within the Chinese community in diasporic space. Boundaries can be conceived as having extended their reach beyond geographies into transnational space. Diverse geopolitical and cultural contexts shape the identities of people coming from different places, cutting across shared ethnic attributes. Among Chinese migrants, 'home' identities influence and may even determine whether one obtains a job, a place to live, has access to certain information, or belongs to a specific social group and, thus, what future opportunities are available. The fieldwork for this study reveals the role of geographic origin in determining where one belongs. This is particularly striking among Chinese from the PRC and Taiwan, who live, in most cases, in separate social circles in Germany. To a large degree, this can be attributed to the historical and political animosity between their two governments. Nationals in the diaspora embody their respective collective memories and reinforce the tensions, conflicting identities and interests between the two homelands.

Nevertheless, we should not overestimate the control of communal politics. The ending of the Mid-Autumn Festival story above helps illustrate the power of the individuals. To my astonishment, this intense nationalist 'Beijing, Please Shut Up!' effort was followed by a performance by a violinist from Beijing. This contradictory programme illustrates that the expected conflicting relationship between communities does not always translate into disharmonious interactions despite active reinforcement of differences at the institutional level. Individuals are also active agents in constructing their identities by the ways they choose to organize their social relationships with others.

Remembering and forgetting as strategies for homemaking

Memories of the homeland are often expected to imply nostalgia and yearning for the home sweet home. Indeed, interviews with migrants often reveal that memories provide a comfort zone and shared memories also offer a foundation for friendship networks and sense of belonging in the diaspora. Ahmed (1999, p. 343) goes so far as to suggest that, 'Acts of remembering [ ] are felt on and in migrant bodies in the form of a discomfort, the failure to fully inhabit the present or present space.'

Whether remembering is *always* a sign of being out of place is debatable. In fact, one should be cautious in making such a deterministic association which can be used as a basis for obsolete concepts of home, belonging and loyalty as singular and exclusive. This section will also discuss the strategy of forgetting in the process of homemaking. My communication with forced migrants offers insights into this aspect. For having been forced to leave, home is filled with traumatic memories and as a place of no return. My conversation with Mr Leung (late sixties) was revealing. He fled Vietnam in the 1970s, spent a few years in a refugee camp in Hong Kong, finally found refuge in Frankfurt. When he recounted his migration experience to me, the part about his original home in Vietnam was brief. Possibly due to my own Hong Kong background, he elaborated on his life in Hong Kong (Interview, 27 Mar. 2000):

> Life was so tough in Hong Kong. People fought all the time. Was terrible. So when the Germans came to collect people, I went to them right away. Many people wanted to go to the USA. So they'd rather wait longer in Hong Kong. But it was so terrible. I just wanted to get out.

He went on remembering fondly and thankfully his new life in the German welfare state: to a certain extent, Leung's life began in Hong Kong in this particular narrative. Vietnam is a home lost, a past forgotten. Leung has been active in ethnic Chinese communal affairs in the Frankfurt area; his attachment to China, more specifically Nationalist China, migrated with him:

> We just do the same thing. In Vietnam, we also taught our children how to read and write Chinese. We meet for the A-Ma's [Chinese Goddess of the Sea] birthday. We celebrate Chinese New Year. So here, we just continue, doing the same thing as we were in Vietnam.

Leung's case demonstrates the multiplicity of 'home' especially among those who, with their family, have migrated multiple times. While historical circumstances have denied Leung a sense of home in Vietnam where he grew up, he circumvents the trauma and connects his soul with the Chinese diaspora. Ironically, China is a place with no concrete memories. In his case, home is an imagined place, a reinvented past in some ways, which is anchored in the Chinese language, religious rituals as well as communal and family memories. My interview with Tina (late twenties), who fled Vietnam with her grandmother to Germany as a child, exposed another strategy of homemaking. Tina recalled with tears in her eyes (Interview, Oct. 2000):

> Have you heard of 'Cap Anamur'?[5] Without them, I would not be talking to you now. They saved us from the sea. It was so dark, windy and I was so scared. Hungry. But I don't remember much ... But now, Hannover is home. I am happy here. Everything I have is here. My grandmother, my husband, and my son [Tina was pregnant then].

Regarding the meaning of Vietnam, Tina reminisced for a while and answered:

> We will bring our son to my husband's hometown [in North Vietnam]. It is very important for them [her parents-in-law] to see the baby.
>
> [What about your home in South Vietnam?]
>
> Well, you see. My father lives in the USA. I have visited him and my [half] brothers and sisters. But I don't like it there. They have a good life there. He asked me to stay and he found me a husband, but I wanted to come back to my grandmother. My mother is in Vietnam and has her own family. I don't really have contact with her.

Tina's narrative provides a rich testimony of the sentiment of a refugee who was forced to establish a new home thousands of miles away from her birthplace. Haunted by the frightening experiences of childhood, Tina chooses to practically erase her home memories – echoing the experience of Mr Leung. Rather, she opts to establish a new home, plant new hopes in the city of Hannover. 'Vietnam' embodies, in the course of her life passage, different meanings. It has evolved from a place (in the south) of fearsome memories to another (in the north) that will, hopefully, carry happy memories of her transnational family.

Sustaining memories and culture

Family is an important space for the (re)production of memories. Childbirth often serves as a special impulse for families in the diaspora to revitalize the past, restructure memories and often (re)invent traditions. Oi Ling (late thirties), a new mother born and raised in Hamburg, considered a longer stay in her ancestral home of Hong Kong with her daughter. She explained (Interview, July 2004): 'I want to let her go to kindergarten in Hong Kong. Just for a few months or a year. That's what

I did when I was a child. My mom took me back to Hong Kong for a few months.' Contrary to her younger brother and sister, who work in Beijing and Hong Kong respectively, Oi Ling had never envisaged a 'return' to Hong Kong. Her short visits to her parents' home city had always been restricted to tourist or work-related nature. After the birth of her daughter, she remembers Hong Kong with a different quality, namely a place with which she affiliates her childhood. These memories are refreshed upon the arrival of her daughter and have consequently reshaped her future plans.

Aihong, a banker in Hamburg (thirties), who went to Germany about ten years before and is now married to a German, repeatedly told me that she was 'not very Chinese anymore' (Interview, 21 Jan. 2000): 'I think I am very Germanised. Sometimes I forget that I am Chinese! [laugh] ... I can't speak [Chinese here at home.] ... But if I have a child, I would for sure have him or her learn Chinese. It is important.' Settling in Hamburg with a German husband has let Aihong 'forget' that she is Chinese. Nevertheless, echoing the case of Oi Ling, Aihong imagined that the arrival of a child would most likely modify the importance of her Chinese background. 'It is important' as language is an effective instrument for the transmission of cultural heritage. As Fortier (2000) argues, 'generations, in migration discourses, are the living embodiment of the past with present living conditions, bringing the past into the present and charged with the responsibility of keeping some form of ethnic identity alive in the future'. By keeping up the common anchoring in a shared past, individual family members from different generations subscribe to membership of a common community. More than being seen as a vehicle of cultural transmission, the Chinese language is also increasingly important, according to many parents, because it helps their children to tap into the burgeoning Chinese-speaking economies.

Oi Ling and Aihong have confirmed Yuval-Davis's (1997) observation that women act as, or are expected to be, the carriers of the 'authentic voices' of a culture and are 'constructed as the symbolic bearers of the collectivity's identity and honour, both personally and collectively'. In line with this remark, all the Chinese schools observed in this research are highly gendered space. Almost all of the teachers and parents are women. While it is easy to slip into an argument that women have subscribed or been ascribed the role of 'upholders of culture', or even are the 'unpaid keepers and embodiments of memory' (Rayaprol 1997, p. 64), a more flexible conceptualization of such cultural and memory work is useful. In their study on expatriate women in Singapore, Yeoh et al. (2000) have pointed out the importance of community work, such as the unpaid or low-paid teaching of Chinese in community schools. This comprises 'a third sphere' that provides 'a viable substitute in place of the advantages and anchorage that waged work could potentially offer, as well as an added strategy to extend the scope of [the women's] identities beyond their roles as mothers, wives and homemakers' (Yeoh et al. 2000, p. 152). Similarly for some mothers, bringing their children to Chinese schools is not only a cultural duty. Carmen (thirties) accompanies her 12-year-old daughter to the Chinese schools every weekend. She explained (Interview, 22 Jan. 2000): 'Actually, Hiu-Ching can come to school by herself. She is old enough. But I usually come with her. I don't mind. Here, I can also see some friends. During the week, I don't have time. Here, we can chat a bit, and gossip a bit.'

My conversations with a few of the older mothers, whose children formerly attended the Chinese schools, also confirmed that the Chinese schools play a key role in bringing people together socially, and, additionally, provide space for the creation of informal networks and communities among women and the children. Mrs Chan (early sixties) recalls with a slight sense of nostalgia (Interview, 19 Nov. 1999): 'I have not been to the Association ever since my kids stopped going to class. No reason to. We used to see friends who brought their kids to school. But we don't see each other that often after the kids have grown.'

The Chinese schools are thus not only places for the transmission of cultural heritage and reproduction of Chinese identities among children. They provide a site where (mostly) women meet, a place where other forms of networks are developed and new memories in the diaspora are created.

Migrant memories and 'business' decisions

Making a jump to another aspect of homemaking, this section explores the connection between two seemingly distant subjects: 'memories' and 'business'. Establishing one's own business is a way for many migrants to make a living in their new homeland. How do migrant memories influence how migrant entrepreneurs organize their businesses?

Chang (fifties), owner of an academic travel agency in Hamburg, offers a rather exceptional reason for his choice of business. He explained how his professional background accounts for his choice of a particular, though probably not the most lucrative, clientele (Interview, 21 Jan. 2000):

> My wife and I were microbiologists before we came to Germany. That is why I'd rather run an academic travel agency. There is a mission.

> I organise academic trips and excursions for schools and universities to visit China. I am not very interested in ordinary travellers.

Chang's example demonstrates that business decisions are not made in an economic vacuum. In our conversation, Chang repeatedly emphasized his and his wife's academic achievements before migration, hinting that the lack of opportunity for them to continue their research careers was a cost they paid in moving to Germany. Providing services for an academic clientele offers them a way of still participating in the academic field back 'home', thus carrying on their career that survives in memory. Though it is an indirect way at best, it nevertheless gives them satisfaction.

Another travel agency operator, Chen (fifties), chose to locate his business in a place filled with family memories. Chen is a third-generation migrant, whose grandfather migrated to the harbour city from China in the 1920s. He resigned his 'very promising' job as a senior engineer in a big shipping company and set up a travel agency 20 years ago. For him, the harbour city is 'home', a home where his grandfather settled and established the Hamburg Chinese Association in 1929. The association was set up to help seamen arrange work trips and provide them with other support when they came onshore. Chen's travel agency is located in the house that his father bought in 1962 as the Home for Seamen. In his explanation of why he chose the site that he did, his family history in the Chinese communities and Hamburg dominated his speech; economic factors were hardly mentioned (Interview, 15 Jan. 2000).

For other first-generation migrants, Hamburg can also embody a homely feeling. A number of my informants also indicated that Hamburg, being a cosmopolitan city where a relatively large number of ethnic Chinese live and work, is appealing. It makes them feel more 'at home'. Ten years previously Susanne Hong's previous employer, a manufacturer of electrical appliances in Taiwan, assigned her to Germany. She chose Hamburg as the location for her office because, to a certain degree, it 'feels like home' (Interview, 4 Dec. 1999). Settling in a place that can arouse home memories is one of the strategies to create a sense of home away from home. In addition to choosing a homely place to make their new home, migrants also manufacture a 'home' through consumption. Classical migrant businesses such as ethnic restaurants, grocery stores and video/VCD rental shops offer a space where sojourners can indulge in the way of life 'like at home'. In the following section, I shall examine more specifically the power of memories in the sector of diaspora tourism, which has boomed in the era of intensified globalization and transnationalism.

Marketing memories for business

An increase in international travelling is one of the characteristics of our contemporary world with intensified transnationalism. Migrants' visits between different homes, as well as to other places where families, friends and relatives around the globe live, provide one of the most cohesive forces that maintain transnational communities. Diaspora tourism has grown into a significant market niche in the tourism sector in recent years. Among the different migrant businesses, travel agencies are one of the 'closest to the heart'. They serve not only functions that facilitate migrants' life overseas, providing spaces where migrants can 'get things done the way like at home' like other classical ethnic businesses. Moreover, they also arrange the sojourners' journeys, physically taking them to, among other destinations, their (ancestral) homes. Hence, Chinese tourist agencies find their niche beyond simply selling far-flung destinations through promoting *Fernweh* ('distance sickness'), as travel agencies usually do, but just as intensively, by marketing *Heimweh* (homesickness) to their fellow co-ethnics in the diaspora. Nostalgia and 'homing desire' (as coined by Brah 1996) are the foci of this sales pitch by a travel agency in Düsseldorf:

> The great Yangtse, the Great Wall,
> Yellow Mountain, the Yellow River;
> Weigh like a thousand stones in my heart.
> At any time, at any place, as close as my heart.
> (Translation)

Here, by painting a beautiful, romanticized (stereo)typical landscape in the reader's mind, the travel agent evokes nostalgic sentiments, and even almost a sense of duty to return home. Advertisements of this nature are particularly visible in community publications a few weeks before festivals such as Chinese New Year or Mid-Autumn Festival that are traditional occasions for family reunions.

During our interview at his travel agency, Li Kai (forties), who had studied German language and literature and worked in tourism in the PRC before migrating to Germany in the late 1980s, pointed out more explicitly the importance of the 'homing desire' to his very successful and expanding business. In answering a question about the stability of the business environment in the travel agency sector, he said (Interview, 3 Dec. 1999):

> How should I say? Put it this way. Among German people, they might not once think of going away. But among Chinese, may they be from

> Hong Kong or China, they want to go home. So I believe that every single Chinese who is running on the street here could potentially become my customer.

With a confident smile, he continued to explain his personal philosophy for business success:

> That was my thinking when I set up my firm [in 1993]. I am cultivating that. Who does not want to go home? If they have the money, when they have holidays, they want to go home. They are there, [the market is] stable. It all depends on how you operate, how you run your business. There are also Chinese travel agents that closed down. So I say, theoretically the business is stable, because the clientele is stable. The point how you get these people who want to go home, that is another question. The stabilising factor is that these people are here, and they want to go home.

Although migrant memories of home assume a variety of different meanings, a homing desire is a heartfelt yearning shared by virtually all migrants. While this desire, coupled with a sense of nostalgia, might not lead them to stay in one 'home' for ever, it nevertheless serves as a potent force to entice migrants to repeat their journeys home again and again.

Nostalgia and home memories are powerful and reliable forces in the tourism industry. Although world tourism in general suffered serious disruption after the terrorist attacks in the USA on 11 September 2001, homeward travel was the portion of tourism that was least affected. As Hsien (forties) observes, 'Business trips have been cancelled. But for those who need to go home, nothing can scare them away' (Interview, 28 Jan. 2002).

At a local level, narratives related to migration are also being revived and repackaged for profit. For instance, Chinatowns have been a major asset for local authorities in many countries around the world (e.g. in Singapore, New York, Yokohama). As mentioned earlier, two geographic centres of Chinese settlement existed in Hamburg and Berlin respectively between the two world wars, where social, cultural and economic contacts between the Chinese and Germans were more intensive compared to other parts of Germany. Memories of these early linkages have been used in advertising efforts by city agencies seeking Chinese investment. The Hamburg Business Development Corporation, for instance, considers the fact that the first German commercial fleet sailing to China began its journey from Hamburg in 1792 to hold symbolic significance for further cooperation between the two economies. While there have not been any efforts to revive these two 'Chinese quarters' on their original site to promote tourism or commerce, projects to create new 'Chinatowns' are in place in both cities, mainly targeted to attract investors and tourists from Chinese-speaking countries, in particular the PRC. In Hamburg, a 'China Town' has indeed been planned 'to enable Chinese to stay close together' (HKHBDC 2004). In Berlin, a sizeable conference and trade centre under the name of 'Asiatown' is one of the priority projects by urban planners (Bregel 2003). The success of the three-year-old Shaolin Temple in Berlin has also prompted business people in the culinary and retail sectors to establish a 'Chinatown' on the Kurfürstendamm, the most popular boulevard in the capital city (*Berliner Morgenpost* 2003). Unlike the case of Singapore where the migration history and cultural heritage of the old settlers are brought out in the new Chinatown, the German projects do not involve any memories from the old Chinese settlements. This can be explained by the discontinuous settlement history of the Chinese in Germany. These efforts can be considered a fabrication to capture the business potential of the increase in trade between Germany and East Asia as well as the rise in popularity of 'Oriental' culture. Yü-Dembski, Chair of the Society for German–Chinese Friendship, is sceptical of these artificial projects. Communications with informants have also confirmed the belief that a Chinatown would not bring a positive impact to the community beyond economic gain for a few business people. Disturbed by narratives of the historical China quarters, an old migrant Liu objected to the idea of rebuilding a Chinatown, 'Why? We don't have to stick together. It would only become a centre of crime and that would hurt our image' (Interview, 11 Jan. 2000). A lack of strong sentimental connection with the early settlers and the overwhelmingly exotic and immoral images lingering in the host society's memories have swayed many community members to let their history sleep and move forward, hopefully with new and more positive images.

Conclusion

In the course of writing this chapter, I referred back to my field notes and interview transcripts – literally digging into my memories. I would share my rediscovery of interesting material about the Chinese in Germany with a German-born friend who has 'returned' to Hong Kong, her ancestral home. She said once, 'Oh yes, I have heard something about that, could you make me a copy of the article?' Another time, she recalled, 'My childhood friend did her school project on the Chinese Quarter in

St Pauli. That's right. I have heard about that.' In some ways, my research has revived community memories that have played rather little impact in shaping the group identities and consciousness among the contemporary migrants. It would be careless, however, to jump to the conclusion that memories are not important among contemporary Chinese migrants in Germany. This chapter has illustrated the power of memories of different nature in the homemaking processes among these migrants.

Firstly, I have emphasized the inclusion of the host society in consideration of memories. While it is logical and commonly practised to focus on what and how migrants remember and forget in their negotiation of a sense of home in migrancy, the host society also controls the space available to the newcomers in claiming home. A survey of the narratives produced by earlier German writers and reproduced by contemporary authors suggests how the Chinese migrants have been perceived and remembered. The choice of reviving exotic narratives of the migrants, coupled with the many 'funny' and 'attention-grabbing' representations of people with different cultural backgrounds, work together to restrain the space for migrants to make a comfortable home in their new place of residence.

Furthermore this research has reconfirmed the dynamics of remembrance. What one remembers is not only a function of the capacity of one's grey cells. Rather, selective remembering or forgetting is also performed strategically in one's negotiation of identity and belonging. Forced migrants represent a good example of those who purposely choose to forget at least the traumatic part of their individual, family, community as well as national history. For many, it is by forgetting that they create space for new memories and belonging in another society, finding another home.

Common memories of the homeland provide the basis for connection among members of a diaspora community. As in other diasporas, the Chinese diaspora is made up of many migration systems. While the different groups within the Chinese diaspora possess a set of shared memories, narratives and heritage as 'Chinese', they embody simultaneously social memories that set them apart from each other. Their anchorage in different diasporic memories might translate to a friendly coexistence of various 'Chinese' migrant communities or to, at times rather politicized, community politics among different diaspora groups. The most obvious examples here would be the relationship between the mainland and Taiwanese Chinese communities. On occasions where the various groups meet to celebrate their 'pan-Chinese' heritage, their conflicting identities also surface. While memories of some kind help to create a sense of home away from home for some, they serve simultaneously to exclude other sojourners from feeling belonged. Communal gatherings are, in other words, time-space where individuals and communities experience their present and past, recall their collective memories and produce new ones. These dynamic processes consequently mould individuals' identities and sense of belonging.

The last section of the chapter examined the power of memories from an economic perspective. Individual and family memories may shape one's decision about where to live or what kind of business to go into. On an extremely pragmatic level, memories and nostalgia have been utilized by migrant entrepreneurs as a marketing tactic for their business. By putting the spotlight also on the economic and pragmatic facade of migrant memories, I aim to highlight the complexity of 'cultural' concepts such as identities, belonging, memories and nostalgia. While these have been topics in the diaspora research explored by cultural geographers, anthropologists and scholars in cultural studies, connections between this realm of literature and other areas, such as the studies on migrant businesses, are still to be made. Interviewees in this study have shown how cultural sentiments and psychological desire can be turned into marketing tactics for businesses. In order to understand the meanings and power of memories on the one hand, and the logic of a specific migrant business and how it fares 'on the ground' on the other, more observant fieldwork-based research should be conducted, making connections among concepts familiar to diverse social science disciplines. It is only by actively and sensibly entwining the economic, political, social and cultural aspects of such understanding that one can begin to decipher the complexity and dynamics of memories and belongingness in the diaspora.

Acknowledgements

The present chapter was written while the author was affiliated with the Department of Geography and Resource Management of the Chinese University of Hong Kong. The research was funded by the German Academic Exchange Service. I am most grateful to my many informants who generously shared their memories and inspiration with me.

Notes

1 Unless otherwise noted, the term 'Chinese' refers to ethnic Chinese, regardless of their national background, throughout the chapter.

2 In addition to prearranged interviews, many more spontaneous communications with Chinese migrants were carried out, which also provide rich material for the research.
3 It should be noted that Weyrauch's views are not considered representative of the positions held by other Chinese Studies scholars in Germany.
4 All informants are given pseudonyms.
5 *Cap Anamur* was a freighter chartered by the committee 'A ship for Vietnam' for a rescue mission in 1979.

References

Ahmed, S. 1999, 'Home and Away: Narratives of Migration and Estrangement', *International Journal of Cultural Studies*, vol. 2, no. 3, pp. 329–47.

Ardnt, U., Duffé, T. and Gerstacker, B. 1995, 'Lächelnd überleben – Das "Chinesenviertel" in der Schmuckstaße der dreißiger Jahre', in S. Pauli (ed.), *Geschichte und Aussichten vom Kiez*, Historika Photoverlag, Hamburg, pp. 113–15.

Barth, A. 1999, ' "Tschin Tschang" und die Opiumhöhlen', in, *Die Reeperbahn: Der Kampf in Hamburgs sündige Meile*, Spiegel-Buchverlag, Hamburg, pp. 52–3.

Berliner Morgenpost 2003, *Shaolin am Kudamm: Der Tempel der Kampfmönche*, viewed 22 Dec. 2006 <http://morgenpost.berlin1.de/archiv2003/030803/berlin/story620626.html>.

Bowles, E. 1992, 'The Chinese of Hamburg, Germany: Migration and Community', Master's thesis, University of Hawaii.

Brah, A. 1996, *Cartographies of Diaspora: Contesting Identities*, Routledge, London.

Bregel, M. 2003, *Investor plant großes China-Handelszentrum, Berliner Morgenpost*, viewed 29 December 2006 <http://morgenpost.berlin1.de/archiv2003/030803/berlin/story620622.html>.

Chamberlain, M. and Leydesdorff, L. 2004, 'Transnational Families: Memories and Narratives', *Global Networks*, vol. 4, no. 3, pp. 227–41.

Ebeling, H. 1980, 'Von der Dame Fortuna, von weißen Pülverchen und den Glückseligkeit der gelben Söhne des Himmels', in *Schwarze Chronik einer Weltstadt – Hamburger Kriminalgeschichte 1919–1945*, Ernst Kabel Verlag, Hamburg, pp. 157–87.

Eberstein, B. 1988, *Hamburg–China. Geschichte einer Partnerschaft*, Christian Verlag, Hamburg.

Fortier, A.M. 2000, *Migrant Belongings: Memory, Space, Identity*, Berg, Oxford.

Giese, K. 2003, 'New Chinese Migration to Germany: Historical Consistencies and New Patterns of Diversification within a Globalized Migration Regime', *International Migration*, vol. 41, no. 3, pp. 155–85.

Gütinger, E. 2004, *Die Geschichte der Chinesen in Deutschland: Ein Überblick über die ersten 100 Jahre ab 1822*, Waxmann, Münster.

Harnisch, T. 1999, *Chinesische Studenten in Deutschland: Geschichte und Wirkung ihrer Studienaufenthalte in den Jahren von 1860 bis 1946*, Institut für Asienkunde, Hamburg.

HKHBDC (Hong Kong Hamburg Business Development Corporation) 2004, *Chinese Have Face in Hamburg China Town*, Business News and Information, viewed 30 Dec. 2006 (Google cached) <http://www.google.com/search?q=cache:PYNjrl9pJ6kJ:www.china.ahk.de/gic/biznews/investment/040420_HWFPR1.htm+%22Hong+Kong+Hamburg+Business+Development+Corporation%22&hl=en&gl=au&ct=clnk&cd=1>.

Hu, T. 1995, *Chenfu Laiyinhe*, Jiefangjun Wenhua Press, Beijing.

Hücking, R. and Launer, E. 1988, 'Chinatown: keine große Freiheit', in R. Hücking and E. Launer (eds), *Tuten und Blasen: Hamburger Hafenrundfahrten durch acht Jahrhunderte*, Galgenberg, Hamburg, pp. 67–72.

Jürgens, L. 1930, 'Chinesenviertel', in *Sankt Pauli: Bilder aus einer fröhlichen Welt*, Hans Köhler Verlag, Hamburg, pp. 14–18.

Knödel, S. 1995, 'Die chinesische Minderheit', in C. Schmalz-Jacobsen and G. Hansen (eds), *Ethnische Minderheiten in der Bundesrepublik Deutschland – Ein Lexikon*, Beok Verlag, Munich, pp. 119–34.

Leung, M. 2004, *Making Home in Transnational Space: Chinese Migration in Germany*, IKO Verlag, Frankfurt.

Morgenstern, H. 1932, 'Hamburgs Chinesen-Gasse', *Niederdeutsche Monatsheft*, vol. July, pp. 195–7.

Rayaprol, A. 1997, *Negotiating Identities: Women in the Indian Diaspora*, Oxford University Press, Delhi.

Rübner, H. 1997, 'Lebens-, Arbeits- und gewerkschaftliche Organisationsbedingungen chinesischer Seeleute in der deutschen Handelsflotte: Der maritime Aspekt der Ausländerbeschäftigung vom Kaiserreich bis in den NS-Staat', *Internationale wissenschaftliche Korrespondenz zur Geschichte der deutschen Arbeiterbewegung*, vol. 33, pp. 1–41.

Safran, W. 1991, 'Diasporas in Modern Societies: Myths of Homeland and Return', *Diaspora*, vol. 1, no. 1, pp. 83–99.

Skeldon, R. 2003, 'The Chinese Diaspora or the Migration of Chinese Peoples?' in L.J.C. Ma and C. Cartier (eds), *The Chinese Diaspora: Space, Place, Mobility and Identity*, Rowman & Littlefield, Lanham, pp. 51–66.

Statistisches Bundesamt 2006, *Statistisches Jahrbuch für die Bundesrepublik Deutschland*, Statistisches Bundesamt, Wiesbaden.

Wang, G.W. 2003, 'Mixing Memories and Desire: Tracking the Migrant Cycles', in *The Second International Conference of Institutes and Libraries for Chinese Overseas Studies 'Transnational Networks: Challenges in Research and Documentation of the Chinese Overseas'*, The Chinese University of Hong Kong,

Wang, S.S. 1998, *Hanbao Sanjii*, The Publishing House of World Chinese Writers, Taipei.

Weyrauch, T. 1995, *Fluchtziel Deutschland: Migranten aus der Volksrepublik China; Hintergrund, Determination und Motive*, Projekt Verlag, Dortmund.

Yao, S. 1988, *Hsi-te, Ao-ti-li, Jui-shih Hua Chiao Kai Kuang*, Cheng Chung Bookstore, Taipei.

Yeoh, B., Huang, S. and Willis, K. 2000, 'Global Cities, Transnational Flows and Gender Dimensions, the View from Singapore', *Tijdschrift voor Economische en Sociale Geografie*, vol. 91, pp. 147–58.

Yü-Dembski, D. 1987, ' "China in Berlin" ', 1918–1933 – Von chinesischen Alltag und deutscher Chinabegeisterung', in H.Y. Kuo (ed.), *'Berlin und China' Dreihundert Jahre wechselvolle Beziehungen*, Colloquium Verlag, Berlin, pp. 117–30.

Yü-Dembski, D. 1997, 'Chinesenverfolgung im Nationalsozialismus – Ein weiteres Kapitel verdrängter Geschichte', *CILIP / Bürgerrechte & Polizei*, vol. 58, no. 3, <http://www.cilip.de/ausgabe/58/china.htm>.

Yuval-Davis, N. 1997, *Gender and Nation*, Sage, London.

Zhu, M. 1995, *Nacuijizhongying de Zhongguonühai*, Hebei Shaonianertong Press, Hebei.

11
A Century of Not Belonging – the Chinese in South Africa

Darryl Accone and Karen Harris

> ... fitting in meant keeping his balance, learning to bend with the changing winds, as his forebears in South Africa had found ...
>
> (Accone 2004, p. 7)

For many South Africans, the closing decade of the twentieth century heralded the end of an era, ushering in new inclusive democratic governance with divisive strictures of apartheid legislation finally annulled. For the suppressed and disadvantaged masses and minorities who now belonged to a new South Africa, it was a time to look forward, but also a time to look back. With the freedom struggle over, victims and perpetrators from a wide spectrum of cultures and classes were able to reflect on what Nelson Mandela termed the 'weal and woe of ... over a century and beyond' (Faber and Van der Merwe 2004, p. 5). Voice was given to individual and community memory, as divergent experiences under the successive authoritarian regimes were recalled. These different memories were shards of the reality which impacted on particular individuals or sections of the multicultural society. For some this memory was, however, still coloured with the sense of not belonging. One such community was the South African Chinese who throughout this hundred-year presence had no sense of belonging. Being neither white nor black, and clinging to their rather insular Chinese community, they were forced to continue to negotiate a precarious position in this African space.

This chapter presents the chequered history of such a Chinese-South African family over the past century. It traces their place – or lack of it – through four distinct chronological phases. This personal story begins in the last phases of British colonialism with its drive for reconstruction and Anglicization; moving into the Union with its divided stance of white conciliation and non-white segregation; onto the evolving structures of apartheid and legalized discrimination; culminating in the new democratic society with its acknowledged concerns for transformation and reconciliation.

British colonialism

At the turn of the twentieth century, the southern tip of Africa was engrossed in a prolonged war between the allied republican Boer states and Britain. In 1902, after two and half years, the war eventually culminated in British Crown Colony rule which was to continue for much of the remainder of the decade. Under the new regime, the position of the black and so-called Asian communities, many of whom had been caught in the crossfire of the hostilities, remained relatively unchanged. The British administration did little to alleviate their prewar subordinate position, and at some levels their situation became even less tenable.

The former Boer republican policy of no equality between *blanken* [white] and *gekleurden* [people of colour] (Artikel 1858) remained virtually intact, as did the provisions of other legislation which specifically deprived the 'native races of Asia' the right to citizenship and ownership of fixed property, except in 'streets, wards and location' which the government assigned to them (South African Republic 1885, Law No. 3). This legislation also called for the registration of all 'Asians' and regulated that they carry a pass. The postwar British authorities re-enacted most of these laws. The Peace Preservation Ordinance of 1903 which denied persons defined as 'undesirable' access to the Transvaal by a permit system was followed by additional regulations which required voluntary 'Asiatic re-registration'. The new administrators established an 'Asiatic Department' to administer 'Asian activities', which subsequently upheld the separate locations for 'Asiatics' and took steps to set up Asian bazaars or locations in every town. The infamous 'Black Act' was introduced in 1906 as the Draft Asiatic Law Amendment Ordinance. It stipulated the compulsory registration of all 'Asiatics' over the age of eight with the 'Registrar of Asiatics'. The certificate registration required additional information including name, residence, age, caste and marks of identification, as well as finger and thumb impressions. The issue of trading licences was made conditional upon the production of such a certificate, and the penalty for failing to comply ranged from a fine to imprisonment and deportation. The implications of this ordinance were to prove far more restrictive than any previous legislation. The British authorities also endorsed the regulations of the 1898 Gold Law which denied any 'coloured person' – which referred to any 'African, Asiatic,

Native or Coloured American person, Coolie or Chinamen' – the right to be a licence holder in the gold mines or to be in any way connected to their operation other than 'as a workman in the service of whites' (South African Republic 1898, Law No. 15). Most of these discriminatory laws enacted under both the Boer and subsequent British rule had primarily been promulgated to control the numerically larger Indian population (Bhana and Brain 1990, p. 78). Thus, sharing a common geographical nomenclature, the small Chinese community prevalent in the region, was subjected to the same discriminatory laws.

Another development in this postwar period of British 'reconstruction' which was to further ostracize the existing Chinese community was the introduction of 63,659 Chinese indentured labourers to work in the gold mines. The South African War had seriously disrupted the gold mining industry through work stoppage and labour dispersal. In order to salvage the situation as quickly as possible, the British government sanctioned a scheme propounded by the mine owners to import Chinese indentured labour. This elicited widespread opposition, both locally and abroad, and resulted in extremely stringent labour importation regulations (Harris 1995, pp. 161–2). It also had a profoundly detrimental impact on the existing free Chinese community. Not only did the Chinese become more conspicuous within society as a result of public anxiety and anger over the importation of thousands of Chinese labourers, but existing restrictive laws were more rigorously enforced and additional ones enacted in the aftermath.

The most consequential legislation resulting from the indentured scheme was the Cape Colony's Chinese Exclusion Act such as the Statutes of the Colony of the Cape of Good Hope, 1904: Act 37, which ranks as one of the first overtly racist pieces of legislation introduced during the period of white hegemony in southern Africa (Harris 2004). Its primary aim was to prevent the entrance of Chinese deserters from the Transvaal mines into the Cape Colony, as well as to prohibit the arrival of newcomers from China. Contravention of the provisions could lead to a fine, imprisonment or deportation to China or the country of origin. Unlike its Australian, New Zealand, American and Canadian counterparts, the Cape Colony Chinese Exclusion Act dealt with 'all classes' of Chinese as opposed to certain labouring classes, and it was to remain on the statute books for an extended period of nearly three decades. Added to this was the resolute and ultimately successful campaign to end the Chinese indentured mine labour scheme. Notions of the 'other' and the 'alien threat' provided powerful imagery to canvass political support in Britain and South Africa (Harris 1998).

The decades of animosity further marginalized the small resident Chinese community, both in terms of their legal status as well as emotive in the public consciousness. It was into this increasingly negative anti-Sinitic environment that the first generation of Darryl Accone's[1] ancestors contemplated going to South Africa. Why would people commit themselves to so forbidding an environment? The answer lies partly in the perceived opportunities offered by Kum Saan ('Gold Mountain' in Cantonese) – Johannesburg and its newly discovered gold reefs – and, primarily, in the widespread poverty in China.

The possibilities of a more comfortable material life motivated Chinese emigration in the nineteenth century to gold-rush areas such as California, South Africa and Australia. In this scramble, Chinese living in the southern province of Kwangtung (now Guangdong) had certain advantages over those elsewhere in the 'motherland'. Its capital Canton (now Guangzhou), an ancient seaport, was a gateway to the world for hundreds of thousands of Cantonese. It was from here that they left directly, or took ship to Hong Kong, on the first stage of their journey to foreign lands. Naturally, people from Kwangtung – and more specifically from the so-called Namsoon villages within a radius of about 12 miles of Canton – had an advantage of proximity to this port.

Many of these 'emigrants' did not plan on becoming settlers; certainly that was not the intention of Accone's great-grandfather Langshi and grandfather Ah Kwok (better known as Ah Leong). Langshi was a traditional Chinese herbalist. It was this skill that he was exporting to set up a practice in the burgeoning Chinese community in the recently founded mining town of Johannesburg. Father and son would work very hard to send money home, planning all the while to follow it back after a short time. The plan was for Ah Kwok to keep up his Chinese studies while in Africa, come home and prepare for further school examinations and then sit entrance exams for higher education or government administration.

The decision to go to Namfeechow (South Africa) had not been arrived at easily. The opportunity had arisen in a letter from Langshi's cousin Ah Sin. Wearied by life in one Gold Mountain – San Francisco – Ah Sin had moved on to Johannesburg. In a very short time – the letter said just over six months – Ah Sin had saved more money than in several years in San Francisco. Would Langshi, the letter asked, perhaps consider coming to South Africa to provide his sorely missed herbalist's skills in the community? It would, of course, be for a short time, only two or three years at most.

Langshi's wife Soi Sien had resisted from the first. Family legend has it that she said: 'If you go to this other Kum Saan, I may become one of those women. I do not want that. Not now, not at my age.' To which Langshi is said to have replied, trying to reassure his wife:

> My idea is to work very hard for a short time, to live frugally and to set aside money to send home. Soon, we will have accumulated the wherewithal to secure a comfortable future. We are growing older and in some years I may not be as hale and able to undertake demanding daily work of the sort that I am sure awaits me in this gold-prospecting place across the seas. So, release me and Ah Kwok for a few years. I promise that his studies will not be neglected. And above all I vow to return to you and Sha Kiu and to our life together, a life that will be amplified by what I manage to do in the time away.

At first the chance to go to Kum Saan was very exciting: a city of gold, where everything was new and anything possible. As his father, mother and grandparents discussed the venture, Ah Kwok was swept along by their sense of possibility. It would be an adventure for the boy, the adults concurred – an opportunity to see some of China and a whole new world too. Surely it would stand him in good stead. Nor were he and Langshi going for ever. This would be a short-term working excursion, to a land not as distant as America, to which some of Langshi's brothers had journeyed. Langshi explained it to Ah Kwok as follows:

> You and I are going to this land far to the west so that I can work among our people there, who have much more money than we here back home. The goldfields in Namfeechow are the richest in the world ... For the present, we T'ong yan [Chinese] will live close by and support each other. One day, that will change. But by then we will be back home, you and I. You will be in Peking sitting your examinations for the imperial administration and I will be passing on my knowledge of medicine to a younger man. In the evenings your mother and I will think of you and remember your grandfather, if he is not with us then. All of this will be possible because of the few years we will spend across the sea.

Soi Sien remained unconvinced by her husband's arguments. But as winter wore on and the matter was discussed again and again, she came to accept that Langshi and Ah Kwok would leave in the spring. Eventually she found herself comforted by Langshi's repeated and confident assurances. Any forebodings she still harboured she kept to herself, or confided to her mother-in-law.

Union and segregation

By the end of the first decade of the twentieth century, the foundation for the future position of the Chinese community in South Africa had been laid. While developments during the next half century would radically reduce their numbers and therefore their political significance, there would remain a lingering legacy of 'Orientalism' in much of the white South African collective memory. This would play itself out in the subsequent phases of constitutional and political change as the Chinese would find themselves in an increasingly untenable position.

These anti-Sinitic and racially intolerant developments prevalent at the start of the twentieth century were by no means unique to colonial South Africa. Western countries, such as the United States, Canada and Australia, had all followed a similar pattern and introduced similar legislation. The Chinese, who formed part of the large-scale international emigration during the second half of the nineteenth century (Pan 1990, p. 43), were increasingly denied admission to these societies, either through complete exclusion or by means of controlling regulations. This situation was generally compounded by 'white supremacism' and Orientalist discourse which regarded all things Eastern as inferior (Dawson 1967, pp. 132–54; Mackerras 1989, pp. 44–5; Worden 1994, p. 65). While much of the discriminatory legislation was repealed in most of these other countries within a few decades of their promulgation, the latter mindset persisted. As members of an identifiable and highly stereotyped minority, the Chinese continued to be victims of discrimination. However, no other country was dominated for so long by such a race-based political system as in South Africa. Until the mid twentieth century, its society was characterized by segregation and later codified as apartheid.

With all four states in South Africa under British colonial rule the consolidation into a single state followed with the founding of the Union. Although the new 1910 constitution set up a highly centralized system, limited powers were retained at the provincial level (Spies 1986, pp. 225–6). This meant that certain pieces of legislation remained on the statute books of individual provinces and local authorities, and therefore many of the pre-Union racially based regulations were perpetuated. This had in fact been the only way to break the numerous deadlocks (Spies 1986, p. 226), particularly around issues related to race such as the franchise, employment, residency and other social amenities.

With the legislation for the new found Union, the Chinese and other people of so-called 'colour', were often subjected to a dual set of restrictions. While they were increasingly legally excluded from the political, social and economic realm at a national level, they were subjected to further local restrictions. People of colour were generally regarded as subordinate, and there was a distinct and concerted effort to enforce separation in all spheres of life at national, provincial and municipal levels.

The introduction of the Immigrants' Regulation Act of 1913 was a case in point. Not only did it compound the existing provincial prohibitions by endorsing the language test and the definition of a 'prohibited immigrant' at a national level, but it also allowed the pre-Union legislation to remain on the statute books. The restrictive efficiency of the law in this regard was evident in the fact that statistics in the first Union year book indicated that by 1917 there were only 711 Chinese in the country (Union of South Africa *c.*1920, p. 192). In the 1930s immigration legislation added further restrictions on immigrants. Thus an end was put to new Chinese immigration, as well as the entrance of the relatives of Chinese in the country for close to three-quarters of a century. This made their numbers entirely dependent on natural increase and the occasional special permit entrant.

The position of the Chinese already resident in the country remained relatively unchanged, except for their dramatically reduced numbers. They were generally treated as second-class citizens with their status of 'non-European' or 'non-white'. From 1910 to 1948, various administrations consistently introduced legislation which drew lines between whites and the rest of society: in 1911 the colour bar was enforced in the workplace (Horrell 1963, p. 8); in 1913 property rights were controlled and territorial segregation enforced; in 1920 mixed marriages were limited with 'illicit' sexual relations following suit in 1927; and in 1923 residential segregation was implemented. All of these statutory restrictions served to further entrench white attitudes of racial superiority.

Most threatening of all the laws that applied to the Chinese were those that restricted their ability to earn a basic living. Economic strangulation was by no means an invention of the apartheid regime of the mid twentieth century. Developed, refined and codified by the initial colonies and republics, these restrictive laws and practices were united in the legal system of the Union of South Africa. Chinese immigrants were confined to a constraining circle of self-sufficiency – business was generated mainly within the Chinese community. Trading licences were often denied if applicants were Chinese. Trading hours, too, were restricted, as was travel for Chinese in the Transvaal. So repressive was the cumulative effect that daily survival was an achievement in itself.

The miniscule size of the Chinese community was also to have far-reaching effects on how they responded to, and dealt with, this discriminatory situation. Too small to lobby independently, they generally complied with the various regulations and avoided confrontations with government. They did, however, have recourse to redress and that was the existence of the Chinese Consul General within South Africa. To a degree this also served to underline the South African Chinese's sense of not belonging – having recourse to and being represented by an official of the country of their birth – China. Nevertheless, diplomatic strategizing did not mean that the Chinese were no longer the subject of discriminatory legislation. Rather, they continued to be implicated in the racial policies of the segregationist years even though their numbers only rose to 4000 by the 1940s (CSS 1946–1954: Population Census, 7 May 1946). They were persistently included with other 'non-Europeans' in broad racial categories or as coloured for the purposes of state legislation and municipal ordinances which denied certain rights to all communities except the whites, such as the use of pavements, parks, benches, beaches and public transport and other facilities (Horrell 1963, pp. 10–11). That the Chinese objected to this treatment is evident in the opinions voiced by the Chinese Consul General in interviews and memorandums to the Union government.

Thus in the second phase of the twentieth century of constitutional development in South Africa the Chinese were not only prohibited from adding to their numbers, but they were literally left in-between. In a system predicated upon race and colour, in which they were neither 'white' nor 'black', they were marginalized.

While Langshi had not been unaware of this sociopolitical milieu before he left China, he concentrated on accumulating capital. He and Ah Kwok travelled for South Africa in 1911, setting off from Sha Kiu village in Kwangtung province. The journey was to take them first to Canton, then by sampan to Hong Kong and finally to southern Africa on board a Japanese steamer. During this long voyage in steerage, Langshi's son had a first and unwelcoming intimation of the new country. As Langshi explained during their sea journey, Ah Kwok would have to be someone quite different in Gold Mountain. Langhi broke the news as follows:

> You see, I cannot bring you in to the new country as my son. If I had been working there, and then gone home to visit and a child had been conceived during that time, it would be different. Then I would have been able to bring that child over at a later stage.
>
> Sometimes people who work in Namfeechow do not send for their children. Others report children who have not been born. Still others lose their children. Many of these people give their papers to relatives or sell them. I bought your papers – gee tsai – from a couple who lost their

> son. That is why you cannot be known by your name, Fok Kwok Ying. You must remember that from now on, until we return to Sha Kiu, you are Ah Leong, not Ah Kwok.

Such was the painful severing of Ah Kwok's identity. He lived the next 73 years under a name that was not his. He lived that time remembering what his grandfather, Tian, had said to him when they parted, on the hill above Sha Kiu. Giving Ah Kwok a red silk cord, the old man had said:

> This cord will bind you in Namfeechow to us in Chung-kwok [China]. It symbolises holding kin together. It is a lifeline to your family that will never break. It will bring you back again. And you must not forget that wherever in the world you are and will be, Sha Kiu will always be your old family home. It cannot be otherwise, for here you have spent the first ten years of your young life. No village, no town, no city can take its place. Sha Kiu has your heart and you have its, forever.

Thus the roots were laid for Ah Kwok's sense of not belonging in South Africa, a profound feeling of alienation and disaffection that afflicted most Chinese immigrants, in greater or lesser degree, that continues among some until now.

Langshi did indeed see Sha Kiu again, but only during a brief visit home after which he returned to South Africa where he died in 1934. Ah Kwok never set foot on Chinese soil again, but never renounced his Chinese citizenship or sought naturalized status in South Africa. The man known as Ah Leong married Yok Laan, better known as Gertie, in 1930. Two children, Hong Hgang (Jewel) and Hong Lin (Mickey), followed, and by 1934 the family settled in Westdene, a working-class suburb in Johannesburg, where they lived in rooms behind their businesses, Ah Leong Family Grocers and Perth Road Fruit Shop.

Despite all the regulations and restrictions the government placed on Chinese traders, Ah Leong and Gertie were able to make a living by selling the necessaries of daily life in small quantities, and often on credit. Since the Chinese traded in working-class areas, many of the inhabitants were regularly unemployed, fomenting contentious relationships between Ah Leong and Gertie and their white working-class customers. On Fridays, pay day for the men of the area, their wives would come to the shop begging for a loaf of bread, half a pound of butter, some cheese and milk on credit for the family at home. Their husbands were at the local bar, their wages washing down their throats. It was at these times that Ah Leong and Gertie were Mr and Mrs Leong, but on other days, whether they were in the street or on a tram, there would not be a word or even a look of recognition for the shopkeepers' Friday afternoon kindnesses.

The other side of Ah Leong and Gertie's shopkeeping had to do with avoiding infringing any of the numerous by-laws to trip up the careless trader. Squads of inspectors patrolled businesses, checking everything, verifying weights and measuring up establishments in a numerous other ways. No items of clothing could be draped or hung anywhere in a shop. If your coat was found on the premises, you were fined. Every item of merchandise had to be individually marked, as well as priced on the shelf. All shopkeepers had to wear aprons; later the dress code was amended to three-quarter-length khaki jackets. There were inspectors for controlling weights and measures and inspectors for keeping the hours of business under observation (Ah Leong's grocery had to shut at 6 pm during the week and at noon on Saturdays). All these daily trials were nothing, however, compared to what awaited the Chinese under apartheid.

Apartheid and discrimination

In 1948 the National Party government won the elections and immediately set about implementing its policy of apartheid, which entailed the separate development of ethnic groups in all spheres of life. This ideology was partly a reaction to what the new leaders regarded as the gradual demise of segregation after the Second World War, as well as an effort to mobilize nationalism among 'Afrikaners across divisions of region and class' (Worden 1994, pp. 90, 95). It was a development that would catapult the country and its people into a new dimension, both in terms of everyday living and international relations. A plethora of racially contrived restrictions were introduced, described as a 'project of social engineering the likes of which had rarely been seen' (Scher 1993, p. 321). Despite their small numbers, the Chinese were also configured into this racially divisive equation, albeit inconsistently, which only served to underline their sense of not belonging.

The foundation of the apartheid system was the classification of the population into distinct racial categories in order to facilitate the fundamental principle of separate development. The Population Registration Act of 1950 initially identified three distinct groups – a white, a black and a more inclusive coloured group – with the latter being subsequently subdivided into subgroups such as Cape coloured, Cape Malay, Indian, Griqua and Chinese, other Asiatic and other coloured. In the case of men, racial grouping depended at first on 'general acceptance', while in the case of women it followed the race of the person to 'whom she is married or with whom she cohabits' (Johnson 1951, pp. 286–8). Although members of the Chinese community had at first requested that they be treated as 'white', they acceded to classification as a separate group as it provided them with the means to differentiate themselves from other groups. However, classification as a specific category did not necessarily mean that the Chinese were treated separately in terms of the various other apartheid regulations. On the contrary, the restrictions were erratically applied, leaving them in a grey area.

One such regulation was the Group Areas Act that was instituted to provide for separate residential areas that were based on population categorization. While the Chinese accepted being constituted as a separate group, they did not want a separate residential area as many Chinese were dependent on trade for their livelihood. Deputations argued that numerically the community was too small to form a viable economic or administrative entity and the creation of separate areas would be contrary to the trend of understanding between South Africa's Chinese and European communities, as well as the racial harmony that existed between them and other racial groups. Despite these requests, for almost two decades the government proposed numerous areas that were ultimately abandoned. Instead, the Chinese were subjected to a permit system, allowing them to live in an area after obtaining permission from the Department of Community Development as well as a 'no objection agreement' from the immediate neighbours. This proved to be both a humiliating and very insecure provision.

Another dimension of the apartheid system were the regulations formulated to enforce separation among the racial groups on a social level, in all public places and in the use of amenities. Already in 1949, the Prohibition of Mixed Marriages Act had been introduced to put an end to 'marriage between a European and a non-European'. In 1953, the 'Reservation of Separate Amenities Act' was introduced as a means to consolidate former legislation and further enforce separation. However, in practice, due to the impracticability of the Group Areas Act as regards the Chinese, they increasingly shared the same public facilities as whites. Many proprietors felt obliged to obtain permits to admit Chinese while others turned them away. Permits were also required for Chinese wanting to attend white state schools, technical colleges and universities (*Citizen*, 30 Oct. 1980; *Evening Post*, 18 Mar. 1980; Horrell 1978, p. 169; *Sunday Express*, 1 Oct. 1982; *Sunday Times*, 29 Aug. 1965).

Although there were unpleasant experiences associated with the implementation of apartheid regulations, the Chinese had very little choice other than to accept the status quo. They realized that their admission and tolerance were very much dependent on the discretion of whites and therefore they generally tried to avoid situations that could lead to problems. Apartheid officials were aware that double standards were being applied – according to some of the law the Chinese were 'non-white', but in society they were treated as 'white'. They were, however, not prepared to reclassify the Chinese as white for fear of the reaction that could emanate from the other 'non-European' communities to such privilege (*The Star*, 19 Feb. 1986). Nevertheless, racial harassment remained a cause of anxiety and humiliation for the Chinese and served to highlight their treatment under apartheid.

From the 1970s onwards there was an official attempt to change the position and status of the South African Chinese. International pressure on South Africa and the Republic of China or Taiwan (ROC), two 'pariah states', drew them economically closer together. With increased contacts at commercial and diplomatic level, the South African government felt obliged to reconsider the position of its Chinese residents. This resulted in an unprecedented focus on the Chinese, who despite their ambiguous legal status, indicated they 'preferred to remain invisible' (*Daily News*, 20 June 1980; *Financial Mail*, 10 July 1981; *The Star*, 19 June 1980). The government persisted and passed an amendment whereby the Group Areas Act ceased to apply to the Chinese community. Effectively 'right by permission' thus ended and the Chinese became the first 'non-white' group to breach the racial divide of the apartheid system. By this time, however, the impact of decades of discriminatory legislation was evident in the dramatic increase in emigration of many young South African-born Chinese graduates to Canada, the United States and Australia (*Die Transvaler*, 2 Dec. 1980; *Sunday Express*, 13 Feb. 1983).

Thus, from the mid twentieth century there ensued an avalanche of legislation which attempted to control society through both race and colour coding. Although the Chinese were seldom the object of apartheid's social plans, they were left in the interstices of a system structured by race and colour, in which they were neither white nor black (nor Indian which comprised a large community). The ambivalence of their status within this divided society, where they were made to feel that they did not really belong, made their position that much more untenable.

A story of exclusion through time

On the morning of the National Party victory, 27 May 1948, a white woman, with curlers in her hair and a net cloth pulled tightly around her head, shuffles in to a grocery shop, greeting the Chinese woman behind the counter:

> 'Morning, Mrs Leong. May I have half a loaf of white bread on tick, please?'
> 'Hello, Mrs Botha. Certainly. Anything else?'
> 'No. We are too happy to need anything more this morning, you know.'
> 'Oh, yes. You must be very happy that the National Party has ousted General Smuts and the United Party.'
>
> In an instant, the sedate Mrs Botha, generally a browbeaten and dishevelled figure, transforms into a whirling dervish. '*Ja*! *Ja*! We won!' she shouts exultantly, waving the freshly-cut half-loaf above her head as if it were a victory banner, and skipping around the shop floor. 'Now we are in charge. We will put all those *kaffirs* and *coolies*, those *klonkies* and *Chinkies* in their place. This is our country now!'
>
> Mrs Leong lets the pejoratives and the irony of the half-loaf bought on credit hang in the air and dissolve. Always the embodiment of graciousness, she smiles at Mrs Botha and says 'Oh, yes. I'm sure things will be much better for you now. You must enjoy the celebrations with the people from the other houses on the hill and we'll see you tomorrow, I'm sure, to talk more. Good morning!'

Moving with rapid speed, the new government introduced multiple laws based on racial classification, vigorously reinforcing the separation of races. Typical were the difficulties experienced by Ah Leong and Gertie's elder daughter, Jewel. After completing her Bachelor of Arts at the University of the Witwatersrand, Jewel spent six months looking for work. Early on, Jewel's university friend, Rosemary Cohen, had told her about a job at the South African Medical Research Institute. Jewel was granted an interview, but it was clear to her when she arrived that her prospective employers had not been expecting a Chinese face. 'It's not possible to employ you as the institute falls under the government,' she was told in the first and last minute of the interview.

It was back to poring over the ads in the daily papers and walking up and down the streets of Johannesburg, on the lookout for job notices. When she was fortunate enough to secure an interview, it was always the same story: 'In spite of your admirable qualifications, it is not possible to employ you because you are Chinese.' One or two places had been prepared to risk taking her on, but when the staff were told, they threatened to walk out or to report their employers to the authorities.

By chance, Jewel met a varsity friend who was working in the library at their alma mater. Approach the Librarian, Miss Elizabeth Hartmann, she advised Jewel. There were no posts at Wits, Miss Hartmann told Jewel, but she promised to let her know if anything suitable should turn up. After almost half a year of disappointments, the undertaking seemed to Jewel merely the most gracious rejection that she had received. But three weeks later, Miss Hartmann phoned with two options: a place at the Wits Library or a vacancy at the Institute of Race Relations, whose research library was housed in the third basement of the Wits Library. When the two met to discuss the jobs, Miss Hartmann recommended that Jewel apply for the Institute post as it was more challenging. Jewel did and was given the job.

Red tape and bureaucracy bedevilled Chinese life in many other ways. Jewel and Giddy's son Darryl had to apply for permission to attend Loreto Convent, a feeder school to the Christian Brothers' College (CBC) in Pretoria. Every year, Jewel had to deal with the Transvaal Education Department's permit, which posed a series of obstacles to applicants. First the head of the school had to signal approval by signing the form. Then there were questions to be answered. How far do you live from the school? How near is the Chinese school to your place of residence? Why have you chosen this school? Last came the interview at the Transvaal Provincial Administration building in Pretorius Street. Always, the rubber stamp would hammer down on the form and the ordeal was over for another year.

When her son moved to CBC, Jewel took a while to become used to the novelty of not applying for a school permit. Brother Smith, the young and determined principal, refused to sign the application. He told Jewel that he would not sign any of the permits for Chinese pupils as the process was degrading, and he would decide whom to accept or refuse, not the Education Department bureaucracy. He added that as Chairman of the Catholic Schools Committee, he had given instructions to that effect to brother and sister schools. Brother Smith's stand brought an end to Jewel's yearly applications, though not to the annual appearance by education officials performing a headcount of Chinese pupils at CBC.

Finding a place to live was also extremely stressful, given the difficulties posed by the Group Areas Act. In 1969, Jewel and her husband Giddy went to the local Group Areas office in Pretoria, seeking permission to move to a house they had found in a non-white enclave about to be declared white. 'If you move in there, girlie, I'll throw your bed, kettle, stove and your arse into the street,' said the short, fat, heavily bearded man behind the desk. Before Jewel and Giddy could respond, he pushed his chair back and walked into the adjacent annexe, shutting the door behind him. Humiliated and angry, Jewel could not help crying. As she and Giddy walked towards the lifts, they passed a man who said:

> I am Nel, the head of Non-European Housing Affairs ... Allow me to make it up by issuing you with an Open Permit which will allow you to live anywhere in the city that you like. And please be in touch with me should you meet any problems.

Jewel and Giddy were grateful. Nevertheless, the well-meaning gesture was empty since there was no prospect of their being allowed to live where they chose, but it was enough that the permit gave them means to continue looking for a house. Indeed, a few days after the visit, they received a call from the housing department offering them a number of houses in Claremont, a derelict suburb on the edge of the city.

When they went out to Claremont, they found all the proffered houses in terrible condition. None had electricity, running water or toilets. Candles, Primus stoves, a backyard tap and a long-drop lavatory outside were how people lived. Best of the four houses was a solitary, square house, with an old poplar tree that shaded the southern side. Here, at 902 Achilles Street, Giddy and Jewel found four families living sharing a kitchen. One of the mothers was in when they visited and she and Jewel exchanged a look of empathy.

> 'Don't be sad about us,' said the Coloured woman. 'We are moving where they say things will be better, there in Eersterus. You will like this place, it has a nice feel, my dear.'
>
> Jewel thanked her and wished her well, and then gently pulled Giddy by the sleeve. Outside, passing under the tree, she whispered to him,
>
> 'I don't know if I can go through with this. It's not the house, it's moving the people who live there.'
>
> 'Look at it this way. They have no choice but to move. The people here are tenants in a place where they don't have any basic amenities. Maybe the woman is right and Eersterus will have lights and water. But we aren't evicting her, the government is. Whether we take the house or someone else won't change what happens to those families back there. It's the way apartheid makes dominoes out of people.'
>
> 'We condone that if we move here,' said Jewel.

Over time, Jewel became reconciled to the idea. Summer eased into its last days as she, Giddy and their son settled in to the house Giddy had spent several months renovating. It had been a long journey to this patch of paradise that seemed to reach, with the purity of fire, from the earth to the sky. Here, Giddy and Jewel thought, it was as if they were living all under heaven.

Democracy, transformation and reconciliation

As a result of economic crisis, international pressure, internal opposition and the general unfeasibility of the apartheid scheme, elements of the legislative system were gradually eroded or abandoned from the late 1980s through to the 1990s. Eventually, various structures were set in place to transform South Africa into a more equitable multicultural society and after 1994 the new democratically elected government made a concerted effort to address the inequities and disadvantages of the past. True to form, the Chinese community was generally disregarded and remained relatively inconspicuous throughout the process. However, once the political tables had turned, the Chinese would, to a large degree, again find themselves in an anomalous position despite the political transition.

From the mid 1980s, the white National Party government began to make alterations to the constitutional structure of government and certain apartheid practices. Yet still disparities remained as the dominant white minority government clung to their privileged position to the detriment of the rest of society. Although the ensuing mass internal unrest was combated with draconian government restrictions and a nationwide state of emergency which amounted to 'legalized tyranny', ultimately the forces of the masses prevailed (Thompson 1990, pp. 235–42).

In 1990 new leadership in the National Party government took the initiative to break the stalemate and, along with the business sector, entered into negotiations with a range of stakeholders. In 1991 the cumbersome cornerstone of apartheid, which had been amended ten times during its four decades of existence, was repealed. This signalled a tangible milestone in an effort to desegregate South Africa. Other discriminatory legislation, which had been linked to the racial categorization of society, was also abolished, such as the Public Amenities Act, the Group Areas Act, the Mixed Marriages Act and the Immorality Act. By 1993 arrangements for a new constitution and transitional government were in place and in 1994 the first democratic elections in a single non-racial unitary state took place.

The new government, dominated by the African National Congress (ANC), was assigned the task of delivering benefits after the political transformation. The 'legacy of apartheid was harsh' (Ross 1999, p. 198), and in an effort to rectify the inequalities and discriminatory impacts of the past, it enacted a wide range of affirmative action policies. These related to issues ranging from land distribution to equity in employment and social services such as health care and education. According to the government, the blacks, Indians and coloureds qualified as beneficiaries of these policies, but the Chinese were excluded as they were not regarded as 'formally disadvantaged' (*Sunday Independent*, 1 Aug. 1999; The Chinese Association 2000, 2002). The community argued that under apartheid they were 'not white enough', and now, under the post-1994 dispensation, they are 'not black enough' (*Saturday Star*, 19 Jan. 2000), and therefore they were 'just as marginalized as they were under apartheid' (*Sunday Argus*, 22 Jan. 2000). Thus the ambivalence and ambiguity that underpinned governmental and societal attitudes towards the small South African Chinese community for over a century continue to persist. As the new democratically elected government continued to attempt to transform and reconcile this multicultural society, the Chinese remained in a liminal position of 'not quite belonging'.

When Accone was 15, he discovered Maxine Hong Kingston's book, *The Woman Warrior.* Its powerful subtitle – *Memoirs of a Girlhood among Ghosts* – resonated within him as the story of the Chinese in South Africa is one of a people always inhabiting a liminal space between acceptance and rejection, privilege and discrimination, freedom and oppression. The Chinese were and are ghost citizens inhabiting a grey zone; damned in the past to be classified non-white and seemingly fated in the future to be regarded as not previously disadvantaged. Home is here, at the tip of Africa, but also across the sea, as it was for their immigrant ancestors.

Briefly, around the time of the first universal franchise elections in South Africa in 1994, hopes flared up of a different position for the Chinese. Accone recalls:

> It is 27 April 1994. All around the country, people are lining up in orderly but serpentine queues outside polling stations, waiting to vote. Mrs Botha, the dervish in the shop of Mrs Leong, my bobo (grandmother), would be less happy today. But she is dead and today the National Party will begin going the same way. This is another country now, with new owners. 'Ah Nung,' my mother calls to me as we wait in line. 'Ah Nung, what do you think bobo would have had to say about today?'

Conclusion

Three distinct Chinas can be said to have sprung up in South Africa. First there is the Cantonese community of initial immigrants, now third- and fourth-generation South Africans who have diversified beyond small family-run businesses into the professions. Next is the Taiwanese community, many still involved as entrepreneurs and industrialists, many others in various professions. Last is the burgeoning presence of Chinese from the People's Republic of China, whose effect on trade and industry is likely to be considerable.

For constant and steadfast community presence, however, it is to the original Chinatown, in Commissioner Street, Johannesburg, that one must turn. Chinese have lived and conducted business here for more than 100 years. This 'old' Chinatown plans to add a new dimension as a tourist attraction. Plans have been submitted to the authorities to turn part of the street into a pedestrian mall, with a moon gate on either side of the proposed walkway. Those gates will not only be connecting with the past; they will be a gateway to the future too, pointing to the continuing contribution of Chinese to South Africa. But whether these gates will lead to a greater sense of belonging in the broad church of the multicultural, multiethnic, multilingual South African community is debatable.

Throughout their time in South Africa, the Chinese have been largely apolitical, undermining their official position under both old and new regimes. This is understandable in at least one vital respect. If politics is rooted in a sense of belonging, it is understandable why the Chinese have been politically uncommitted; simply put, they have never felt that they really belonged on this southern tip of Africa.

Note

1 This and other oral testimony used in this chapter formed part of the research for Darryl Accone's book (2004).

References

Accone, D. 2004, *All under Heaven: the Story of a Chinese Family in South Africa*, David Philip/New Africa Books, Cape Town.

Artikel 1858, *Grondwet van die Zuid-Afrikaansche Republiek*, Artikel 9.

Bhana, S. and Brain, J.B. 1990, *Setting Down Roots: Indian Immigration to South Africa, 1860–1911*, Witwatersrand University Press, Johannesburg.

CSS 1946–1954, *Population Census, 7 May 1946*, Central Statistics Service, Pretoria.

Dawson, R. 1967, *The Chinese Chameleon: an Analysis of European Conceptions of Chinese Civilization*, Oxford University Press, London.

Faber, P. and Van der Merwe, A. (eds) 2004, *Group Portrait South Africa*, Kwela Books, Johannesburg.

Harris, K.L. 1995, 'Chinese Merchants on the Rand, c.1850–1910', *South African Historical Journal*, vol. 33, pp. 155–68.

Harris, K.L. 1998, 'A History of the Chinese in South Africa to 1912', PhD thesis, Unisa, Pretoria.

Harris, K.L. 2004, 'Encouraged and Excluded: the Chinese at the Cape a Century Ago', in *The Historical Association of South Africa Conference*, University of Stellenbosch.

Horrell, M. 1963, *Legislation and Race Relations*, South African Institute of Race Relations, Johannesburg.

Horrell, M. 1978, *Laws Affecting Race Relations in South Africa*, South African Institute of Race Relations, Johannesburg.

Johnson, C.J. 1951, 'The Group Areas Act – Stage 1', *South African Law Journal*, vol. 68, p. 286.

Mackerras, C. 1989, *Western Images of China*, Oxford University Press, New York.

Pan, L. 1990, *Sons of the Yellow Emperor*, Kodansha Globe, London.

Ross, R. 1999, *A Concise History of South Africa*, Cambridge University Press, Cambridge.

Scher, D. 1993, 'The Consolidation of the Apartheid State', in B.J. Liebenberg and S.B. Spies (eds), *South Africa in the Twentieth Century*, Van Schaick, Pretoria.

South African Republic 1885, 'Law no. 3', in, *Statute Laws of the Transvaal.*

South African Republic 1898, 'Law no. 15: the Gold Law of the South African Republic', in *Laws of the Transvaal up to 1899*, South African Republic.

Spies, S.B. 1986, 'Reconstruction and Unification, 1902–1910', in T. Cameron and S.B. Spies (eds), *An Illustrated History of South Africa*, Jonathan Ball, Johannesburg.

The Chinese Association 2000, *Gauteng: Newsletters*, vol. August.

The Chinese Association 2002, *Gauteng: Newsletters*, vol. June, July, August.

Thompson, L. 1990, *A History of South Africa*, Yale University Press, New Haven.

Union of South Africa *c*.1920, *Union of South Africa Yearbook, 1910–1917.*

Worden, N. 1994, *The Making of Modern South Africa*, Oxford, Oxford.

12

Look Who's Talking: Migrating Narratives and Identity Construction

Amy Lee Wai-sum

Multiple Chineseness: voices from far and near

Although it is commonly iterated that the twenty-first century putatively belongs to China[1] in terms of its dynamic economic growth and political role it plays on the international stage, China has already enjoyed millennia of a colourful and rich history. Possessing one of the longest recorded histories, China and 'Chineseness' seem eternal, unquestionable and unquestioned. With a vast territory clearly demarcated on the map, and a large concentration of people clustered in cities as well as scattering throughout its rural regions, China has long served as an anchor to root Chinese to a common heritage. The history, the culture, the now uniform language and writing script, all seem to coalesce into a collective feeling of a people united as a single cultural entity.

With the revolution in international travelling and information technology propelling globalization, China as a geographic entity and, perhaps more importantly, a historical–cultural framework may no longer provide adequate containment of a contingent collective identity of Chineseness. Today, although the term 'Chinese' is still used to refer to a set of qualities and values, increasingly we are forced to confront the problematic of treating this adjective as a simple and transparent description, something that is collectively agreed and endorsed. Born and raised in Hong Kong, a Special Administrative Region[2] of China since 1997, I have numerous experiences of telling foreigners while travelling that I am 'from Hong Kong'. I also felt it necessary to qualify this by saying 'I am a Hong Kong Chinese'. Paradoxically, I had never been to mainland China in the first twenty-two years of my life, and still have not mastered the national language, and read English (a second language in SAR) more quickly than simplified Chinese characters, the official script of China today.

Chineseness, therefore, for a person in my situation, is an elusive and complex word embodying a range of, and sometimes even contradictory, feelings, affiliations, values, historical facts and meanings. Viewed from the margins in a place such as Hong Kong, with its future now firmly linked to China, the core constructs of Chineseness embodying the complexities of Hong Kong life are enormously intimate yet bewilderingly foreign. Perhaps it is the century-long political and cultural detachment from its 'motherland' due to its colonial heritage with its history of entrepreneurial capitalism steeped in the shadow of Westminster; but for someone positioned in liminality such as those in Hong Kong (or Macau) to understand the content of Chineseness, the near-yet-so-distant China is far from a fixed entity representing a clearly marked identity.

While the 'outside world' marvels at the dramatic and remarkable transformations China has undergone through its long history, for those living in the shadow of the mainland, the identity of Chineseness, on reflection, has never been unproblematic,[3] made more so by the tumultuous transformations China has undergone in the short period of what is termed 'modern China'. The question then becomes – if the core, if the foundational entity of Chineseness comprises a site of multiplicity, how do we conceptualize belonging, especially when identity is situated somewhere and somehow away from this indescribable Chinese core? The ambiguities of Chineseness point to the dilemma of contextualizing the Chinese diaspora.

Voices of remembrances

The second half of the twentieth century gave rise to a flourishing of voices from those living at the ideational margins, outside their ancestral 'homeland'. A gradual need for a stronger sense of self-awareness developed among émigrés, reflecting their different diasporic experiences. With the end of colonialism across the world, many émigrés stepped onto a postcolonial stage fashioned from their respective colonial encounters. Migrants in their host countries increasingly made their personal reflections of identity more audible. Literary expressions of memories affected an understanding of their identities and situations. These collectives of voices evidenced both a break with imposed and inflicted identities of colonial selves, with an equally substantial movement to negotiate identities in relation to their 'motherland'. Reflecting on their relationship to their ancestral homelands, migrants in the former colonies reconstructed themselves, often in the language of English or French, but certainly in the name of the mother(land). Root-finding and reidentification usually took the form of a deep submergence into a common pre-colonial and pre-separation history, and re-established this immersed or severed connection through a systematic tracking down of pre-separation history, or through a reappreciation of the significance of the motherland as a means to reidentify and remember themselves. Hong Kong was no exception, but in multiple mimetic ways began deploying Chineseness in alternative discourses that captured their cultural practices formed from shared memories of ruptured boundaries.

Those socially and politically marginalized from the Chinese centre emerged from their silence and voiced their personal stories against the background of a more open and receptive environment. Since the 1980s, a relatively more personal approach in writing can be found in literary writings by Chinese writers, both inside and outside the mainland. Many personal narratives during this period recounted the experience of the Cultural Revolution, placing the individual self alongside the collective historical social self in such a way as to understand the traumatic experiences of this period, as well as to secure a sense of individual identity in the face of the dislocation and unremembering associated with this traumatic time. There existed a parallel trend with the increasing urbanized readership. Root-seeking, in the sense of tracing one's familial ancestry and, perhaps more importantly, the reappreciation of Chinese heritage, spurred a powerful movement in the 1980s. A remembering process, however, was not simply a straightforward filling of memory gaps, but a process of reinterpreting memory creatively for the constructions of a multifaceted cultural identity.

Memory assumed the locus of this host of narratives embodying the personal, the historical, the political and the cultural threads which, when woven together, formed the various ways that linked the individual back to the motherland identity. For the postcolonial selves, a collective cultural memory provided a site of rejuvenation of the present selves. The 'mother culture', together with the motherland, lost in the period of colonization, staked a new presence in the postcolonial reworking of age-old narratives and beliefs. Survivors of political and social marginalization turned their personal memories into written records, which together formed an alternative picture of 'the collective experience'. This rendition of past memory served as a site for the individual to re-evaluate his/her relationship with the motherland, as well as giving the narrator a critical distance to reconsider his/her own identity.

For the migrants, connection with the motherland held a continuous though perhaps intangible presence in their life in the host country, manifested either visually through family photos, heirlooms, or verbally through the endlessly repeated family narratives, which very often were interwoven with stories of the meticulously kept traditions from the homeland. This memory-as-narrative in a variety of forms and media, a presence whose nature by definition depended on the loss of the 'real', offered a tool with which the diasporic souls reflected and possibly reclaimed their belonging to a mother culture which they might never have and had never seen.

While it is clearly impossible to generalize diasporic writings, or even to frame the various diasporas into well-defined fields, I propose here a seemingly common trend in many of the diasporic writings as the starting point of this discussion. The attempt to write the diasporic self is a journey through history, from present to past, and back to the present, a process of detection and interpretation. Through the creative incorporation of the past, the diasporic identity comes out as a hybrid entity, constructed on the site of the intersection of different historical, cultural and personal narratives. Thus, it is interesting to find that many narratives of the diasporic self – fictional or otherwise – are narratives containing allusions to a mythical past, but somehow surviving 'real' history while sustaining the present.[4]

This memory of a mythic past, long before the birth of those away from home, and far away from their current abodes, provided a potent element in what is popularly termed the Chinese diaspora, although the representative narrative has a different story to tell. While many Chinese have been forced by circumstances to leave their homeland, they are not slaves in the literal sense of the word. Still, like many Africans, they bring with them the treasured memory of their homeland, along with thoughts of return, but a return more glamorous than their departure, and ready to live the 'good life' once back in the homeland. The long journeys these hopeful Chinese made were always assumed to be temporary.[5] This assumption of a temporary journey imbued a particular feeling in the memories of the sojourners, in their almost fixated attitude towards the content of their memories. They were going to return, move back to a more comfortable existence of their original life.

This picture of an inadequate life waiting to be improved by the temporary journey to another country is a regular feature in many Chinese diasporic representations. San Francisco, a popular place of settlement for Chinese 'fortune seekers' in previous centuries, was referred to by the Chinese as the *jiu jin shan* [old golden hill], for both its literal and metaphorical meanings.[6] The desire to return home with new-found wealth and the uncertainty of whether that could be realized transformed memories of the homeland into sacred scripts, to be memorized and rehearsed in one's daily life, as if the power of memories would ensure one's ability to return. Unfortunately, many were unable to return. For those with a knowledge of Chinese history in the recent century, it is perhaps not surprising that many of the sojourners become permanent residents in other lands, although they continued to circulate their personal memories and collective narratives among the younger generations, for whom this 'motherland' had never been a reality.

These tales of belonging, originally a symbol of these sojourners' identity, became something entirely different for the next generation who had no personal knowledge of the motherland or the mother culture. They became folk tales and myths marking a double loss between the generations. For the sojourners whose chance of a return became increasingly remote, it was a loss of an identity which at one time was at the centre of their daily lives in the homeland. In recent decades especially, China has undergone such far-reaching and foundation-shaking changes that it was no longer possible to call it the same 'home' that the people had left. For the generations born in the host country, China was more a symbolic loss of a root which many could never reclaim. The very act of having these tales of 'once upon a time' and 'in a land faraway' being repeated in the domestic space only enhanced the rootlessness of the new generations, for even in their most intimate space, they were made to feel the distance between themselves and their immediate root, and from their parents who once belonged to a home country and who probably insisted on the possibility of returning some day.

The study of emigrant parents' memories of their cherished and perhaps embroidered past reveals that memory is also very much about forgetting. Oppressed women's memories of a time and place of strong patriarchs maintaining strict life routines; memories of a golden period when rigid hierarchies gave rise to a stable order; or memories of a land filled with inexplicable wonders served as powerful reminders of the 'good old days'. Yet at the same time, memories were mental creations emerging from the desperate need to claim a 'home' when the body exists in a faraway locale. Although the reliability of memories and the very fabric of which they are made are themselves intriguing topics for research, the aim of this discussion is not to contest the validity of these memory-narratives of the Chinese diaspora, but to take them as they are and examine in what ways they are negotiated for the storyteller and, in particular, with the state of belonging or unbelonging. Memory, in its immediacy and its infinite stretchability, in its individual specificity as well as its possible collective generality, plays many roles in the unfolding drama of human identification.

Women's memories and memories of women

In the opening section of Maxine Hong Kingston's *The Woman Warrior* (1975),[7] which is entitled 'No Name Woman', Brave Orchid says to her teenage daughter Maxine, who is about to menstruate, that she is going to tell her a story, but that she 'must not tell anyone' (Kingston 1975, p. 17), not even, or especially not, Maxine's father, for he knows the story and has vowed not to mention it within the family. This is one of the examples of the curious logic appearing in many places in the book, and not surprisingly, in the genre of Asian-American narratives. Here was a mother about to tell her teenage daughter a cautionary tale to accompany her daughter's stepping into puberty. The daughter's entrance into the threshold of womanhood was seen to be an important but threatening event, so much so that the mother felt it her duty to pass on an important warning to her daughter – but a warning which was exclusive to the girl, not to be shared with other members of the family. The air of secrecy surrounding the telling of this anecdote was such that one wonders what the daughter was supposed to do. When one examines the actual words of the mother, it is at once noticed that her 'story' was mythic. Brave Orchid related a story of an unnamed aunt, about the absence of the husband, then the pregnancy of this aunt, and the villagers' raid on their house. The cautionary tale ends with the aunt's suicide after the birth of the baby girl. The last sentence Brave Orchid uttered was that 'The villagers are watchful' (Kingston 1975, p. 13). What was the moral of this cautionary tale when mother and daughter were now thousands of miles away from the villagers?

As a reproving tale, this secret story failed as it did not contain any clear indication of what the teenage Maxine should not do. There were facts enough in the tale, the absence of the husband, the growth of the aunt's belly, and, of course, the horrible vengeance expressed by the villagers over the aunt. But the cause and effect connections were missing and Maxine was discouraged from asking questions. The story also did not seem to fare any better as a tool of communication between mother and daughter. The story did not lead to any enlightenment for the daughter and it pre-empted any possibility of effective communication by the mother's repeated prohibition of voicing: 'Don't let your father know what I told you' (Kingston 1975, p. 13). The mother was not even interested to know how the daughter understood this tale. Although the telling and the content of the narrative may have seemed to suggest an exclusive female space of private communication, it actually began and ended with the ultimate patriarchal stricture of discommunication and subservience.

This pattern of the private exchange between a mother and a daughter was in fact a general pattern found in many similar Asian-American writings. In the narrative space, the women talk, exchange advice, opinions and sometimes personal feelings, in the forefront of the narrative, although the presence of patriarchal control was never entirely unnoticed. The space where mothers and daughters talk was out of the sight and the hearing of the patriarchs because it dealt with the forbidden, the mysterious, the guilty, the shameful, all mixed together in the memories carried by the mother. Memories in this sense are female, and so is the narrative that records such events and unfolds in front of the readers. But this feminine quality of memory is not only a private presence; it has a more collective function in Chinese society(ies) as well. Chinese women have traditionally been given the task of memorizing the customs and ceremonies to be performed in the domestic space.[8] Women have to remember both private and collective narratives to ensure that they are perpetuated into the next generations.

Women's memories form the basic structure of Maxine Hong Kingston's *The Woman Warrior* (1975) and Amy Tan's *The Hundred Secret Senses* (1995). In *The Woman Warrior*, subtitled 'Memoirs of a Girlhood among Ghosts', it was not only the mother who imparted memories and life experiences from the mainland to the American-born daughter, but the girl's first personal narrative began with her own personal memory, ending at a point of reflection on the past. Between the beginning of the memoir, when Brave Orchid commanded 'you must not tell anyone' (Kingston 1975, p. 13) and the end of the book when Maxine the (adult) narrator commented on the story of Ts'ai Yen, authentic and embellished women's experiences present a flow of mother's recounting and daughter's responding. Mother and daughter negotiate their relationship with one another through their mutual responses to each other's memories. The dialogical framework between these two females, when read in a particular way, provides a meaningful exchange between different histories, cultures, and valuation of identity, slowly percolating to a convergence at the end.

The matrix of the intergenerational communication and cross-cultural translation of experience in *The Woman Warrior* finds quite a different form and style of existence in *The Hundred Secret Senses*. The binary of mother and daughter is replaced by sisterhood, although Olivia and Kwan were very unusual sisters, and the interaction between two generations gave way to a narrative of multi-life reincarnation through one of the most exciting periods in modern Chinese history. While Brave Orchid's cautionary tale may have been practical advice from one generation to the next, Kwan's fantastic tales of reincarnation seem beyond any application to the exigencies of life in contemporary America. In this sense, Kwan's 'memories' from her different lives were retold with the intention of awakening Olivia to her 'real' identity. The fictional discourse of Tan's *The Hundred Secret Senses* was thus much more obviously motivated to portray 'the discovery of the true (Chinese) self' in a fantastic but interestingly accessible multicultural narrative of memories.

These two texts of 'memories' present interesting examples of how the main character in the story, a second-generation American-born Chinese woman, negotiates between her mother's memories and her own American reality to build for herself an identity in the new society. Tan and Kingston, however, demonstrated in the respective narratives two different strategies for dealing with memory flows from one generation to the next. While Tan's more self-professed fictional narrative offered a route towards self (re)discovery of the Chinese 'soul' at the end of the journey taken by the American-born Olivia, Kingston's protagonist emerged at the end of the journey possessing a method for reading identity rather than the 'facts' of her identity. Tan's Olivia learned to retrieve and read her memories from previous incarnations and created a translated (re)reading of the original Chinese texts which empowered the liminal status of a Chinese woman born in America. The understanding of identity, if it comes, is a formidable translation, not of facts, but of meaning.

Storytelling as mother–daughter dialogue

Admittedly, *The Woman Warrior* opened with a gap, a secret, an absence forbidden to be filled. Not only was the first episode of this memoir about a 'no name woman', but it comprised a story one must not tell, a life that can be summed up in four lines. But very quickly this command of silence, like many other episodes of personal and collective memories recorded in the book, was transformed into something different. Immediately after Brave Orchid related the fate of the aunt – 'as if she had never been born' (Kingston 1975, p. 11) – Maxine, the young narrator, proceeded to expand the story and imagine a myriad of possibilities omitted from the bland cautionary tale. Although the teenage daughter regretted that she 'had to figure out how the invisible world the emigrants built around our childhoods fits in solid America' (Kingston 1975, p. 13), Brave Orchid had, by relating her the story, consciously or unconsciously provided an example of what she can do. The visions of her aunt who 'could not have been the lone romantic' (Kingston 1975, p. 14), who 'was the precious only daughter' (Kingston 1975, p. 17), who 'looked at a man because she liked the way the hair was tucked behind his ears' (Kingston 1975, p. 15), and who 'kept rollicking company' (Kingston 1975, p. 16) were but possibilities enriched by Brave Orchid's simply framed memory.

By imagining different details to fill in the gaps of the cautionary tale offered by her mother, Maxine made the story of the aunt whose name has been denied a site of freedom and liberation into a point where an identity can be constructed according to the desires of the subject. Rather than being a fixed subject with a clearly identifiable name, the story of the no-name aunt was turned into a celebration of the multiple personalities of the aunt, and finally memories that Maxine was able to embrace and cherish. By giving voice to the aunt's life, Maxine the storyteller devoted 'pages of paper to her' (Kingston 1975, p. 22), elevating her life into a myriad of models of femininity, each embracing a different meaning. Perhaps it was a need borne from her status as the first-generation American born in her family; or perhaps it was a survival skill the immigrant mother passed on to the daughter. What the narrator had done was to translate what looked like a factual warning of silence into a flexible and creative tale. In this complex space of the cultural dislocation, where mother–daughter (mis-)communication formed part of everyday life, translation proved itself to be an important means of understanding and a strategy to create meaning out of the originary crucible of the mother–daughter relation – (mis-)communication, here exacerbated by migration.

Migration is not simply a physical change of location, but for those involved it engenders psychological movement as well. It is through the demands of migration that migrants find they must refashion memories and meaning-making from the old to the new environment. Brave Orchid burdened herself with a static image of Chinese life and confined herself to a stagnant existence by holding on to the literal facts of her memories in mainland China. She herself remarked that '[t]he difference between mad people and sane people, is that sane people have variety when they talk-story. Mad people have only one story that they talk over and over' (Kingston 1975, p. 143). The seemingly rigid migrant mother, however, did not appear to be resolutely rigid. Brave Orchid's observation suggested that Maxine's ability to create meaning out of the seemingly irrelevant memories of the mother echoed her mother's ability, demonstrated in the memories she related and how they were related. Instead of a fractious miscommunication, mother and daughter actually engaged in a cultural and linguistic creative translation of memories when they conversed.

The much discussed episode of 'White Tigers' offers a telling example of translations creating understanding. While some may agree with Frank

Chin that the narrative is 'historical facts and legendary heroes and touchstones violated beyond recognition' (Wong 1999, p. 27), it is also possible to consider the incorporation of these legendary heroes and stories in the light of an engendered and ethnically informed discussion. Maxine, nurtured by her daily chanting of the Mu Lan song, which sings of the heroic deeds of this Chinese woman, engaged in daydreams like this one:

> The call would come from a bird that flew over our roof. In the brush drawings it looks like the ideograph for 'human', two black wings. The bird would cross the sun and lift into the mountains (which look like the ideograph 'mountain'), there parting the mist briefly that swirled opaque again. I would be a little girl of seven the day I followed the bird away into the mountains. (Kingston 1975, p. 26)

This daydream of the American-born Maxine entailed a cultural hybrid constructed from various memories. The bird, which is an important component of the legendary life of the historical Chinese hero Yue Fei, was incorporated into Maxine's dream, as the guide to take the girl to a life of heroism similar to that of the Southern Song hero. Moreover, the use of an animal to lead a child destined for an unusual life supplied a standard motif in popular kung fu movies. Thus, the American-born girl's dream was a melange of remembered Chinese history and popular cultural elements. Mother's Chinese memory and knowledge also translated into the daughter's unconscious and formed part of her cross-cultural or hybrid identity.

This cross-cultural rereading and reinterpretation runs throughout the American daydream of the daughter. As part of her training, words had to be inscribed on her body:

> My father first brushed the words in ink, and they fluttered down my back row after row. Then he began cutting; to make fine lines and points he used thin blades, for the stems large blades.... The list of grievances went on and on. If an enemy should flay me, the light would shine through my skin like lace. (Kingston 1975, p. 38)

Once again, hybridity informed the episode resulting from the mother's memory and the daughter's infusion in American culture. The inscription on the back of Yue Fei reads *jing zhong bao guo*, which means 'serve the country loyally'. But in the daydream of Maxine, inspired by the chanting of Mu Lan's song, the words to be carved on her body signify more – the action of 'serving' the country (*bao* in Chinese) turned into 'reporting' (same Chinese character with a different meaning). Instead of serving and repaying the mother country by her efforts, Maxine the imagined heroine related the vengeance of numerous silent people and thus provided voice to these silent people by telling their stories.

The power of the remembered words: storytelling

Storytelling serves as the point of convergence, weaving together the various strands in this autobiographical novel of memory and cultural differences. The collection began with Brave Orchid's recounting of the no-name aunt's story, fulfilling her maternal duty to warn her daughter about the dangers of her female body; yet at the same time breaking the taboo by not keeping quiet. While she safeguarded this secret by silencing Maxine, her terse storytelling ironically fuelled Maxine's curiosity and imagination, generating even inquisitiveness. These stories embraced the tools of communication mother and daughter used to transcend the cultural, historical, geographical and generational fissure between them. The mother wove her knowledge and memory into stories, whereas the daughter interpreted and responded by creating further stories constructed from the merging of what she remembered and from her American reality.

As in the case of 'White Tigers', the American-born Chinese Maxine found it difficult to choose between the reality of her daily life and the stories of a faraway land told by Brave Orchid. What resulted was a Hua Mu Lan (Fa Mu Lan in Kingston's text) figure that was intelligent, patriotic, self-assertive and heroic. Like Brave Orchid, Maxine was nurtured by the traditional stories and memories from China, but she was also in touch with the feminine self-awareness which is often considered a distinct Western feature absent in the Chinese. The 'report' carved on the back of the self-fashioned heroine of Maxine's dream brings up a very contemporary issue. With her newly gained individual voice, the greatest service that she can provide to her people is the service of voice. Thus row after row of names were carved on her back, symbolizing her responsibility to embody the stories of these silent people. Written on her body, these unknown biographies found substance through the process of translation – both linguistic and cultural.

Interestingly, this newly fashioned hybrid identity of Maxine as the translator and storyteller is not represented as the opposite of what Chinese women are deemed to be. The insight of this autobiographical narrative was not American versus Chinese. Rather it was the celebration of the fluidity of the seemingly rigid categories usually held. Although

Brave Orchid appears to be the stern mother whose job was to uphold the patriarchal order which was deemed an important basic structure of the Chinese society, she was portrayed increasingly as an independent, intelligent and empowered woman not unlike, and sometimes even more so than, the ideal held in Maxine's America. In fact, the unfolding of the mother's story revealed that female self-respect was not restricted to a particular time or culture, but was a common quality pertaining to the valuation of the self.

The in-between: shaman and translator

As if to right the misconception that Brave Orchid was the opposite of the independent American spirit Maxine aspired to, and to bridge the gap between the mother and daughter, Brave Orchid's personal memories highlighted the importance of the woman's name (identity) and induced Maxine to revere other women's names and comradeship as a response. In the episode of 'Shaman', Brave Orchid's memory of her venture to the medical college commenced with the detail of her name being recognized. On arrival at the dormitory, she 'spotted the name she had written on her application pinned to a headboard' (Kingston 1975, p. 60) before she quietly settled into the community of other female doctors. Even in the life and death situation when she stayed a night in the haunted room, the chanting of her name by her fellow classmates offered the final means of securing her safety and sanity, reaffirming her identity. Her name, as chanted by the classmates, 'Come home, come home, Brave Orchid, who has fought the ghosts and won.... Come back, Doctor Brave Orchid, be unafraid' (Kingston 1975, p. 69) was the equivalence of her presence.

This respect shown to a woman's name as a personal mark of presence proved a very powerful connection between Brave Orchid and her daughter, despite the difference in generation and the culture they grew up in. If not the best, it still provided an exemplary example of female power in China, and a counter-example to the stereotype of submissive and silent Chinese women, too weak and ignorant to fend for themselves. Even in Brave Orchid's memory of buying a slave girl at a market back in China, the spontaneous but secret understanding the mistress and maid held pointed out that female camaraderie of a kind was present in the oppressive patriarchal Chinese society. After the transaction, Brave Orchid congratulated the slave girl on her quick wit: 'we fooled them very well' (Kingston 1975, p. 78). The employment of 'we' sealed both parties in a moment of mutual respect and understanding, seldom mentioned among women from different backgrounds.

Immersed in her mother's recounting of personal memories in China, although Maxine had no way of knowing whether they were authentic records of what really transpired, or how to 'separate what is peculiar to childhood, to poverty, insanities, one family, your mother who marked your growing with stories, from what is Chinese' (Kingston 1975, p. 13), it does not matter. Authentic or not, personal or collective, the mother's stories were narratives told to express wishes, values, beliefs and all that she was, and told to someone from whom she wants a response. Maxine's confusion, bitterness, fear and imaginative interpretation shepherded the mother and daughter relationship through different stages, but finally coalesced in collusion. Only at the conclusion of the narrative journey, in the last episode, Maxine realized her mother and herself had always shared the same understanding, although not using the same language. She concluded the narrative by saying: 'Here is a story my mother told me, not when I was young, but recently, when I told her I also am a story-talker. The beginning is hers, the ending, mine' (Kingston 1975, p. 184).

Mother and daughter engaged in a collaboration which required imaginative understanding of the many facets of their memories and experiences. Just as Ts'ai Yen's 'Eighteen Stanzas for a Barbarian Reed Pipe' worked for the Chinese and their instruments, Brave Orchid's memories of a faraway land and experience also aided her foreign-born daughter when she translated the memories into a common frame of belonging which united mother and daughter. If translation of memories is the penultimate answer to the issue of how to belong, this type of translation assumed a very different turn in Amy Tan's *The Hundred Secret Senses*. Her rendering of China's Taiping Rebellion and its connection to present American society suggested an infinitely playful translation of collective memories, perhaps because she believed that the essence of belonging was automatically there at the heart of the diaspora. One needed only to seek to find it buried inside.

Compared to Brave Orchid and Maxine, Olivia and Kwan shared no generation gap although 12 years separated the two half-sisters. What lay between them, ironically, was not just the early years of separation when Kwan was in the mainland and Olivia born in a conventional middle-class Chinese-American family, but also Kwan's knowledge of the yin world[9] and a personal memory of the Taiping Rebellion. The bond uniting Olivia and Kwan was much more complicated as revealed towards the end of the novel. Not only had the two gone through life together for a lifetime, but also through several reincarnations. While Olivia was at another critical point of her life – divorce from her husband Simon – Kwan took matters into her hands and reminded her: 'I have something must tell you, very important news. This morning I talk to Lao Lu. We decide: You and Simon shouldn't get divorce' (Tan 1995, p. 22). Lao Lu belongs to Kwan's world of previous reincarnations and she continued saying to Olivia '[y]ou remember him', hoping that Olivia would rediscover their shared world of memories.

Reincarnation as translation

Kwan's memories of her several lives, which she attempted to awaken in Olivia throughout their present life, became an obvious tool built into the novel in order to reclaim Olivia's 'real' identity. Different from most Asian-American narratives of root finding, Kwan and Olivia's roots go a long way back and the drama of memory and remembering was not lost in its transference through reincarnations. Although some critics remark that Kwan's characterization and her memories are farcical, read another way the idea behind the 'literal facts' offered in the novel presented the view that a person's essential identity can survive through lives and reincarnations. Identity, in this perspective, was knowable and traceable, and with this came the assurance of a sense of belonging. Olivia was one of the many lost souls in contemporary American society; she did not know her father, her unsettled mother enjoyed a series of boyfriends, her own marriage lay in ruins through suspicion and paranoia, and she lacked any knowledge of her 'roots' beyond her Chinese father's name, which turned out to be stolen. She was a person deeply in need of a sense of identity and thus belonging.

Even before setting off for Changmian village in China, Olivia's journey of rediscovering herself had already begun. She needed to decide what name to use, now that she is about to divorce. Kwan's memories, and her insistence that Olivia should join her in remembering, afforded a practical tool which pushed Olivia to reflection and a gradual realization of her identity: 'As I think more about my name, I realize I've never had any sort of identity that suited me, not since I was five' (Kingston 1975, pp. 140–1). As she tried to resume her Chinese ancestry – Olivia Yee – it sounds 'alien' to her, because she did not feel Chinese. Thus she concluded: 'Being forced to grow up with Kwan was probably one of the reasons I never knew who I was or wanted to become. She was a role model for multiple personalities' (Kingston 1975, p. 141). This is in fact more true than Olivia understood, for Kwan was indeed comprised of multiple selves in the history of her memories, as is Olivia, although she has to be reminded. The trip to the origin – Changmian – provided an experience of time and space travel, back to the realm of the memories where they belonged.

The journey back(wards) via memories was indeed required, especially when Olivia realized that even Jack Yee, the name she used to refer to her father her entire life, was a stolen name and her fate a stolen fate. Her father migrated to America only because he stole a jacket from a drunkard. Her attachment to China came to nothing but a story about her father who had stolen another person's jacket and name and ultimately fate. Once the long-held family myth was revealed to be nothing but a lie, Olivia lost her orientation with the exception of Kwan. When her own memories proved to be implanted, she relied on Kwan and her memories to come to an understanding of her roots. As Olivia claims:

> I absorbed her language through my pores while I was sleeping. She pushed her Chinese secrets into my brain and changed how I thought about the world. Soon I was even having nightmares in Chinese. (Kingston 1975, p. 11)

Exaggerated as it sounds, Kwan's memories sustained Olivia throughout her teenage and adult life, and they were to be the source from which the adult Olivia located her 'real' identity.

Changmian, the source from where Olivia's memory was refreshed, was the mythic site where memories originated. Changmian was not portrayed as a straightforward record of history; rather it embodied uncertainty and fluidity, qualities which strengthened cultural translations. The name itself, Changmian, denotes 'long sleep' or 'long cotton yarn' when translated into Mandarin, although both are appropriate signifiers of the place. While the 'long sleep' may have indicated its status in Olivia's mind concerning her previous lives, the 'long cotton yarn' signified an apt description of the entire tale centring on the place. In fact, throughout their time together, before her actual visit to Changmian, Olivia treated Kwan's stories told from memory as nothing but a tall story.

This was no ordinary story though, but one which wielded immense power of manipulation that became a tool for survival. Kwan told Olivia of the curse of Changmian, how everyone had been killed in the village so that stories flowed about Changmian being 'a village of ghosts' (Kingston 1975, p. 305). No one knew what happened to the villagers and why people reappeared in Changmian as if nothing had occurred. Olivia proposed that 'I think Changmian became a village of liars. They *let* people think they were ghosts. Less trouble than going to the caves during future wars' (Kingston 1975, p. 305). Liars or not, the yarn of Changmian manifested the possibilities potential in a creative interpretation of memories.

It did not matter whether Kwan remembered the facts or not, as long as what she remembered could be creatively interpreted.

The trip to Changmian not only proved the phantasmic episodes Kwan recalls from her 'previous lives' to be historical facts, but also revealed how they were Olivia's memories as well. When finally Kwan asked her half-sister, 'you remember how we die?' (Kingston 1975, p. 303), Olivia recalled what she 'always thought was a dream' (Kingston 1975, p. 303) but in fact were flashes of memory from her previous lives. In the land of Changmian, Olivia awoke from her long sleep and brought back her memories, revealing to her the roots of her identity in the Chinese land and legends. When she single-handedly unearthed the duck eggs buried in their previous lives, Olivia knew that she irrevocably touched her roots and knew that she belonged. Although the eggs crumbled, 'disintegrating into gray chalk', Olivia no longer worried as she had regained the essence of her belonging and, more importantly, that she would never feel lost again.

This new identity resided in her after she returned to her American life and discovered herself pregnant by Simon (who was allegedly sterile). She understood the conception of the baby girl as a consequence of the disappearance of Kwan, and took Kwan's surname for the girl – 'What's a family name if not a claim to being connected in the future to someone from the past?' (Kingston 1975, p. 320) – in recognition of Kwan's role in her self-discovery. Having a sense of belonging was knowing that one was connected to someone in the past. Olivia's understanding of belongingness, interestingly, was not an attachment to the land, or to objects located in a specific time or place. At the end of the narrative, she remarked: 'I think Kwan intended to show me the world is not a place but the vastness of the soul' (Kingston 1975, p. 320). In other words, feeling a sense of belonging was not dependent on possessing heirlooms or official records of familial links, rather it was a matter of the soul connecting to other souls.

Conclusion

The Woman Warrior and *The Hundred Secret Senses* constructed narratives as a network of the various functions of memories in facilitating the negotiation of a sense of self for the individuals in the respective stories. Although by definition memories are a record of lived experience and happenings, themselves the fabrics from which history is made, memories as used in written narratives can be manipulated playfully, as in the quasi-authentic transliteration of Amy Tan's detailing of various Chinese concepts and words, or in Kingston's large-scale parodying of famous legends and figures in Chinese history for contemporary consciousness. Yet the playfulness of the constructed memory does not detract from the value of the narrative as it reveals the individual strategies narrators adopt to handle their relationship with the people and society in which they are immersed.

While Olivia's physical journey to China closed with a (re)awakening of the deeply buried 'Chineseness' within herself as Kwan disappeared into the secretive hills of Changmian, Tan's narrative portrays a harmonious merging of the Chinese and the American qualities into a comfortable new ethnic identity. The numerous descriptions of the surreal Changmian fail to provide a convincing image of what authentic Chineseness is, rather it offers a site which symbolizes a wealth of ideational possibilities. This kind of closure may be comforting, especially when recalling the instant sense of identification that Jing-mei in *Joy Luck Club* finds when putting her feet on Chinese soil, but China and thus Chineseness are far too heterogeneous to inhere an essentialized identity, made especially problematic across time and space.

Kingston, on the other hand, admits to modification of traditional Chinese myths and legends into a unique rendering of postmodern gender and ethnic consciousness parodied in her autobiographical fiction. Knowledge of myths and legends by themselves was insufficient to create a sense of belonging, rather a personal interpretation and translation of such collective memories into a comprehensible narrative rendered intimacy and attachment. What Brave Orchid bequeathed to her foreign-born daughter was the ability to translate and sustain memories. Belonging did not mean being rooted to a particular place or life; rather belonging depended on the translatability of memories. Maxine the adult storytalker inherited her mother's memories and translated them just as Ts'ai Yen merged the experiences and memories of two cultures.

The human faculty of memory is fallible. Yet this quality makes memories infinitely manipulable. We have witnessed in two autobiographical–fictional narratives how memories, in all their different enactments and degrees of authenticity, have served as a primary tool for individuals to negotiate belongingness from the margins. Whether as a site map for travel book reference, or as a flexible field of interpretation, memories have proved elusive but inescapable. Memories are our keys to becoming and ultimately to belonging. In their own way, they have provided a bridge for me from Hong Kong to the motherland.

Notes

1 China, as used here, refers to the People's Republic of China (PRC), generally regarded as the 'official' China. To people in my part of the world (Hong Kong),

PRC is usually referred to as the mainland, or, the motherland. From 1 July 1997, Hong Kong has been officially a part of China, a Special Administrative Region (SAR) which enjoys a high degree of autonomy in its political and cultural lives.

2 Hong Kong was made into a British colony by the 1842 Treaty of Nanking, after the Opium War. In 1984, the Chinese and the British governments issued the Joint Declaration about the return of Hong Kong to Chinese sovereignty in 1997, and to still enjoy a high degree of autonomy under the one-country two-system scheme.

3 The People's Republic of China covers a vast territory with a population of more than 1.3 billion, composed of 56 ethnic groups.

4 Although this chapter is not a discussion of the African diaspora, it is still relevant to mention one of the common features found in different diasporic writings. The discovery of an intergenerational narrative, sometimes going back to a mythical time unknown, can be found in many African diasporic writings such as in the works of Toni Morrison, Alice Walker, Gloria Naylor and Maryse Conde.

5 Large-scale migrations of the Chinese from the mainland had been intended to be temporary, a matter of seeking better job opportunities in the hope of saving enough money to build a better life back home. Thus even after a long time these Chinese people from different parts of China still maintained the same habits and customs of their home province, and did not adapt the so-called Hong Kong way or sojourners' mentality.

6 San Francisco has been referred to as *jiu jin shan* in Chinese, which means the old golden hill. After the gold had been exhausted, it became the 'old' gold hill to the Chinese.

7 Published to enormous popularity and critical acclaim, Kingston's book aroused almost unprecedented discussion among Asian-American writing concerning its genre. It was put in the category of non-fiction, and thus many take it as an authentic autobiography; although many have contested its validity as faithful documentation of real happenings in previous times. (Refer to Wong 1999.)

8 Domestic ceremonies and rituals in the Chinese family are mainly the responsibility of the women of the house. Although in some cases, the master of the house will preside over the rituals, the person who has to remember all the details concerning the preparation is always the woman.

9 The 'yin' and 'yang' are opposite qualities which keep each other at a perfect balance in the Chinese culture. 'Yin' can be used to represent the feminine, the hidden, and in general the not-often-seen side of things. In this case, the yin world is the underworld, the world of the dead.

References

Kingston, M.H. 1975, *The Woman Warrior: Memoirs of a Girlhood among Ghosts*, Picador, London.

Tan, A. 1995, *The Hundred Secret Senses*, Flamingo, London.

Wong, C.S.L. (ed.) 1999, *The Woman Warrior: a Casebook*, Oxford University Press, New York.

13

In Love with Music: Memory, Identity and Music in Hong Kong's Diasporic Films

Esther M.K. Cheung

Music, film and diaspora

James Clifford's essay 'Diasporas' (1994), which discusses the need to move from the 'ideal type' of 'diaspora' to non-Jewish kinds of migratory experiences, casts significant implications on the study of Chinese diasporas. We can follow this stance to assert that 'diaspora' as an analytical category must be referred to in the plural form and with a lower-case 'd'. In many instances, while such broader usage then implies that the term is more or less interchangeably used with what is 'migratory', it normally does not include the more individually based and politically motivated types of movement such as forced and self-imposed exiles. As exile often refers to 'banishment for a particular offense, with a prohibition of return' (Naficy 2001, p. 11), the migratory experiences explored in this chapter are closer to what is preferably called the 'diasporic' ones. Although the feelings of homesickness, loss and displacement are common to both the exilic and diasporic experiences, this essay concerns itself more with a 'fluid, deterritorialized mobile mechanism of national affiliation' (Lu 2001, p. 276) among displaced Chinese people. Such diasporic experiences are primarily preoccupied with what Benedict Anderson calls 'the horizontal comradeship' (1982, p. 7), as a kind of multi-sited cultural imaginary against the norms of nation states.

In this chapter, at least two major patterns of Chinese diasporas, among others, will be discussed, both of which focus on Hong Kong as the focal location of dispersal and gathering. The first pattern is characterized by the dispersal of Chinese people to Hong Kong due to political upheavals and economic instability in the mainland. Ever since Hong Kong became a British colony, migration from China has been 'an integral part of Hong Kong's development' (Skeldon 1994, p. 21). The disruptions and instabilities caused by the Sino-Japanese War, the Second World War, and the change of sovereignty in China in 1949 created massive population flows from mainland China to the then colonial city. During these decades, Hong Kong became a place of exile, composed of people fleeing from either a war-torn China or a communist regime. Ronald Skeldon describes these Chinese people in Hong Kong as 'exiles *in* China' with a 'refugee mentality' (1994, p. 8). The second type concerns the emigration of Chinese people out of Hong Kong to the rest of the world since the 1980s. This strand is tied closely with, but not restricted to, the 1997 handover which at one time caused Hong Kong people's anxiety about the capitalistic city's reintegration with a communist regime. In such cases, Hong Kong is indeed aptly situated in the 'international migration system' (1994, p. 121). This focus on Hong Kong does not suggest that the Chinese diasporas can be reduced or restricted to examples of these kinds; what intrigues us is the crucial role Hong Kong plays in the Chinese diasporic experiences. The phenomenon shows that Hong Kong can be regarded as a space of flows which is more complicated than merely a space through which human beings move in and out. As Arjun Appadurai's (1990) well-known five-scape model suggests, disjuncture and difference in the global system are created by the cross-border travels of humans, media images, ideologies and capitals. Films from contemporary Hong Kong cinema, which have clearly captured the dynamic flows of this spatially mobile city, have picked up the theme of diaspora as a favourable topic of exploration (see Cheung and Chu 2004 for their discussions of the Hong Kong diasporic cinema; Lu 2001; Marchetti 1998). The study of the Chinese diasporic experience, therefore, will not be complete without the examination of how the flows of people are intricately tied with other kinds of cultural landscapes that Appadurai discusses. In this essay, the ethnoscape of the global system will be explored in accordance with what I would call the 'musical landscape' which moves across geopolitical boundaries. While diaspora is intimately associated with the development of a cosmopolitan consciousness, a study of Hong Kong films will enable us to explore how a sense of belongingness is negotiated by the flows of different cultural artefacts in a transnational context.

Music is always an integral part of film as in the case of the use of background music in film. In this chapter, however, the link between music and film is not to be understood in this formalistic relation; instead, what is at issue is how music, particularly popular music, is represented in our selected films as playing a significant role in shaping collective memory among people in diaspora. This kind of collective memory cemented by musical affect is often in a contradictory relationship with the cosmopolitan dimension of the diaspora discourse. From the two chosen films, Ann Hui's *Song of Exile* (1990) (hereafter called *Exile*) and Peter Chan's *Comrades, Almost a Love Story* (1996) (hereafter called *Comrades*), it is interesting to note that popular music that people consume is also a medium that ties their love together. To twist the argument slightly, I would venture to say that people in diaspora do not so much fall in love with each other as to fall in love with the musical medium itself – with the sounds of music. This is, of course, not a twisted argument to de-emphasize the importance of agency. On the contrary, the intimate relationship between pop music and collective memory illuminates the power of the affect of music. In an essay debating musical value judgments, Simon Frith (1987) argues that music, whether it is pop or classical, creates and constructs people rather than expresses or reflects what people are like. He describes this as the 'cultural placing of the individual in the social' (1987, p. 139). The best example, in his view, can be found in the relationship between music and the constructions of collective identities:

> The role of music is usually related to youth and youth culture, but it seems equally important to the ways in which ethnic groups in both Britain and the United States have forged particular cultural identities.... In all these cases music can stand for, symbolize and offer the immediate experience of collective identity. Other cultural forms – painting, literature, design – can articulate and show off shared values and pride, but only music can make you feel them. (Frith 1987, pp. 139–40)

In fact theoretically this kind of 'cultural placing of the individual in the social' by way of musical mediation can be analysed with regard to two opposite theses: the manipulation/domination thesis vis-à-vis the appropriation/reception thesis. For the critics who support the manipulation thesis, popular music, like other commodities of the culture industries, may be manipulated by the ruling class and the industrialists as what Louis Althusser (1971) would call 'ideological state apparatuses' for 'interpellating' and producing subjectivities. Examples can be shown by the ways nationalistic and patriotic sentiments are 'interpellated' by national anthems in ceremonial occasions (see Adorno 1990).[1] On the other hand, critics such as Frith (1987) who place emphasis on consumers and listeners' active reception perceive the process of consumption of pop music as experience of meaning-construction and appropriation. When the 'placing of the individual in the social' exists in the reception of pop music, it functions in a disorganized and fragmentary manner, out of the willingness of the consumers or listeners' own choice in their everyday activities. In Frith's view, on a personal level, music enables people to create self-identification and 'the pleasure of pop music ... does not derive in any clear way from fantasy: it is not mediated through daydreams or romancing' (1987, p. 14), like other mass cultural forms. On a social level, pop music provides listeners a chance to manage the relationship between their public and private emotional lives. The way pop songs allow listeners to express themselves without embarrassment, for example, in matters about romantic love, is a case in point. In addition to this, as pop music shapes collective memory by organizing the listeners' sense of time, the listeners' sense of self-consciousness is strengthened because music is what one can 'possess' to build up a sense of identity, in the most literal understanding of what 'possession' means (1987, pp. 144–8).

Despite their differences, Frith's sociological view of the aesthetic of pop music shares with John Shepherd and Peter Wicke's argument that music, like language, is a signifying practice. Both groups of critics agree that music plays a significant role in constituting the world, just as language does to construct reality. In addition to lyrics, there is clearly an 'asemantic' dimension in music, which is differentiable from sounds in language. Musical sounds possess an affective power because of their melody and the use of voice, both of which are to be found in the bodily and material dimensions of culture. Frith discusses the tone of voice which is often more important than the actual articulation of particular lyrics (1987, p. 145). In one Hong Kong film, the singing voice of Southern Music, *nanyin*, is indispensable as the use of musical instruments is minimal. The significance of the voice in *nanyin* lies in the evocation of affect at the moment of rendition. At other times, when the voice is tied with a particular singer, for example in the case of a Taiwanese singer in another chosen film, identification with the public personality functions like the workings of stardom. As Shepherd and Wicke claim, music has 'a special capacity to evoke and symbolize the emotional and semantically experienced dimensions of people's lives' (1997, p. 183). It is through this capacity that listeners are able to create symbolic aspects of their social world through music. 'Music,' they further assert, 'can emphasize the relatedness of human existence with a directness and concreteness that language cannot easily reproduce. Through its fundamentally iconic and concrete functioning, music can foreground the character of people's involvement with their biographies, their societies and their environment' (1997, p. 183). In this chapter, collective identities which belong to the symbolic dimensions of our social and cultural reality are rendered direct and concrete by the musical medium in activities like consumption and entertainment.

If 'diaspora' can be aptly understood with reference to its etymological root to mean the scattering and gathering of people, the diaspora of cultural products such as pop music can be viewed similarly. In Benedict Anderson's *Imagined Communities* (1982), the diaspora of nation-statehood is intricately tied with cultural forms/products, the institutions of which have enabled the constructions and mediations of identities across geo-cultural boundaries. Other critics have also observed that this kind of 'mass-mediated public subjectivity', which has not completely eradicated face-to-face communication, is produced by transportable forms such as novels, newspapers and the mass media (Lee 1993). This mass-mediated public subjectivity is based on an interesting relation between community and strangerhood. Imagined communities, which are constructed by dispersed strangers at the margin of nation-states, shape new kinds of deterritorialized and transnational 'structures of feeling' in our contemporary world. The diasporic structures of feeling, mediated by music, belong to what is emerging, unlike the dominant and residual social formations which have been precipitated or solidified. There is a certain structure to this form of emergent cultural formation. Clifford calls it 'the duality of consciousness', combining 'roots and routes to construct ... forms of community consciousness and solidarity that maintain identifications outside the national time/space in order to live inside, with a difference' (1994, p. 308). Clearly this structure of feeling is made up of a sense of attachment and a cosmopolitan consciousness outside the norms of nation-states. Raymond Williams, who first formulated the concept of 'structure of feeling', emphasized the need to deal with 'elements of impulse, restraint, and tone' which can be considered as 'affective elements of consciousness and relationships'. Such relationships are better understood as 'thought as felt and feeling as thought in a living and relating community' (Williams 1977, p. 132). In diasporic cultures, this corresponding relationship between thought and feeling is easily recognized. However, due to the asemantic nature of musical affect, displaced people who are affected by the same song might be emotionally linked but ideologically estranged. It is true that the popular musical medium is a powerful form mediating collective memories, but music's specific nature adds new dimensions to our study of this kind of 'diasporic structure of feeling'.

Diaspora and family melodrama: Ann Hui's *Exile*

When migrants, particularly those from the lower socio-economic groups, have no choice but be caught up in the post-Fordist modes of flexible accumulation, the massive transnational flows of capital and labour may result in racial and economic marginalization, gender subordination and blocked social advancement. Although many diasporic people transcend their confined condition by way of what Clifford calls 'the skills of survival' (1994, p. 312), they are inevitably subject to the negative experiences of loss, displacement and marginality. It is true that segregation and displacement may lead to the formation of new coalitions and solidarities as most migrant communities have shown, but the condition of estrangement and alienation is the basis for the dramatic action to unfold in films. In this essay, the selected films provide us with a chance to see the ambiguous relationship between intimacy and strangerhood mediated by music. The condition of alienation in the larger context of diaspora is often either allegorized or simply intertwined with experiences on the personal and familial level. Writing about *Exile*, Ackbar Abbas claims that in family romance, there is always a specific structure of a discordant human affective relationship: 'We see this first in the presence of a structure that can be identified as family romance, the fantasy that our parents must be more interesting or worthwhile than our actual parents' (1997, p. 37).

The film is a family melodrama dealing with estranged relationships in the family caused by the migration of people. The Chinese title of the film, *Ke tu qiu hen*, taken directly from a well-known Southern tune, literally means the melancholy of being in the condition of exile; the English title thus captures the essence of this melancholic song, an issue which will be explored below. As Hui's semi-autobiography, the film tells the life of the protagonist up to the year 1973. Hueyin (Maggie Cheung), a young Hong Kong woman of a Chinese father and a Japanese mother, returns from London to Hong Kong for her sister's wedding. At odds with her Japanese mother, Aiko, Hueyin's homecoming revives memories of her unhappy childhood.[2] Later accompanying Aiko to her hometown in Japan, Hueyin finally realizes that her mother has also had a sense of displacement and alienation ever since she was married to her father. Set in different locations and times, the film addresses the concept of exile from different personal experiences and vantage points. It raises issues concerning what one has to do with history and one's own position in society. The political and social upheavals in China before 1949 had caused different generations of characters in the film to be estranged from each other. In the first instance, like many Chinese people, migration was clearly caused by warfare. Ironically it was also warfare that made Hueyin's Chinese father and Japanese mother fall in love with each other. The wide cultural rift between Aiko and Hueyin's grandparents is a major contributing factor to Hueyin's alienation from her mother because the protagonist was raised by her grandparents. The grandfather especially has a strong affiliation with the sense of Chineseness. His political allegiance is portrayed by his decision to move back from Macau to Guangzhou during the time of the Cultural Revolution. In this way, the larger question of the Chinese diasporas is interiorized in the context of generational differences in the same family. If exile and homelessness constitute the theme song of the Chinese diasporic experience, the characters' generational and cultural differences in terms of their varying degree of affiliation to the Chinese nation state can be regarded as variations of this 'song of exile'.

As a family melodrama, *Exile* deals with the ways the personal and the familial dimensions have provided the crucial tropes for understanding the tensions between blood-tie affiliation and cosmopolitan consciousness. Most Hong Kong films are not overtly politically motivated; consequently, the emphasis on the negative side of diaspora does not emerge as dominant concerns for economic exploitation and racial discrimination.[3] It can be observed that the emotional side of the diasporic experience has informed many film texts; *Exile* is a typical example. As a kind of structuring principle, the covert politicization of the condition of diasporic estrangement in both family melodrama and romance has become a recognizable trait of Hong Kong diasporic films. To further explore this covert level of politicization, it is necessary to examine how the musical medium functions to affect people in diaspora, mediating cultural memories and constructing collective identities.

The song, 'Ke tu qiu hen', sometimes translated as 'Melancholy on an Autumn Trip', sometimes as 'A Wanderer's Autumn Grief', is a popular song of the *nanyin*.[4] The Southern Music in Guangdong is a vocal art form dating from the early Qing Dynasty.[5] Since the beginning, the *nanyin* musicians were mostly blind and they used to make their living by divination and fortune-telling. The kind of *nanyin* sung by the blind was also called *di shui nanyin*. *Di shui* is a term used in divination (Hugo Production 1996, p. 17; Urban Council 1988).

The popularity of this song can be demonstrated by its frequent adoption in Hong Kong cultural texts, not to mention its being well liked by listeners of Cantonese opera. The piece began with the words: 'The faithful cool wind keeps its words, the autumn moonshine is boundless. I reminisce my lover, feeling one day like a year' (my translation). The story is about a poor scholar who met a singer and fell in love with her. But he was forced to join the army to defend the country. Later when he had lost track of his girl friend's whereabouts, he was extremely dejected. This piece is often sung in a melodic way; as one critic puts it, it has 'a long melody that can bring tears to one's eyes' (see Programme Notes in Urban Council 1988). In addition to its explicit borrowing as the Chinese title of Hui's film, it is also cited in Stanley Kwan's film *Rouge* (1987) as the love-at-first-sight song that draws the two protagonists together. In Hong Kong writer Dung Kai-cheung's short story entitled 'Yongchengjie xing shuai shi' ('The Rise and Fall of Wing Shing Street'), this song provides a sub-textual layer of meaning to the main narrative of the short story.

The most interesting thing about the impact of the song lies in the appropriation of the song for one's own use without direct reference to the original content of the song. In fact the function of the song in the film narrative is significant because its romantic narrative mirrors that of the family melodrama. In *Exile*, the process through which the song acquires new meanings for people in diaspora illustrates what we might call 'recontextualization' in cultural transmission and adaptation. There are two occasions where the song is sounded in the film. In both cases, the song is cited as a kind of non-diegetic sound when the protagonist Hueyin recollects her past. The recollections are intimately associated with Hueyin's grandfather and the Chinese identity of people of his generation. In the first instance, the song plays a significant role in exposing the differences between two generations of Chinese people at the outset of the film. The film opens with the portrayal of Hueyin's experience of studying abroad in the United Kingdom. Although the film is based on the film-maker's personal experience, this detail is not just autobiographical but also a common experience of those people born and bred in Hong Kong seeking overseas education. This is particularly true of what David Faure calls the 'generation of the 1970s' (1997, p. 103). As a representative of the Hong Kong New Wave Cinema which emerged in the late 1970s, the film-maker has an international outlook which is shared by other contemporaries of her time (see examples in Li 1997, p. 160).[6] The protagonist's integration into foreign culture as an overseas student is revealed by her eagerness to get a job at the BBC and her reception of foreign popular culture. Bob Dylan's 'Mr. Tambourine Man' that arouses great pleasure in her contrasts with 'Ke tu qiu hen' which is sounded at the moment of return to Hong Kong from the UK. 'Mr. Tambourine Man' is performed by a singer on campus as a kind of diegetic sound on screen. The physical locale and concrete presence of the performers and the students convey an ambience of youthful energy and a yearning for a forward-going life although a similar sense of rootlessness and homeless is also present.[7] The lyrics of the song also express such a state:

> My toes too numb to step, wait only for my boot heels
> To be wanderin'.
> I'm ready to go anywhere, I'm ready for to fade
> Into my own parade, cast your dancing spell my way,
> I promise to go under it.
>
> (Dylan 1964)

In contrast to Dylan's song, the exilic, melancholic *nanyin* song performs a metacinematic function as a kind of commentary on the film narrative, like what all non-diegetic sounds often do. The disembodied, nostalgic singing voice creates a haunting feeling associated with a distant past; it indeed turns backward. When Hueyin returns to Hong Kong, it is also the time when she has to deal again with the long-term estranged relationship between herself and her mother. The melodic and melancholic lines of the beginning sung with minimal musical accompaniment help to underline Hueyin's emotional bond with her grandfather: the images of trustworthy cool autumn wind and boundless autumn moon always bring back of remembrances of things past. Hueyin reminisces about the time when she was nurtured by her grandfather to be familiar with Chinese literature, culture and nationalistic thinking. Even without a lot of elaboration, her grandfather's patriotic nationalism as a form of vertical identification among diasporic people is clearly revealed to the audience. While Hueyin has a more intimate relationship with her grandparents than with her Japanese mother, her colonial education and upbringing in Hong Kong in one way or another estrange her from her grandfather whose unyielding patriotism for 'China' cannot arouse her total identification. The emotional bond is thus at odds with the cultural and ideological differences between them. It is through the use of the song that such a contradiction is exposed.

This contradiction is further enhanced when the song is sounded the second time towards the end of the film. After Hueyin has been reconciled with her mother and gained a better understanding of her uprooted experience in China, she visits her dying grandfather in Guangzhou. At the sight of him in the present, the protagonist reminisces about her earlier happier days with her healthy grandfather in a beautiful Chinese garden when 'Ke tu qiu hen' is played on the soundtrack again. The emotional tie is clearly strong and touching as we see Hueyin's tears roll down her face. When Hueyin becomes more and more involved in the local political events in Hong Kong as she has become a TV journalist, her distance with China has also increased. It is the time of the Cultural Revolution when the grandfather has suffered a stroke because of the Red Guards' persecution, while Hueyin is increasingly committed to the betterment of Hong Kong society through the modernization of its bureaucratic and political system. The nostalgic tune of the song signifies a time when the return to the (Chinese) origin has become impossible. The sense of homelessness evoked by the nostalgic song is more 'reflective' than 'restorative' in Svetlana Boym's terms (2001, pp. 41–55). It does not help to construct a sense of continuity and stability with one's origin in a restorative manner; on the contrary, nostalgia plays a reflective and critical role of exposing the impossibility of a 'homecoming' for both the young woman and the old man, but for different reasons. While Hueyin's colonial experience and Western-style education have distanced her from China both culturally and politically, the old man's sense of homelessness and uprootedness is enhanced by the political upheavals of the Cultural Revolution.

The function that this pop song from the Southern Music plays in *Exile* demonstrates an intriguing case about the musical mediation of collective memory. As the use of the song illustrates the process of recontextualization in cultural adaptation, the split between nation and state in the hyphenated word 'nation-state' is disclosed by the gap between an emotional bond and political affiliation. If 'statehood' refers to the machinery for maintaining political sovereignty, 'nationhood' signifies the sense of identification which cuts across geopolitical boundaries. The functioning of a modern nation-state often requires the workings of both within and across national terrains. Just as the first sounding of the song in the film exposes a generational difference between Chinese people, the second time indicates a clearer split between 'nation' and 'state'. The content of the song is thus not important, but what is interesting is the way the song participates in the shaping of a 'diasporic structure of feeling'. The power of affect does not lie in the lyrics in this ambiguous relationship of intimacy and strangerhood created by the diasporic experience. If we can talk about the social and cultural placing of individuals by music, it is important to note that musical affect transcends ideological differences because of its asemantic nature. The next question that follows is: how is the sense of belongingness negotiated by musical affect reconciled with cosmopolitan consciousness in diaspora discourse? The next film provides some clue to this intriguing question.

Diaspora and romantic melodrama: Peter Chan's *Comrades*

Comrades also deals with the condition of rootlessness associated with diaspora. The film is about two people, Li Xiaojun (Leon Lai) and Li Qiao (Maggie Cheung) who migrate to Hong Kong from different provinces of mainland China, in search of a better life in the capitalistic city. At the outset, the representations of the two characters are quite stereotypical and symbolic: Xiaojun represents the frugal, naïve and idealistic northern Chinese, whereas Qiao's calculating and pragmatic character is closer to the southerners who are relatively more urbanized. In fact this set of rural and urban binary oppositions is not an innovative mode of representation; it has informed many earlier Hong Kong films about the cross-border movement of mainland Chinese to Hong Kong.[8] The focus of these films is to highlight the contradictory identities borne by Hong Kong people and their mainland counterparts. This awareness of the conflict, aroused and deepened by the change of sovereignty in 1997, was broadly felt on the societal level and often referred to as 'the China syndrome' (Lu 2001, p. 137). Chan's film, however, plays with this binarism differently, bringing about a shift to a discourse of transnationalism and cosmopolitanism (Curtin 2002, p. 202; Lu 2001, p. 137). It focuses on the sense of homelessness shared by migrants of all kinds. This interesting detail reminds us of Chan's own migratory experience. Chan was born in Hong Kong but migrated with his family to Thailand when he was 12 where he grew up. In the early 1980s after studying abroad, he returned to Hong Kong to work in the film industry. Sharing the drifting sense of diasporic life, he remarks in an interview:

> There are a lot of descendants of Chinese immigrants within the Hong Kong population who are just like me. Basically, we all share an identity crisis because we are going round in circles.... I consider myself a Hong Kong person, but that does not mean I consider myself Chinese. I am Chinese by ethnicity but not by nationality. (Tsui 1997, p. 26)

In the light of this, the rural–urban binarism in the film aims primarily to set up an initial dramatic conflict in the narrative of this romantic melodrama to prepare the audience for a final moment of resolution. If family melodrama like *Exile* is an ideal genre for the exploration of generational differences among diasporic Chinese, generic elements in romance such as romantic encounters and unrequited love provide details for allegorizing the 'identity crisis' that Chan speaks about. Despite their different backgrounds and inclinations, the two characters form a love-cum-friendship bond in Hong Kong and overseas. Their relationship has been intermittently linked by the popular Taiwanese singer Teresa Teng's song. It is such a strong bond that even though they traverse different paths and experience different ups and downs of life, they encounter each other again in New York a decade later. In an almost symbolic moment in the film when the two diasporic characters coincidentally grieve over the death of Teng in a New York street, the film finally reaches its denouement where diasporic experience is preferably perceived as a time of gathering. Although the film seems to be another old-fashioned love story of separation and reunion, it places the romantic encounter in the broader context of the multiplicity of the Chinese diasporic experience. From the characters' initial estrangement in Hong Kong to their final reunion in New York, the film attempts to articulate 'diaspora' as a duality of scattering and gathering. Very interestingly, similar to the melancholic *nanyin* song in *Exile*, music again plays a significant role in mediating a sense of togetherness among diasporic people.

The central figure in this process of musical mediation is a Taiwanese singer named Teresa Teng (Deng Lijun). Teng was one of the most famous singers in Asia and different Chinese communities all over world. Born to a mainlander family in Taiwan and spending her early life in Japan, Teng made herself famous by perfecting a musical style based on traditional Chinese ballad and contemporary pop music. Her popularity took an interesting historical and cultural turn when the People's Republic of China was opened up after the Cultural Revolution. Even the famous economist Steven N.S. Cheung made the following remarks when he analysed the economic transformation in the PRC:

> What happened was that after Deng Xiaoping introduced reforms in 1979, Teresa's popularity soared in the Mainland. Pirated copies of her songs were selling like hot cakes, and to attract even more customers, music shops in Chinese cities took to broadcasting Teresa Teng loud and clear every evening. Then came the 'Anti-Spiritual Pollution Movement' at the end of 1983, when Teresa's songs were singled out as a pollutant and banned. My article explained that this happened because she was a living proof that Marx was wrong. (Cheung 1998, p. 126)

He said that Teng was not a 'capitalist' in the Marxian sense, but she was a 'labourer' who happened to make millions because of her fame. Her reputation thus gave rise to a popular saying in the PRC, 'Deng Xiaoping rules by day, Teresa Teng rules by night.' She was nicknamed the 'Little Deng' in the so-called 'Deng Dynasty' in the 1980s.[9] The widespread circulation of Teng's songs in the PRC shows the power and impact of popular culture even in the most ideologically stringent environment. Her popular reception in the overseas communities was enhanced during and after the Tiananmen incident in 1989. She performed in Paris in 1989, declaring her support for the pro-democracy movement. As she spent her life mostly in the diaspora, her death from an asthma attack while on a trip to Thailand in 1995 caused worldwide mourning, especially in the overseas Chinese who could easily identify with her. Despite her death, she continues to enjoy her fame posthumously: busloads of visitors frequent her Hong Kong residence (see, for example, Ritter 2004); her tomb in Taiwan is another favourite site for her fans (North Coast and Guanyin Mountain Travel Network n.d.); her wax portrait was officially unveiled at Madame Tussaud's in Hong Kong in 2002 (TeresaTeng.com); not to mention the setting up of transnational fan clubs and websites under her name (see 'Teresa Websites' at TeresaTeng.com n.d.). It is within this special historical context that her cultural role in the film is represented.

In the film, Teng is used as both a marker of cultural difference and sameness. The film opens in the mid-1980s, a time during which popular Hong Kong singers such as Alan Tam, Anita Mui and Leslie Cheung had made Teng's singing style outmoded in the city. Interestingly it was also the time when Teng's popularity in the PRC was gaining its momentum. As a result, the presence of Teng in Hong Kong has become a marker of cultural and regional difference. This cultural difference is dramatized when the two characters join hands but fail to sell Teng's records in a flower market on the Chinese New Year Eve. This initial reference to Teng's cultural role in Hong Kong functions paradigmatically in the film narrative to echo with the rural–urban split that was discussed earlier. While the new generations of Hong Kong singers in the 1980s were more westernized than Teng, her waning popularity in the city also signifies Hong Kong people's growing sense of detachment from traditional Chinese culture, which is in one way or another, identified with a rural imaginary.

Teng's initial role as a marker of cultural difference in the film soon gives way to the portrayals of her powerful, unifying impact on the worldwide transnational Chinese communities. In fact even in the first part of the film, when Xiaojun and Qiao are seen cycling together in the streets of Hong Kong, Teng's sweet love song 'Tian mi mi' is heard on the soundtrack to signify a sense of togetherness. The most symbolic and dramatic moment in the film belongs to the time when the news of her death is broadcast on television; it is also the time when the two characters are physically reunited in New York – a city of multiculturalism, division and diaspora. The fact that this moment of hope and reunion in diaspora is mediated by her love songs which do not contain any political content is suggestive. Similar to the *nanyin* song in *Exile*, they only acquire political connotations when they are appropriated and recontextualized in the film-discourse level. The politicization of her songs in this case echoes with the way an émigré Chinese artist responds to her songs. Ju Dahai, a pro-democracy activist, makes the following connection between Teng and the process of democratization in the PRC:

> On the New Year Day in 1979, I had a chance to listen to Teresa Teng's 'He ri jun zai lai' ('When Will You Be Back') in a new students' orientation day at the Peking University, I was very excited and curious. Apart from Teng's songs, we were also exposed to the influence of democratic thought through American broadcasting and Hong Kong political magazines. (Ju 1993, p. 415)

It is perhaps not a coincidence to find that this activist's personal reflections converge with the economist's analysis cited earlier. In Cheung's view, when the PRC was opening itself up to the outside world in the early 1980s, the flow of cultural commodities were more powerful than ideological control and propaganda. At this time, Teng represented new and democratic culture from the outside. As a popular icon whose drifting and diasporic life is well known, Teng later played an important role in mediating a sense of belongingness among diasporic Chinese. The way Teng's image creates identification among Chinese people is similar to how stars function in the culture industries. As Richard Dyer observes, stars are iconic representations of 'recognizable social types' which carry 'social and ideological meanings' (1982, p. 111). Because of these meanings, the audience can create identification through their deep affection for their stars. On another level, however, this iconic signification of her image with covert political overtone is at odds with the totally apolitical content of her lyrical songs. A few lines from 'Sweet Honey Honey' will illustrate this contradiction: 'Oh, the sweet one, your smile is so sweet / Like the blossoming flowers in the spring breezes' (my translation). As one critic has noted, because of 'its simple melody and its plaintive, throaty renditions by Teng', her songs unite people together by sentiment, not by ideology (Curtin 2002, p. 283; Davis 1998, p. 60). If music as a cultural form mediates collective memory, it is found in the *feeling* of being Chinese rather than any overt articulation of ideology. The power of musical affect, as argued before, lies in its 'asemantic' content but it has the capacity to evoke 'the semantically experienced dimensions of people's lives' (Shepherd and Wicke 1997, p. 183). In this way, musical consumption and reception are a process of meaning production and appropriation. The way the 'asemantic' musical affect brings out or concretizes listeners' 'semantically' lived experience demonstrates that the diasporic structure of feeling can be effectively mediated by the musical medium. There might not be a direct, corresponding relation between 'thought' and 'feeling', as Williams suggests, but the way 'feeling' functions to affect thought is remarkable.

In a more historical sense, Darrel Davis implies such a connection, or rather disconnection, between 'thought' and 'feeling'. He observes that those who identify with Teng's voice are the 'new China' (1998, p. 60). *Comrades* indeed inflects a series of unprecedented changes in the PRC since the 1980s: from the 'Four Modernizations' in the 1980s that opened up China economically to the outside world to the recent escalating progress towards modernization and commercialization. At the same time, when such forces of marketization and globalization are at work, the flows of cultural artefacts and commodities are as active as the cross-border travels of humans. The economic liberalization in the PRC inevitably provides chances for Chinese people, especially for those who are on the move, to develop a cosmopolitan consciousness. Michael Curtin asserts that *Comrades* does not resort to the pursuit of a 'distinctive Hong Kong identity', nor does it promote a return to a Chinese nationalist paradigm. Instead it expresses 'a cosmopolitan consciousness that is grounded in the lived experiences of the Chinese diaspora' by erasing the boundaries of identities (2002, pp. 265–6). To a large extent, this assertion in the light of a historical reading of the film in the broader global context of the Chinese diasporas is well taken. What remains to be discussed is the question of identity crisis in the film within the complex, intertwined relationship between cosmopolitanism and global capitalism.

Xiaojun and Qiao in the film represent this new kind of personality after the 'new China'. It can be observed that people in the PRC in the Reform Era have increasingly been subject to the market economy and its logic. Some people call it the 'post-Cultural Revolution personality' which is pragmatic, capitalistic and anti-revolutionary. Similarly the characters' life trajectories are inseparable from what we can now understand as 'global capitalism'. On the one hand, they have no choice but to be assimilated into the capitalistic way of life in Hong Kong. The recurrent motif of the Opportunity Furniture Shop in Tsim Sha Tsui serves as a subtle visual backdrop to comment on how the two mainlanders' have been preoccupied with the need to seek new opportunities to pursue a better material life. Although the characters, especially Xiaojun, have their concerns other than what is economic, they are portrayed more or less as fortune-seekers, more or less like Aihwa Ong's *homo economicus* desiring 'flexible citizenship' in a post-Fordist world of flexible accumulation (1993). On the other hand, their close association with capitalism is mediated by their consumption of cultural commodities such as Teng's songs. While the migratory experience nurtures a cosmopolitan awareness, the sense of affinity mediated by the mass media indicates what David Morley and Kevin Robins call 'globalization as identity crisis'. They assert that 'there is a desire to be at home in the new and disorienting global space.... Home in a world of expanding horizons and dissolving boundaries' is constantly being shattered and reconstructed (1995, p. 10). It can then be argued that the pan-Chinese consumption of Teng does serve as a symptom to indicate a kind of 'diasporic malaise' – a kind of homesickness which does not seek a cosmopolitan outlook if cosmopolitanism is understood as 'a willingness to engage with the Other', in Ulf Hannerz's articulation (1990, p. 239). On the contrary, what is revealed in the film is an urge for the reconstitution of an endangered sense of Chineseness by way of collectively remembering Teng's music. This threat to identity is perpetually being experienced by border-crossers of all kinds, and an analysis of the binding power of Teng's songs illustrates this cultural need. In a subtle manner, the film renders a *symphony* of diaspora as a *cacophony* of euphoria and elegy.[10] If there is a cosmopolitan dimension in diaspora, it is at best understood as one side of the root–route duality (Clifford 1994, pp. 307–8). The musical affect generated by Teng's songs has been a useful clue to the understanding of this duality.

Music and diasporic structures of feeling

The above analysis sheds interesting light on the study of the Chinese diasporic experiences and their close relationship to global capitalism. While *Exile* is more reflective on the notion of nation-state, *Comrades* charts a transnational path which draws our attention to issues in connection with imagined communities and the flows of cultural landscapes (Appadurai 1990). Although the protagonist in *Exile* is cosmopolitan in her outlook, other characters in the film express more exilic than diasporic feelings because of their constant desire to return to their homeland.

At one point in their lives, the issues about allegiance to one's own country are concerns for both the Japanese mother and the patriotic grandfather, despite the constant shattering of such illusion of homecoming in the film. By contrast, the vertical relationship with the nation-state is never an issue in the latter film; what is at stake is comradeship which is constructed horizontally across geopolitical boundaries. The representative song from *nanyin* belongs to an older form of popular entertainment where face-to-face contact is primary, whereas Hueyin's consumption of Dylan is then closer to the way Teng's songs function in the latter film. They construct a transnational imaginary which is intricately rooted in the development of the mass media in a global context. It is also this latter form that has given rise to what Benjamin Lee calls 'the mass-mediated subjectivity'. In his discussion of pop cultural commodities like film, he argues that cinema creates an imaginary space of spectatorship which is characterized by a potentially infinite differentiation of desire:

> The fascination created through visual imagery links the specificity of consumer choices to the body as signs of individual interest, desire, and subjectivity, but the publicity of mass-mediated choice creates the image of an imaginary public other (i.e. that which is other than me is what is public); one's individual choice stands in contrast to all other similarly mediated desires. (Lee 1993, p. 171)

Music plays a similar role in negotiating different desires in audio reception in everyday life. The power of musical affect excludes 'the imaginary public other'. This exclusionary characteristic of music is also where its binding power lies. One is simply *in love with the music* that negotiates one's own public and private lives. The 'root' side of the diasporic structure of feeling helps to shape alternative public spheres which are outside the confines of the nation-state but at the same time they form communities of their own among strangers who construct similar collective memory through the musical medium. In a similar vein, identity politics, new types of nationalism, new social movements such as feminism or gay rights, cannot be understood without the understanding of these new forms of mass-mediated publicity. Whether a community thus constructed will be able 'to engage with the Other', and to establish 'an intellectual and aesthetic stance of openness toward divergent cultural experiences' (Hannerz 1990, p. 239) still remains to be seen. Will the 'contrapuntal' consciousness of diaspora (Edward Said) be of any use to the reconciliation of ethnic attachment and cosmopolitanism? Or is it true that all displaced people can only live with such a tension without the need to look for a resolution or a synthesis? Has such a duality indeed become their ontological condition in the midst of the great currents of history, and last but not the least, in the private moments when *they fall in love with music*? What insights can we get from the 'musical landscapes' mediated by the Chinese diasporas?

Notes

1 See Adorno (1990) as well for his Frankfurt School critical position, but his argument is different from Althusser because he places emphasis on the aesthetic form of pop music.
2 See Hui's autobiographical documentary *As Time Goes By* (1997).
3 Mabel Cheung's *Illegal Immigrants* (1985), Clara Law's *Farewell China* (1990), Stanley Kwan's *Full Moon in New York* (1990) and Evans Chan's *Crossings* (1994) are exceptions.
4 The song was often believed to be written by Miao Lianxian from the mid-Qing Dynasty. Recent researches, however, have shown that the writer should be Ye Ruibo (1780–1830).
5 The text of *nanyin* has rhyming lines of seven characters each. The singer develops the music from the text according to a scheme of melodic, metric and transitional interlude patterns.
6 Examples are Ann Hui, Yim Ho, Allen Fong and Tsui Hark.
7 See also Tony Williams's discussion of 'Mr. Tambourine Man' in *Jump Cut* (Williams 1998).
8 For example, Johnny Mak's *Long Arm of the Law* series (1984–90) and Alfred Cheung's *Her Fatal Ways* series (1990–94) portray mainland Chinese as either invasive outlaws or rural country bumpkins.
9 The so-called 'Deng Dynasty' refers to Deng Xiaoping, Deng Lijun and Deng Yingchao, the widow of Zhou Enlai.
10 See Cheung and Chu's 'Introduction' to *Between Home and World* in which the original discussion is in the broader context of globalization. The original sentence reads like this: 'We are thus not surprised to hear the *symphony* of globalization as a *cacophony* of euphoria and elegy' (2004, p. xxx).

References

Abbas, A. 1997, *Hong Kong: Culture and the Politics of Disappearance*, Hong Kong UP, Hong Kong.
Adorno, T.W. 1990, 'Adorno, Theodor W', in S. Frith and A. Goodwin (eds), *On Record: Rock, Pop, and the Written Word*, Routledge, London, pp. 301–14.
Althusser, L. 1971, 'Ideology and Ideological State Apparatuses', in *Lenin and Philosophy and Other Essays*, New Left Books, London, pp. 127–86.
Anderson, B. 1982, *Imagined Communities*, Verso, London.
Appadurai, A. 1990, 'Disjuncture and Difference in the Global Cultural Economy', *Public Culture*, vol. 2, no. 2, pp. 1–24.

Boym, S. 2001, *The Future of Nostalgia*, Basic Books, New York.
Cheung, E.M.K. and Chu, Y.W. (eds) 2004, *Between Home and World: a Reader in Hong Kong Cinema*, Oxford UP, Hong Kong.
Cheung, S.N.S. 1998, 'Deng Xiaoping's Great Transformation', *Contemporary Economic Policy*, vol. 16, no. 2, pp. 125–35.
Clifford, J. 1994, 'Diasporas', *Cultural Anthropology*, vol. 9, no. 3, pp. 302–38.
Curtin, M. 2002, 'Sweet Comrades: Historical Identities and Popular Culture', in J.M. Chan and B.T. McIntyre (eds), *In Search of Boundaries*, Ablex, Westport, pp. 264–90.
Davis, D.D. 1998, 'Comrades: People on the Make', in *Cinedossier: the 34th Golden Horse Award-Winning Films*, Golden Horse Film Festival, Taipei, pp. 56–61.
Dyer, R. 1982, *Stars*, BFI, London.
Dylan, B. 1964, *Mr. Tambourine Man (Bob Dylan's Lyrics)*, Special Rider Music, viewed 3 January 2007 <http://www.bobdylan.com/songs/tambourine.html>.
Faure, D. 1997, 'Reflections on Being Chinese in Hong Kong', in J.M. Brown and R. Foot (eds), *Hong Kong's Transitions, 1842–1997*, Macmillan Press, London, pp. 103–20.
Frith, S. 1987, 'Toward an Aesthetic of Popular Music', in R. Leppart and S. McClary (eds), *Music and Society*, Cambridge UP, Cambridge, pp. 133–49.
Hannerz, U. 1990, 'Cosmopolitans and Locals in World Culture', in M. Featherstone (ed.), *Global Culture*, Sage Publications, London, pp. 237–52.
Hugo Production 1996, *Notes (in the accompanying booklet of) the sound disc 'A Wanderer's Autumn Grief: Au Kwan-cheung sings nanyin'*, Hugo Production (HK), Hong Kong.
Ju, D. 1993, 'Wo can jia min yun de jing guo', in H. Mai (ed.), *Zhongguo de liang xin*, Xianggang zhi lian hui, Hong Kong, pp. 414–17.
Lee, B. 1993, 'Going Public', *Public Culture*, vol. 5, no. 2, pp. 165–78.
Li, C.T. 1997, 'The Return of the Father: Hong Kong New Wave and its Chinese Context in the 1980s', in N. Browne (ed.), *New Chinese Cinemas*, Cambridge UP, Cambridge, pp. 160–79.
Lu, S. 2001, 'Hong Kong Diaspora Film and Transnational TV Drama', *Postscript*, vol. 20, no. 2/3, pp. 137–46.
Marchetti, G. 1998, 'Plural and Transnational', *Jump Cut*, vol. 42, pp. 68–93.
Morley, D. and Robins, K. 1995, *Spaces of Identity*, Routledge, London.
Naficy, H. 2001, *An Accented Cinema: Exilic and Diasporic Filmmaking*, Princeton UP, New Jersey.
North Coast and Guanyin Mountain Travel Network n.d., *Teresa Teng's Grave*, North Coast and Guanyin Mountain Travel Network, viewed 26 December 2006 <http://www.northguan-nsa.gov.tw/en/view_detail.php?id=13>.
Ong, A. 1993, 'On the Edge of Empires: Flexible Citizenship among Chinese in Diaspora', *Positions*, vol. 1, no. 3, pp. 745–78.
Ritter, J. 2004, *Savvy Traveler – the Graceland of Asia*, American Public Media, viewed 26 December 2006 <http://savvytraveler.publicradio.org/show/features/2001/20010413/feature2.shtml>.
Shepherd, J. and Wicke, P. 1997, *Music and Cultural Theory*, Polity Press, Cambridge.
Skeldon, R. 1994, *Reluctant Exiles?: Migration from Hong Kong and the New Overseas Chinese*, Hong Kong UP, Hong Kong.

TeresaTeng.com 2002, *Madame Tussaud's Officially Unveils Teresa Teng Portrait*, Teresa Teng's Fan Club, viewed 26 December 2006 <http://www.teresateng.com/main.php?act=article&id=8>.

TeresaTeng.com n.d., *Teresa Websites on the 'Links' Page*, Teresa Teng's Fan Club, viewed 27 December 2006 http://www.teresateng.com/main.php?act=links>.

Tsui, A. 1997, 'Comrades, Almost a Love Story – Interview with Peter Chan', in *Hong Kong Panorama 96–97*, Urban Council, Hong Kong, pp. 26–7.

Urban Council 1988, 'Programme Notes for the Nan Yin Concert in the City Hall on Oct 14–Nov 2, 1988', Urban Council, Hong Kong.

Williams, R. 1977, *Marxism and Literature*, Oxford UP, Oxford.

Williams, T. 1998, 'Song of the Exile: Border-Crossing Melodrama', *Jump Cut*, vol. 42, pp. 94–100.

14

Conclusion: through the Diasporic Looking-Glass

Andrew P. Davidson

> In another moment Alice was through the glass, and had jumped lightly down into the Looking-glass room. The very first thing she did was to look whether there was a fire in the fireplace, and she was quite pleased to find that there was a real one, blazing away as brightly as the one she had left behind. So I shall be as warm here as I was in the old room, thought Alice: warmer, in fact, because there'll be no one here to scold me away from the fire. Oh, what fun it'll be, when they see me through the glass in here, and can't get at me!
>
> Lewis Carroll, *Through the Looking-Glass* (1991)

Diasporic communities and their concomitant trajectories provide critical spaces to examine and come to terms with the dramatic migrations that have defined recent human history and appear to continue unabated in this century. Like Alice in *Through the Looking-Glass*, movement is about constructing narratives of self and 'home'. In Kondo's (1996, p. 97) words, home 'stands for a safe place, where there is no need to explain oneself to outsiders; it stands for community'. In this respect, memories as narrative and 'things' establish a bridge between the old and new life worlds, as well as provide a bond between the past, present and future. But migration is seldom a simple matter of undisturbed movement as Alice discovered when admonished by the Queen, 'It's a poor sort of memory that only works backwards', a point made in *Memories of a Future Home: Diasporic Citizenship of Chinese in Panama*, where Lok Siu explores how diasporic Chinese in Panama constructed a home and created a sense of belonging while inhabiting the interstices of multiple cultures.

Memories of diasporic communities frequently consist of reinvented stories characterized by processes such as syncretism and cultural infusion of metaphors of home. Typically, a sense of cultural ethos reconstructs a complex past in order to reinvent a sense of present identity. While memory is typically taken as something remembered or recalled it is also part of imagination; to separate the two forces a Cartesian split between the objective and subjective worlds of thought that marks a further distinction between history and memory. To the contrary, imagination is the propellant of memory and as Appadurai (1996, p. 7) writes, 'the imagination is today a staging ground for action, and not only for escape'. It is in this respect that Alice had her 'leap of faith', and migrants in this volume migrated to places they knew but had never been. Then too, modern media and telecommunication enabled the imagination to actively remember the imageries of home, both of origin and destination (Sun 2002).[1] Like Alice, few made that leap through the looking-glass without their memories and narratives of migration. Imagined memories thus perform at the crossroad of space and time. Once through the looking-glass, memories of the past home are blurred as they are reconstructed and take on new meaning. And with the new home, imagined memory and 'reality' are seldom uncontested.

The study of diasporic communities also offers a primary means to de-essentialize the nation-state by opening it up as an ongoing process rather than an end-point, or what Osborne (2006) terms a 'nationalizing-state'. As with Alice in *Through the Looking-Glass*, the trick of relationships for migrants is 'displaced and transformed' such that the mastery of meaning and power are dislodged and contested (Cixous 1982, p. 242). Memories express variant elements of intensity in relation to a diasporic imaginary as well as different concepts of spatial relations, and with how diasporic migrants engage the politics of cultural and political belonging in a transnational context. So too with the Chinese diaspora, made evident by the number of scholarly writings, novels, films and dedicated web pages.[2] *At Home in the Chinese Diaspora* took on the task of exploring the variant Chinese diasporic communities through the resonant theme of memory and how memories are deployed and negotiated to re-establish a sense of identity and, ultimately, feelings of belonging. Focusing on the power of memory and how movement across international borders affects myths of homeland and return, the authors set out to consider how identities are constructed, lived, transformed and passed on. To this end the chapters in this volume explored the varied relationships between migrants' adjustment and remembering home through the focal point of memories.

Place also is a vital crucible of memory. As noted by Bender (1993, p. 3), space 'is never inert, people engage with it, re-work it, appropriate and contest it' [as] 'It is part of the ways in which identities are created and disputed, whether as individual, group or nation-state.' The encounter between place and history and between memory and identity destabilizes the migrant and thus the diasporic community. But with the migrants' recreation of places of home as nodes of identity in a disparate landscape, migrants provide communal solace and meaning. Imagination in the interplay of memory looks to place as an agent of deterritorialization and reterritorialization according to the prevailing political discourses and how these are subsequently inscribed on identities (Osborne 2006). In other words, 'Tradition can now become a way of conceptualizing the fragile communicative relationships across time and space that are the basis not of diaspora identities but of diaspora identifications' (Gilroy 1993, p. 276). Here memory is given voice in place through identification that can serve as a means to create new relationships and solidarity among members of the diasporic communities.

The power of memory also lies in its capacity to both compel and dispel identities and identification: here Chineseness. But Chineseness is both accepted and problematic as a constructed idealized identity through hypervalued memories. Nevertheless, 'Our understanding of the present is invariably predicated on actual or imagined links to, or ruptures from, a recalled past' (Seyhan 2000, p. 1). Memories can tell us about the ways in which diaspora is experienced subjectively and, perhaps more importantly, intersubjectively. Thus identities are never stagnant but as Hames-García (2000, pp. 111–12) so aptly notes:

> To account for multiplicity, social identities can never be viewed as static entities sutured at all ends. However, despite this emphasis of revision and transformation, claims and references to these identities can be justified because the causal features of the social world that give rise to them and that give them their political salience are not arbitrary . . . even if their *exact* contours remain indeterminate, like those of a family resemblance.

What the chapters in the volume made clear was the heterogeneity of identities in Chinese diasporic communities scattered throughout the world, as well as in any single country. Social or collective memory, after all, cannot be readily or easily unscrambled from individual memory. Social memories are important, but the final meeting point lies within the individual who reinterprets memories according to personal circumstances and emotional discourses. In other words, 'recollections of the past serve as the active ideological terrain on which people represent themselves to themselves' (Ganguly 1992, p. 29).

Gender, class and hybridity

> In this paper I will rethink social stratification away from the polarity between the material and the symbolic, and argue that material inequality, as a set of outcomes relating to life conditions, life chances and solidary processes, is informed by claims and struggles over resources of different types, undertaken in terms of gender, ethnicity/race and class. This formulation allows us to include these categorial formations, alongside class, as important elements of social stratification i.e. as determining the allocation of socially valued resources and social places/locations.
>
> (Anthias 2001a, p. 368)

The decision to migrate is rarely if ever taken lightly and is in effect where necessity ends and possibilities begin. Migrants move for a variety of reasons, including family, education, employment, sociopolitical freedom, and so on. Seldom is the migration experience as migrants anticipated. For some life is better, for others worse. Watkins et al. (2003), for example, note this for Vietnamese migrants to Australia while Begum (1999) draws similar conclusions in his study of migration to Dhaka. The point is, once a migrant relocates they are subject to new cross-cutting structural pressures of variant correlates of stratification and then typically in multiple layers.

Ethnicity or race – Chineseness – is not the only form of hegemonic practice of interest in exploring diasporic communities and its interpolation with memory. Gender and class situations represent others. Recognizing that these relations, like any other, are embedded within institutions lays the foundation for analysing the structural factors that condition social relations, in addition to other social relations and ideological factors. Social relations are about power that is organized according to dominant discourses and shot through with conflicting interests and hierarchies of power and privilege (Glenn 1999). Power comes to the fore in a multiplicity of discursive elements that coalesce in diverse social situations. Thinking through these registers allows for some of the more paradoxical and contradictory aspects of identities in diasporic communities to be more easily taken apart and understood.

But if our stories of Chinese migrants shared a common theme, it was of migrants located in patriarchal worlds, patriarchal worlds that were nonetheless a fluid and shifting set of contextualized social relations with men exercising varying degrees of power and control over women.

Of course women resisted male oppression in diverse ways, engaging in subversion, collaboration, acquiescence and manipulation, animating the hegemonic power relations between men and women in a dialectic of force and consent. According to the 'patriarchal bargain' for example, 'women strategize within a set of concrete constraints that reveal and define the blueprint of ... the *patriarchal bargain* of any given society' which will of course exhibit variations according to other power relations such as ethnicity and class (Kandiyoti 1988, p. 275). Migration, however, decentred and opened up new sites of contestation and resistance in gender relations. Nevertheless, as Zhou (2000, p. 445) reminds us, in a study of Chinese women migrants in New York, that women, by virtue of migrating, 'enjoy more liberty, freedom, and equality than in their country of origin'. Still others such as Sun (2002) argue that Chinese transnationalism (or diasporic communities) is constructed on the power of the Chinese state and the potency of a collective memory of the Chinese nation, putatively retaining gender relations as well.

Class too punctuates gender and affects migrants' life chances. Certainly migration opens up opportunities for many migrants but migration is not always the story of a successful migration experience. Downwards mobility is not uncommon in an otherwise invisible minority. The literature on Chinese migration is replete with documented evidence 'of immigrants' experiences with downward mobility, gender role reversals, and immigrant women's improved social status on arrival in their new homeland' (Yick 2001, p. 555).[3] The 'fall from grace' can be particularly stressful for men given their prominent position in Chinese society. A friend of mine in Sydney, a 'successful' migrant from Shanghai, shared a story with me about three male migrants who journeyed to Sydney while in their mid-thirties to study English and stayed on. The first had been a journalist and newspaper editor in Beijing and now works as a cleaner; the second held a medical degree and currently works in a Chinese restaurant chopping vegetables; and the last had been a music conductor in a Beijing orchestra and presently labours as a dishwasher. Each in a bittersweet memory of the confluence of old and new identities commented on their present circumstances. The first replied 'the floor is a big paper and the mop my big pen', the second said that 'I still wield a "knife", but now I operate on carrots'; and the last commented that 'with the chopsticks I conduct the bowl and the plates'.

So how can we reconceptualize Simmel's stranger, the 'person who comes today and stays tomorrow'? How can we make sense of and talk about hierarchies of power as relational constructs that are contextually and situationally realized? Hybridity as a construct of transnationalism entered the vocabulary of cultural critique as a defining signifier of the postmodern condition, associated with the diasporic condition of post-modern life with its emphasis on deterritorialty and difference. Despite certain misgivings, this concept has opened up approaches to identity and migration that involve the deconstruction of identity through anti-essentialist projects and critiques of static notions of culture (see Ngan this volume). Initially, the concept of 'marginal man' implied a situation where people were involved in two or more culturally distinct societies or groups and where value conflicts were being experienced (Park 1928). Hybridity arose in response to marginal man to designate new identities that are of a more transethnic and transnational character. Hybridity is a complexity in its own right, comprised of variant asymmetric power relations producing cultural hierarchies of class gender, and ethnicity. More appropriately, Anthias (2001b, p. 629) advances the notion of 'transnational positionality' as a more adequate means to address a range of issues relating to hybridity, to effectively draw on subject-agency and, more importantly, with how that agency is exercised within a system of structural constraints and 'linked to the positionality of actors (both individual and collective) within specific social contexts', allowing us not only to explore gendered identities, but class as well.

New Racism or 'the more things change, the more they seem the same'

> For many years we have been concerned with issues around migration, the economic, the social and political realities of transnational communities and the making of national identities. Throughout this period we have been concerned to show how each of these processes is constituted in racialised, gendered and class relations which are by no means static, not least because of the ways in which individuals and collectivities contest certain boundaries and carve out new spaces of identity and control for themselves.
>
> (Westwood and Phizacklea 2000, p. 2)

At the close of the twentieth century the word 'multiculturalism' gained prominence in both political and public discourse, especially in Western countries. Multiculturalism assumed the abandonment of the myth of a homogenous nation-state as an epistemic shift towards a heterogeneous unified nation-state (Castles 2002). Nevertheless, current history reveals that cultural exclusion is difficult to dispel. In practice, by stressing cultural difference, minority cultures can readily become differentially marginalized from the dominant centre. The cumulative effect of cultural homogenization is to reify boundaries, to give life and meaning to imagined communities of cultural collectivises. It is these cauldrons of exclusion where diasporic communities take life, shape and root. Still, it is precisely in reading between the borders of authority and community that we begin to see how a superfluity of identities emerges within a range of discourses of power. In effect, migrants carve out niches – a *home* – and develop a feeling of belonging that are succoured by memories.

Both migrant and host routinely essentialize and fix the other's identity, trapping each other in strictures of stereotype. Stereotypes today, however, are different than in the past, far more subtle although still as binding. This new situation is part of what Balibar (1991) argued was the decentring and superseding of older forms of racism based on biology and genetics to '*differentialist racism*' or the primacy of cultural differences. In other words, racism or ethnic deprecation has shifted from notions of biological essentialism to constructs of cultural purity (such as Chineseness). Thus, biology is not the only a means of naturalizing human behaviour, culture too can also be naturalized and 'function as a way of locking individuals and groups a priori into a genealogy, into a determination that is immutable and intangible in origin' (Balibar 1991, p. 12). The results are no less confounding. Rey Chow's (1991, p. 5) insightful critique of Bertolucci and his film *The Last Emperor* goes to the heart of this with Bertolucci's description of the differences among Chinese and Japanese members of his film crew:

> They are very different. The Chinese, of course, are more ancient. But also the Japanese have this myth of virility. They are more macho. The Chinese are the opposite, more feminine. A bit passive. But passive, as I say, in the way of people when they are so intelligent and so sophisticated they don't need machismo.

The idealization of ethnic identity still has a powerful subversive potential, even in a supposed compliment. For better or worse, stereotypes essentialize and fix an individual's identity and dictate the individual's performativity and performative value.

The poetics of memory and the mirrors of identity

Memories are the mirrors of life. As such, memories are fragmentary moments that are selectively remembered and forgotten, ordered and reordered and reminisced and related. Memories too are dancing phantasms that entice, inspire, cajole and awe. As part imagination, memories are emotionally driven in shaping personal identities and histories. Who we are then is as much about fact as it is fiction. It is in this respect that we depart the realm of the historian and anthropologist (see Berliner 2005) and settle into cultural discourse. Here we become Alice trying to find meaning in the looking-glass and ask: Who is the master of meaning? The deep reach of memory positions cultural identities and informs us who we 'really' are, and often in spite of whom we want to be identified as. Hence the common retort to the migrant: 'Where are you really from?'

It is in the interstices of memory and identity that the past provides a crucial discursive terrain for reconsolidating selfhood and identity. Then too, the axis of deep cultural memory shifts from the initial migrant to subsequent generations. Memories and identities change. Social or collective memories are important but the final meeting point is, in the end, within the individual who reinterprets those memories according to personal circumstances, and here memories are as much about what is forgotten as how memories are recalled. Thus the diasporic identity is a flood of contradictions, full of beginnings and hope, as well as despair and anguish. Perhaps memories are best summed up by Alice: 'Now, Kitty, let's consider who it was that dreamed it all.'

Notes

1 'Those who wish to move, those who have moved, those who wish to return, and those who choose to stay rarely formulate their plans outside the sphere of radio and television, cassettes and videos, newsprint and telephone. For migrants, both the politics of adaptation to new environments and the stimulus to move or return are deeply affected by a mass-mediated imaginary that frequently transcends national space' (Appadurai 1996, p. 6).

2 See for example, http://www.gseis.ucla.edu/faculty/chu/chinos/diaspora.html, *Chinese Diaspora Websites, Bibliography, and Other Interesting Facts about the Chinese Diaspora* (viewed 25 December 2006). The connection between the Internet and diasporic communities (digital community) is an increasingly important line of research.

3 Yick presents an insightful article on gender, mobility and domestic violence in the US among Asian immigrants, including Chinese.

References

Anthias, F. 2001a, 'The Material and the Symbolic in Theorizing Social Stratification: Issues of Gender, Ethnicity and Class', *British Journal of Sociology*, vol. 52, no. 3, pp. 367–90.

Anthias, F. 2001b, 'New Hybridities, Old Concepts: the Limits of "Culture"', *Ethnic and Racial Studies*, vol. 24, no. 4, pp. 619–41.

Appadurai, A. 1996, *Modernity at Large: Cultural Dimensions of Globalization*, University of Minnesota Press, Minneapolis.

Balibar, E. 1991, 'Is there a "New-Racism"?' in E. Balibar and I. Wallerstein (eds), *Race, Nation, Class: Ambiguous Identities*, Verso Press, London, pp. 17–28.

Begum, A. 1999, *Destination Dhaka: Urban Migration: Expectations and Reality*, University Press Ltd, Dhaka.

Bender, B. 1993, *Landscapes: Politics and Perspectives*, Routledge, London.

Berliner, R. 2005, 'The Abuses of Memory: Reflections of the Memory Boom in Anthropology', *Anthropological Quarterly*, vol. 78, no. 1, pp. 197–211.

Carroll, L. 1991, *Through the Looking Glass*, Project Gutenberg and Duncan Research Shareware, viewed 20 January 2007 <http://www.cs.indiana.edu/metastuff/looking/looking.txt.gz>.

Castles, S. 2002, 'Migration and Community Formation under Conditions of Globalization', *International Migration Review*, vol. 36, no. 4, pp. 1143–68.

Chow, R. 1991, *Woman and Chinese Modernity: the Politics of Reading between West and East*, University of Minnesota Press, Minneapolis.

Cixous, H. 1982, 'Introduction to Lewis Carroll's: Through the Looking-Glass and The Hunting of the Snark', *New Literary History*, vol. 13, no. 2, pp. 231–51.

Ganguly, K. 1992, 'Migrant Identities: Personal Memory and the Construction of Selfhood', *Cultural Studies*, vol. 6, no. 1, pp. 27–50.

Gilroy, P. 1993, *The Black Atlantic: Modernity and Double Consciousness*, Harvard University Press, Cambridge, London.

Glenn, E. 1999, 'The Social Construction and Institutionalization of Gender and Race: an Integrative Framework', in M. Ferree, J. Lorber and B. Hess (eds), *Revisioning Gender*, Sage Publications, Thousand Oaks, California, pp. 3–43.

Hames-García, M.R. 2000, '"Who are our own People?": Challenges for a Theory of Social Identity', in P. Moya and M. Hames-García (eds), *Realist Theory and the Predicament of Postmodernism*, University of California Press, Berkeley, pp. 102–9.

Kandiyoti, D. 1988, 'Bargaining and Patriarchy', *Gender and Society*, vol. 2, no. 3, pp. 274–90.

Kondo, D. 1996, 'The Narrative Production of "Home", Community, and Political Identity in Asian American Theater', in S. Lavie and T. Swedenburg (eds), *Displacement, Diaspora, and the Geographies of Identity*, Duke UP, Durham, pp. 97–118.

Osborne, B. 2006, 'From Native Pines to Diasporic Geese: Placing Culture, Setting our Sites, Locating Identity in a Transnational Canada', *Canadian Journal of Communication*, vol. 31, no. 1, pp. 147–75.

Park, R.E. 1928, 'Human Migration and the Marginal Man', *American Journal of Sociology*, vol. 33, no. 6, pp. 881–93.

Seyhan, A. 2000, *Writing outside the Nation*, Princeton University, Princeton.

Sun, W. 2002, *Leaving China: Media, Migration and Transnational Imagination*, Rowman and Littlefield Publishers, Lanham, Maryland.

Watkins, R., Plant, A.J., Sang, D., O'Rourke, T., Le, V., Nguyen, H. and Gushulak, B. 2003, 'Research Note. Individual Characteristics and Expectations about Opportunities in Australia among Prospective Vietnamese Migrants', *Journal of Ethnic and Migration Studies*, vol. 29, no. 1, pp. 157–66.

Westwood, S. and Phizacklea, A. 2000, *Trans-Nationalism and the Politics of Belonging*, Routledge, London.
Yick, A. 2001, 'Feminist Theory and Status Inconsistency Theory: Application to Domestic Violence in Chinese Immigrant Families', *Violence against Women*, vol. 7, no. 5, pp. 545–62.
Zhou, Y. 2000, 'The Fall of "the Other Half of the Sky"? Chinese Immigrant Women in the New York Area', *Women's Studies International Forum*, vol. 23, no. 4, pp. 445–59.

Index